My Psychosis,
My Bicycle, and I

My Psychosis, My Bicycle, and I

The Self-Organization of Madness

Fritz B. Simon, M.D.

translated from the German
by Sally and Bernd Hofmeister

JASON ARONSON INC.
Northvale, New Jersey
London

Production Editor: Judith D. Cohen

This book was set in 11 pt. Bodoni Antiqua by Alpha Graphics of Pittsfield, New Hampshire, and printed and bound by Book-Mart Press of North Bergen, New Jersey.

Library of Congress Cataloging-in-Publication Data

Simon, Fritz B.
    My psychosis, my bicycle, and I : the self-organization of madness /
  by Fritz B. Simon.
        p.   cm.
    Includes bibliographical references and index.
    ISBN 1-56821-647-5 (alk. paper)
    1. Psychoses—Etiology.   2. Self-organizing systems.   3. Chaotic
  behavior in systems.   I. Title.
  RC512.S54   1996
  616.89—dc20   95-21424

Manufactured in the United States of America. Jason Aronson Inc. offers books and cassettes. For information and catalog write to Jason Aronson Inc., 230 Livingston Street, Northvale, New Jersey 07647.

CONTENTS

1

Introduction

A DIAGNOSTIC TEST

Let us begin with a simple test. Suppose you have just opened a book entitled *My Psychosis, My Bicycle, and I: The Self-Organization of Madness,* and you begin to read the first chapter.

Suppose you are at this moment (right now) reading the first line (?) of the second paragraph. See, that is what I was afraid of. You give free rein to your imagination and let it run away with you. You are obviously a person with far too vivid powers of imagination. You might as well admit it—you really do have the impression that you are reading such a book. You even believe you are holding this book in your hand and can actually feel it.

It is quite alarming that someone like you, who considers yourself enlightened, critical, and rational, is so easily influenced and impressionable. Your independent powers of judgment and autonomy seem to be in a bad way. Not only do you blindly obey a stranger's promptings to abandon yourself to some fantasy—no, even worse, you become so absorbed in this world of daydreams that you really believe you live in it. Or are you going to deny that you actually feel you are reading this fictitious book?

The symptom is obvious to every psychiatrist. You cannot distinguish between your imagination and your perception. Does this happen often? Do you always obey the orders of all your fellow men? For how long have you been unable to dissociate yourself from others to this extent?

You really believe you are holding this book in your hand. In general psychiatric experience, this belief signifies that you have lost your connection with reality. After all, you are only following instructions to imagine something.

Should you now be toying with the idea of closing the book in frustration, it would be evidence that you react with a tendency to flight whenever you do not immediately understand a basic idea. You probably tend to break off relationships in situations you cannot fathom too.

On the other hand, it is also an alarming sign if what has just happened to you leaves you absolutely cold and unmoved: that means you dismiss all feelings that might shake your confidence in yourself and the world and instill you with a sense of fear. So you do not let yourself become really involved in relationships (not even in one that is objectively harmless, like the one to this imagined book).

Are you a bit confused and wondering what this is all about? Are you even asking yourself whether you are being manipulated, whether someone is playing games with you? It is so easy to see through you.

However, you probably really believe that you are reading this book right now. How can you convince yourself and the diagnostician who claims you are the victim of an optical illusion and entangled in systematized delusions that this book in front of you really exists?

To tell you the truth, my impression is that you must be out of your mind at the moment (please excuse the stark wording—it is not intended personally or indeed pejoratively). On the other hand, do I actually exist? Am I too just a product of your egocentric sick fantasy that sees itself surrounded by psychiatrists and other pursuers and takes every book, the news on television, and the texts of pop songs personally?

The answer to the question whether the book in your hand really exists has wide-ranging consequences. It says more about you and your mental state than about the book. If it is a hallucination, you are probably mad at the moment. To use a medical term: you are probably psychotic, whatever the reason. According to psychiatric experience you will probably come into conflict with your fellow men soon, because your perception, your view of the world, and your patterns of behavior, thought, and emotion deviate from those of your fellows. And since the majority will not be on your side, it might well be your fate to be removed from society and sent to a clinic or an asylum in which you will be provided with some form of therapy.

How do you and others come to consider some views and statements about the world as true or false? How can you test your perception and distinguish illusion, hallucination, deception, imagination, dream, and all the other monstrous products of your fantasy from reality? What separates mad thinking, feeling, and acting from normal thinking, feeling, and acting? But above all, how can the emergence of one or the other be explained?

Should you be a little confused by what you have read so far or by what you have not read (God knows what you expected!), then you have been allowed a little taste of the confusion into which those who occupy themselves intensively with madness and madnesses are plunged. Of course, the helplessness aroused by a written text can transmit only a vague idea of what happens to the social existence of people who mean something to each other when they confront or experience madness. Nevertheless, this modest attempt to give you a slight and harmless idea of some of the interactional and logical aspects of madness is undertaken for a simple reason: speaking, writing, or reading about madness is something quite different from inducing and experiencing it. It is the kind of difference that exists between a menu, the preparation of the meal, and the meal itself.

Anyone who eats recipe books is mad.

PSYCHOSIS OR MADNESS? ON THE DIFFICULTY IN FINDING THE FITTING TERM

To limit this book's and to preclude misunderstandings, the term *madness* is used here to express types of behavior, thinking, and feeling that are described in psychiatric textbooks as an expression of mental illness and emotional disorder, as psychopathological symptoms of so-called endogenous psychosis. People who behave in such a way that they are finally given a diagnosis covering this spectrum seem to have lost or left the reality that is so self-evident to the rest of us. Their experience deviates from that of their fellows in a characteristic way. They seem to think and feel in a way others can barely or absolutely not comprehend, and their behavior is less predictable than that of other people. Their thinking, feeling, and behavior seem not to be determined simply by chance, but ordered differently—not normally. When one observes the various, externally perceptible aspects of such patients' behavior and includes those patients' own reports on their self-observation and experience, typical patterns and rules of internal emotional processes deviating from the norm can be distinguished. Over the past century traditional psychiatry assumed (and still assumes) that these complexes of psychopathological symptoms can be dissociated from one another, diagnostically assigned to different basic illnesses, and given different names.

In this book, diagnostic labels such as schizophrenia or manic-depressive disorder are used merely to describe characteristic phenomena—patterns of behavior, feeling, and thinking—in contrast to the tacit bias of the concept of the illness. They do not imply any kind of explanation in the sense of an organic model of pathology. This dissociative preliminary remark is necessary since the description of phenomena is so easily and fatally equated with, and mistaken for, its explanation when such medical terms are used.

The question of how these phenomena emerge goes beyond the limited frame of medicine to the field of elementary intellectual, ethical, and political problems. It is a question of what is deemed true, beautiful, and good in society. One cannot speak of madness without saying something about normality, nor about normality without saying something about madness. Only by being dissociated from each other do madness and normality gain contour and content. The question of the development of madness is thus a question of the origin of normality. Every attempt at a global and complete answer to these questions would be megalomaniacal, that is, rather mad. The complexity one is confronted with in such a case is too great. However, what can be attempted, and is attempted here, is the development of a model that simplifies this complexity enough to enable the construction of correlations of meaning and explanations useful in day-to-day life. It intends to provide all who have anything to do with madness(es) (and who hasn't) with a frame of orientation for behavior in day-to-day life and for dealing with it.

Unfortunately a model like this cannot be put together using a fretsaw, like the model of a house, and thus rendered concrete and understandable. It has to be produced by means of language. As in the construction of all such models, the question of the choice of suitable building materials—that is the fitting term—arises. The fact that here the expression "madness" is given preference over "mental disorder" or "psychosis" has to do with the magical effect of words: they change what they name, and sometimes they even give rise to it.

If you say, for example, "Mr. Smith has psychosis" or "He has a mental disorder," you give the impression that Mr. Smith and his mental disorder are two separate things. Just as Mr. Smith can own a bicycle or a house, he can also call a psychosis his own. It only seems logical then to come to the conclusion that he can be freed from his psychosis in the same way that his bike could be stolen or his house seized. Strangely enough, the use of the term "psychosis" or "illness" only seldom seems to suggest the equally plausible idea that Mr. Smith could simply leave his mental disorder somewhere by mistake like he could his bicycle, leave it on the subway like an umbrella, or sell it like his house. The term "illness," this magical formula that seems to explain everything, makes him a passive minor character in the story.

As we usually believe that what has a name exists, the choice of words determines what we consider to be an object for independent contemplation or examination. If we separate Mr. Smith from his psychosis or his mental disorder, we find ourselves in Alice's Wonderland where the ever-smiling Cheshire cat suddenly disappears, leaving only its smile (Carroll 1865). We let Mr. Smith simply disappear while preserving his psychosis. Then we can study it independent of Mr. Smith, his life history, and conditions, cut it into small pieces, and, when we finally believe we have understood its mechanism, try to put it back together again.

It is difficult, though, to find a better phrase or a more fitting term. If we replace "to have" with "to be," we change the tacit bias in the meanings of our words and the indirect suggestions connected with them ("If you've got something, then you are someone!"). Changing the words in this way does not improve the situation very much though: "If you've got a psychosis or a mental disorder, you're psychotic, mentally ill, a psychotic, a mentally ill person." Tell me what you are and I'll tell you who you are—that is the rule according to which a person is given a certain identity in our daily language and the logic it entails. The separation of the person and the psychosis we just lamented is indeed offset by such a choice of words; instead, a no less lamentable lasting identification of a person with his or her often merely temporary way of thinking, feeling, and behaving comes into force.

Although in the former case we were dealing with a relationship between partners in which one of the two partners (the patient) suffered under the other (the mental disorder), they are now indistinguishable, the best of friends. In the first case at least there was still a possibility, as in other partnerships, that they would separate and go their own way in peace or that one would leave the other amicably or in hostility. However, in the latter case there is a danger that the phenomenon named "ill" becomes the person's identifying characteristic recorded in his passport. This causes them to fuse into an inseparable entity (until death do us part).

There is a further risk connected with the use of the terms "mental disorder" or "endogenous psychosis." They might give rise to the impression that someone knows exactly how madness originated. If we look more closely at what is actually meant by the term "psychosis," it is rapidly seen to be a false pretense. In the code language of doctors, the suffix "osis" always implies that it is a case of something that falls outside the frame of normality, that illness is attached to it. "Endogenous" is merely a nice-sounding word to veil

the fact that nobody really knows how to explain this occurrence.[1]
So when a doctor determines that a patient has an endogenous
psychosis, all he is really saying, in a way that will harm himself
and his future as little as possible and will benefit his prestige, is
that he knows as little as his colleagues about why the patient behaves the way he does.

In this case illness is not only a metaphor of questionable value
but also a program for the future, an instruction for action and
treatment. If you look for explanations for it, you naturally use
methods that have proved useful for explaining other illnesses. As
in the case of syphilis, one tries to expose and isolate the cause of
public offense, namely psychosis. The hunt for the offender (the
notorious schizococcus) once again starts from the assumption of a
division in at least two distinguishable entities: psychosis and its
cause.

The advantage of the term "madness" is, first, that it is barely
charged with medical bias. The aureole of meaning surrounding
madness derives from much more mundane fields. How often do
we find ourselves saying "you must be mad" as a reaction to behavior or ideas that deviate ever so slightly from what is considered
the norm? In the same way that loose screws are a sign of disorder,
madness implies that a kind of disorder has developed—suddenly,
with no gradual transition, just like that. Madness means then that
someone's standpoint, the spatial or temporal order in which he
orients himself and lives, has changed.

Screws that fit tight and are fastened properly are indeed a sign
of the order of the human mind, but are certainly no measure of it.
The models of explanation and solution contained in the metaphor
of the loose screws are a little bit simple: "Who loosened the screws?"
and "Who is going to tighten them back up again?" are the questions that arise immediately. Where such a static form of disorder
rules, it is only too easy for those who bring order and those who
make sure of order, with their terribly simplifying and easy answers,

---

1. From the Greek *éndon* in, inside and *génos* cause, create.

to believe their time has come. There is good reason to doubt that their methods of action (treatment) are preferred to that of the doctors.

So let us turn once more (torn this way and that) to the term "illness" to see whether the dangers linked with its use are not outweighed by the advantages. Its main advantage is that the disorder it describes is dynamic. Health (order) and illness (disorder) are both linked with the life process, which is the prerequisite for both. A person can be critically ill, but when he is finally dead he is no longer ill (but not well either, of course). Thus illness and health are not only opposites but they also have a common basis: the living organism.

Having established that, the disorder of illness is not a medley of odd things thrown haphazardly on a garbage heap; it is rather an ordered disorder. If an observer sees the same physical changes (symptoms), their origin, their peak, and their disappearance in different people, he can regard them as distinguishable entities and give them an independent existence following certain laws. Just like living beings or persons they seem to have an unmistakable character, differentiated by race and class, and equipped with more or less good or bad traits. Measles and mumps, chicken pox, and acne can thus be identified as recognizable entities and given unmistakable names. However, doing so does not name things; it names specific differences in bodily functioning.

One could, of course, equally well imagine classifying the various ways in which "the screws are loose": wear and tear, broken off, simply missing, and the like. However, it is considerably more difficult to apply autonomous laws, characteristic and recurrent attributes, and a distinguishable identity, independent of the arbitrary decision of the observer, to these different types of disorder.

The meaning of the term "illness" that directs attention to patterns of dynamic processes could be an argument for regarding madness as an illness. But are we dealing with the same patterns of processes here? Is it really a question of physical processes whose order has gotten mixed up? Can, should, may, or must the social and medical evaluation and treatment of physical illnesses simply be transferred to madness?

The people in his environment do not generally make a patient who has measles responsible (blame him or regard him as the cause) for the red spots on his skin. His behavior, though, is quite a different matter. Over and above all the symptoms of so-called endogenous psychosis are deviating behavioral patterns. Is deviating behavior always the symptom of an illness then? If one measured the blood pressure, the adrenocortical hormone level, and similar physiological values of the members of the famous gang of safe-busters whenever they were occupied in opening the main safe of a bank, one would be able to register specific physical changes in them too. But does this mean that they have or even suffer from some kind of "-osis"? There are undoubtedly many examples where human behavior can be explained by physical processes. So what distinguishes criminality from illness? Should we close down the prisons and build psychiatric hospitals instead?

Making the right decision here has wide-ranging consequences. It is an ethical, political, and legal question that touches on the main areas of our social life. How much responsibility can, should, or must we attribute to a person for his way of thinking, feeling, and acting?

The answer to this question is a fundamental philosophical problem that has lost none of its relevance over the centuries. As Kant (1789) pointed out, it falls neither within the competence of doctors nor of lawyers:

Ranting (delirium) in a person who is awake but in a feverish condition is a physical disturbance and requires medical precautions. Only someone who rants and in whom the doctor can find no such signs of disease is called mad; whereby the word disturbed is merely a milder expression. So when someone has deliberately caused an accident and the court is now called upon to determine whether, and in what way, blame can be attached to him, the question which must consequently be determined beforehand is whether he was mad at the time or not. In this case the court cannot refer him to the medi-

cal faculty but should (due to the incompetence of the court of justice) refer him to the philosophical faculty. For the question whether
the defendant was in possession of his full mental faculties and powers of discretion at the time of his crime is absolutely psychological
and, although a physical eccentricity of mind might well be the cause
of an unnatural violation of the lawful duties (inherent in every
human being), the doctors and physiologists in general cannot yet
look so deep into the mechanics of man as to be able to explain the
impulse to such an atrocity or (without the anatomy of the body) to
see it beforehand. [p. 528]

Those who occupy themselves with the origin of madness and
normality—that is, the putative natural intelligence and/or legal
obligations inherent in every man, and the putative abnormality of
intelligence and the violation of legal obligations—soon are caught
up in a gray area in which the borders between territories and areas
of competence of the various sciences and social institutions are
mutually exclusive or overlap. The representatives of these specialized fields use their inevitably limited perspectives as a base and
thus develop their specific explanations and treatment models. One-
track physiologists thus come into competition with one-track psychologists, sociologists with theologists, and psychiatrists with law
specialists and their respective one-track specialist truths. Each uses
his own code language, which makes it impossible for the uninitiated to join in.

Over the past forty to fifty years, however, a scientific model has
been developed that provides the opportunity to combine all involved
areas, to cross the barriers of various fields, and develop a common
metaperspective and language: the model of systems theory and
cybernetics, especially that of self-organization. This model is concerned with the general origin and maintenance, the disturbance,
change, and disintegration of order. At present no other scientific
approach is equally capable of doing justice to the complexity of
the phenomenon of madness. Systems theory can be used in biology as well as in psychology and sociology, in physics as in philosophy. Its main advantage is that it provides not only new answers to
old questions but, far more importantly, new questions to old an-

swers; what has been self-evident up to now becomes incomprehensible. The fact that something is self-evident does not mean that we understand it, merely that we do not question it. All of a sudden not only the exception to the rule needs explaining, but the rule itself. The inevitable question arises as to how normal structures develop, how they are established and maintained.

One of the advantages of this theoretical approach is that it shifts the viewpoint of the observer to things that were self-evident up to this point. In this way problems can be explained in unusual ways, and new ways out of old impasses are revealed that were previously undreamt of. For the treatment of madness in particular, this shift in viewpoint seems desperately necessary in the face of the enormous helplessness and despair of patients, relatives, doctors, therapists, and helpers of all kinds.

Contemplating madness can also be of value to those not directly affected by it, however, since the principal difference between the madness of our private, social, and political lives and the madness observable in asylums is not so very great.[2]

------

2. The sparse footnotes that name and cite only a few people whose ideas and works have contributed in some way to this book are really intended only for those readers who read it for scientific purposes. All the others need not bother about the footnotes—with the exception of this one and the very last one.

2

A Model of Self-Organization

MIND AND BODY: DIVISION OF THE INDIVIDUAL

Whether the spirit is considered willing and the flesh weak or the flesh willing and the spirit weak, one always distinguishes between body and spirit. This seems to be one of the self-evident truths in our use of language. The division between the two is immediately clear to anyone who has ever absented himself spiritually from boring company in spite of being present in body. But even if—or because—it corresponds to our everyday experience, the question of the relationship between mind and body, body and soul, idea and matter arises nevertheless. It arises in particular, of course, when the role of bodily and spiritual, nonmaterial and material processes in the origin of madness is to be examined.

The mind–body question has a long tradition in philosophy and science. From time immemorial, philosophers (in earlier times this category included natural scientists as well) have been occupied with the problem of what relation the world as it is bears to the knowledge of the world. Descartes was one of the most important thinkers in the development of our present, largely scientifically influenced view of the world. He made a clear dissociation between the spiritual and material field, which has helped determine not only the division between Science and the Arts up to the present day but also our everyday ideas about the relationship between body and soul, between things in the world out there and our view of them.

Descartes divides the world into "res cogitans" and "res extensa," into something like thinking and extended matter or extended thing,[1]

---

1. From the Latin *res* meaning thing, matter; *cogitare* meaning to think; and *extensus* meaning extended.

that is, mind and body. For him, both are substances existing independently of one another that express themselves through their attributes (i.e., their characteristics, their essence, their nature) and
can be understood on their own, without the prerequisite of other
characteristics. He sees thought, or rather its modes of feeling,
wanting, desiring, imagining, and judging (in the affirmative and
in the negative) as an attribute of mind. He sees the extension, or
its various ways of appearing, as an attribute of body; for example,
position, shape, movement, and size.

The basis on which Descartes' system stands is the assumption
of innate concepts (*idea innatae*). Such concepts enable reality to
be described and explained. Since they are innate, they need not be
questioned—they cannot be anyway. One of these concepts is God.
Others are the logical fundamental principles—the cause, extension,
number, but above all the idea of substance (of a thing). It is important to remember this idea of innate concepts as they are of
essential importance for the sequences and phenomena combined
with madness (this is also the reason for devoting so much space to
Descartes at this point).

Starting from these prerequisites, this actual state, Descartes
outlines his model of human cognition. His method is doubt. He
only accepts as true what is clearly comprehensible as the essence
of an object. His doubt is aimed above all at the senses. What they
feign cannot be accepted as real. As a doubting subject, however, I
cannot doubt myself, for I have to be in order to doubt. The self-
reference of my thinking gives me the certainty that I am. *Cogito
ergo sum*; I think, therefore I am.

By the way, this self-reference implicitly means that I, as a doubter
finally convinced of my being, identify myself with the *res cogitans*.
My body is thus, as a part of the *res extensa*, separate from me and
has become an object outside myself.

Descartes compares the substance of thinking, in which a fixed
point has been found by the self-certainty of the thinker, to the
substance of extended things. He uses God to connect both substances and to re-establish the wholeness of the world. God created
the world as a whole (for Descartes this is a given truth inherent in

the idea of God), so physical reality cannot be doubted as a fact. God is perfect (for Descartes this again is a self-evident truth inherent in the idea of God), so He cannot be evil or deceitful. As He gave man reason, man can rely on the results of his rational thinking. In this respect a conclusive relationship can be established between objective reality and the results of rational thought (compare von Aster 1932, p. 200 and Jaspers 1937, p. 10).

This line of argument no longer appears quite as cogent as it did in Descartes' time. In particular the explanation about why man can rely on the results of rational thought, but not on his sensory perception, although both come from God, leaves many questions unanswered.

Conceding rationality a special position in cognition of the world has widespread consequences. Rationality's claim to truth and power was originally legitimated by its doctrine of divine right, as was worldly power. Even if this explanation for the truth of rational cognition is no longer used, the claim of comprehending the truth has remained. It is particularly important that even the outer perspective of observation conceded to God, as the creator of all things, is taken for granted as the basis of rational thought. The understanding subject is not of this world; it stands outside the things that make up the world, it is separate from them, and it looks on their surface from the outside.

This split between subject and object in Descartes' model of cognition pervades the body and mind of man as a whole. Thus he can, and must, face and interact with an object called the body that is separate from himself. It is a split in which it definitely makes sense to fight against the impulses and wishes coming from the body, to discipline, subject, and control it; during his daily toilet man only needs to wash his body, not himself. Descartes did not invent this split between body and soul; the idea of wandering souls, of souls going from one body to another, of their living on after death, and similar concepts have existed for thousands of years and form the basis of many great world religions. This distinction is even an important element of Christianity, whose God plays such an important role in Descartes' connection between *res cogitans* and *res extensa*.

Should one wish to bring the Cartesian model of cognition and world view together, it must first be ascertained that Descartes starts from a world that is as it is. It has been created by God in the same way that a machine is constructed and assembled by an engineer. Its parts are separate things whose characteristics cannot be traced back to each other. This machine runs, but its mechanisms are static and unchangeable. The correlation of these objects, which by nature exist independent from each other, is determined by mechanical laws. Cause and effect are combined in such a way that the cause determines the effect. The mind striving for cognition stands opposite this machine. In principle its observations have no effect on the material processes being observed. The rules of mechanics in the outside world correspond to the rules of reason inside. The truth can only be found by following these rules. Cognition is, when successful, a reproduction of reality. The aim is to make this clockwork world calculable and predictable.

With his distinction between *res cogitans* and *res extensa*, between observer and observed object, Descartes made a clever move. He prevented the *res cogitans* from ever being made the object of cognition. If concepts are innate and God makes sure that the relationship between them and their meaning is appropriate, we no longer need to concern ourselves with the question of the relationship between body and mind. The problem of the self-reference of cognition, of cognition that tries to understand itself and that has helped a good many philosophers to the gray hair befitting their rank, does not occur.

The split between the subject and the object of cognition inevitably gives way when a person observes himself. The indivisible (individual) is divided when one deals with one's own body, one's own experience, thinking, feeling, and behavior in accordance with the Cartesian pattern. If we pose the question about the relationship between body and soul, between mind and matter, between idea and body, we cannot accept the division of an individual into two areas of reality that are dissociated from each other and yet immediately next to one another as God given and self-evident. We need a theoretical model that can overcome this split and can grasp not merely the characteristics of any isolated substances standing next to each other but also the characteristic of these characteristics relating to one another.

PART, WHOLE, AND ENVIRONMENT

In nearly all traditional scientific fields—in natural sciences as well as the humanities—the models of cybernetics[2] and systems theory have found widespread use since the Second World War. They can be seen not only as new sciences apart from those already existing but also as a new view that transcends the conventional borders of individual disciplines without ignoring them. At first they developed in the same tradition as the Cartesian world view. Their prerequisite was that the observer perceive the examined object (called a *system*) from the outer perspective, the well-known and well-established split between the subject and object of cognition. As this method was first developed by engineers concerned with the construction and control of machines, this outer perspective was natural and useful. Systems were constructed or examined, that is, objects were put together from several pieces, and their behavior was a result of the combination of all of the parts. The material characteristics of this whole and its parts were not of interest, but rather its behavior, regulation, and control.

When engineers then started constructing machines such as the thermostat, which worked wonderfully, it was established that the explanation of the method by which they worked clashed with several well-loved ideas about the relationship between cause and effect. It is one of the bases of our scientific view of the world that an event that wants to be considered the cause of another event should kindly take place before this effect. In contrast, machines such as the thermostat are able to control certain behaviors—for example, that the heat comes on when the room temperature cools down—

2. Cybernetics from the Greek *kybernétes* meaning helmsman; system from the Greek *syn* meaning together and *histanai* meaning put.

because the interaction of their parts is organized in such a way that a clear distinction between effect and cause is impossible. A course of action is dictated by a certain behavior. It is able to correct itself, as it were, by compensating for disturbances and deviations from a desired nominal value.

Biologists who investigated how certain bodily structures and forms of balance are maintained in organisms found such feedback loops wherever the stability of life processes was concerned. The maintenance of body temperature at 37°C is an example of this principle of control.

An observer who wishes to analyze the dynamics of such events will find it impossible to describe a direct cause–effect relationship with a good conscience. He can neither blame the high room temperature for the heat not starting up (after all, the heating system itself made sure that it had nothing more to do), nor can he accuse the heating system for warming the room up so much (it was the cooler room temperature that switched the heat on in the first place).

Where the link between a certain condition or event (E) and other events or conditions $(E_1 \ldots E_m)$ is such that it forms a circle, these other events are not only the adequate (eventually even necessary) conditions for E but E is also a condition for $E_1 \ldots E_m$. The events or conditions taking place can be described by a law, by which the original and caused events are connected recursively, that is, running back in a circle. Their interaction is organized in such a way that they stabilize each other. Every effect can be regarded as the cause of an effect that itself is the cause of this effect. Of course such a circle is often considerably wider, and quite a number of such causes and effects are involved, so that finally one loses track. Yet even in much more complicated dynamic systems, this same circular form of organization can be found in which the events and conditions that form it develop a self-referential effect.

Even if cybernetics and systems theory do not allow the cause–effect relationships to be established in a conventional sense, they do make the description of logical links and patterns (if/then) possible. As opposed to the causal explanation, the responsibility or blame for other events and conditions or the behavior of the other elements of a system is not attributed to an event or condition or to the behavior of an element of the examined system. Instead, an entity is taken into consideration, the elements of which are combined in a net of interrelationships in which each determines the conditions of all others. Accordingly, the objects of examination are structures and functions, the relationship of elements within a whole structure, the rules of interaction, and the transformation and change of conditions and structures in the system.

However, the question of the relationship of the parts to the whole is only one aspect of cybernetics and systems theory. The second main emphasis, one that has come very much to the fore in the past few years, is the examination of distinctions between system and environment (Luhmann 1984). What influence do changes in the environment of a system have on processes within the system? How does a system emerge as a separate and distinguishable entity, that is, how does the difference between system and environment arise, how is it preserved in the interaction of the system with its environment, and how does the system develop and preserve its structure and form?

The fact that systemic concepts are so abstract and not tied to specific material content allows them to be used in almost all fields of science. They thus can be compared to mathematics, which does not stipulate that, when three and four are added together, this always means apples or pears. The principles of counting and basic arithmetic can be applied to all other concrete objects without specialized knowledge of them. In the same way you can apply the systems and cybernetic concepts in specialist fields that have nothing to do with one another at first glance. Just as the three apples and four pears amount to something new when counted together (seven, a different number of fruit), in the question of the relationship between mind and body it is possible to study the interrelations between bodily and mental processes, transformations of one into the other, dissociations from one another and from a common environment, the development and maintenance of specific structures, the formation and dissolution of units, and similar concepts. The question is no longer one of the relationship between two different substances, but of the relationship of control mechanisms, of the development and preservation of order, of its change and destruction. From this viewpoint mind and body belong to a unified field.

LIVING SYSTEMS

What needed no explanation for Descartes is highly mysterious from a cybernetic perspective: the fact that something stays as it is, or at least appears to, for us as observers.

Descartes describes a world that is (God-)given as it actually is. Man has been set in this world of things and objects and has to think about their being (the state of being). As well as his dealings with these things, this thinking is characteristic of *res cogitans*, the mind. He tries to find out the plan according to which God, that great designer and sculptor, created this world. Mechanical laws form the classic example of this building plan. When you have grasped them, you can handle things better and subordinate them. The static order of this world is one of its self-evident truths. It is always the changes, the movement, the dynamics that need explaining. The tacit bias of this world view is: everything stays as it is, unless someone makes it change.

From the cybernetic-systemic point of view, in contrast, the movement of all that exists and its continuous change are self-evident. When dynamics and change are taken for granted, constancy and statics become a mystery. How can you explain that we as observers have the impression that we live in a world of things and objects? After all, many of the objects that furnish our environment preserve their forms and characteristics quite reliably.

Undoubtedly the traditional model, tacitly presupposing statics, has proved its worth in many areas of day-to-day life as well as in science. In dealing with life processes, its usefulness is limited, however. It is linked with the risk that one abstracts from just what characterizes life processes, their dynamics, and the fact of their being a process. An example will clarify the difference between static systems to which the laws of mechanics can be applied effectively and living systems.

Let us look at the car as an example of such a static system. A designer conceives it and prepares a construction drawing; then workers and machines construct its parts (engine, gear box, body work, seats, windows, wheels, and ashtray). It is made up of a great number of individual pieces. When this wonder of human creation has finally been completed, it remains as it is, unless some kind of outside force affects it. The wing preserves the wonderful roundness that transports the proud car owner into deep reverence until the nice neighbor decides he does not like it any more and dents it with his old scrap heap that only reaps scorn and pity. The paint work retains its gloss until wind and weather weaken its luster. And the car as a whole dissolves into its various parts (which frequently change shape too) when interaction with a tree is too fierce or occurs at too high a speed. Even if it was still mobile until it became a write-off, the observer had good reason to consider the car as a static system. The relationship between its parts remained constant, just as its creators intended. Any change required an outside force to have an effect on this system. In this way the dent in the wing could only be removed by the outside force of a rubber hammer. Without its beneficial effect, the dent would have stayed where the traumatic, and thus impressive, meeting with the neighbor had created it. The system of the car was just as passive during the repairs as during its creation, which it also suffered without active resistance.

The situation is quite different in a living system. If, for example, a human being gets a lump on his forehead after bumping into a cabinet door, this lump disappears on its own after a few days. Man's living system does not need a rubber hammer to work on it from the outside or a mechanic to actively remove damage while the damaged system remains passive. It repairs itself. However, if someone were to go around with a lump on his head for a long time, the question would arise as to how this could happen, in contrast to the case of the car. The answer is probably that he bumps into the cabinet once a day. In this case the preservation of a certain structure (the lump) needs explaining, as it normally disappears quite naturally. The same applies to scratches in the paint work of a living being.

The difference between the two lumps and their history ought to be obvious. In practice this difference becomes important where the art of therapy is concerned; where dealing with people and human systems, education, psychotherapy, or organizational behavior is concerned; where the difference between the mechanic and the doctor, but also where the explanation of chronic disorders, that is, long-term deviations from a biological or behavioral norm, is concerned.

Inevitably the question arises as to how normal structures are produced and maintained. To use Lichtenberg's words: "It's really amazing that the cat has two holes cut in its fur right where the eyes are."

The most striking difference between a static and a living system lies in the fact that living systems have to be actively maintained. Constancy and lack of change require activity: everything changes unless someone or something makes sure that it stays the way it is.

A well-shaven man is only a well-shaven man as long as someone makes sure that he stays that way (nowadays it is usually himself and his razor). In this case the morning shave is the activity required to maintain the status quo. A never-ending, regularly recurring necessity that deserves comparison with the trials of Sisyphus.

A living organism requires certain activities to remain a living organism. On the one hand are processes that take place within it, such as circulation and metabolism; on the other hand there are closely related behaviors that it must carry out, such as eating, drinking, and excreting. The individual bodily functions preserve the main structures. The biologists Humberto Maturana (1975, 1982) and Francisco Varela (1979) give this process of self-creation and self-preservation of the organism the term *autopoiesis*.[3] They describe life as a process in which living systems produce themselves as entities. Even if the term suggests it, autopoiesis does not mean the production of something by something else, as a car by the designer

---

3. From the Greek *autos* meaning self and *poiesis* meaning product, work, poem.

and the mechanics with their machines, as described above, but a process in which the difference between the one who designs and what is designed, between the tools and the product, between the factory and the brand, is dissolved.

As in the case of the thermostat, a feedback loop is involved in autopoiesis; the self-reference of the effect of processes can be described from the perspective of the external observer. Only in this process it is not a value as trite as room temperature that is kept constant, but a physical structure. A creation takes place in which one can no longer distinguish between subject and object, between the creature created and its creator.

DEVELOPMENT AND AUTONOMY OF THINGS

According to the assumptions of the Cartesian view of the world, the relationship between things, articles, objects, and their characteristics, behaviors, and effects are independent from the observer. Objects are considered as isolated units and examined for their features and characteristics. In Figure 2–1 the connection between the structure and function of an object is outlined as assumed in this concept.

The observer can say nothing about the thing as such, only about its externally perceived form, its characteristics, and structure (whereby these terms are mostly used without clearly distinguishing among them). He can also say something about the behavior of this thing, its effect on another thing, how it functions, and its purpose. He can separate structure and function, that is, the method of construction and the way it works. This separation usually occurs in such a way that the peculiarities of the construction method give the explanation for the particular way it works. A washing machine is constructed in such a way that it can do the washing. The way such an object works connects it with the objects in its environment on which it can work (the washing machine with the washing).

The difference that is produced by the self-reference of the way living systems work is illustrated in Figure 2–2.

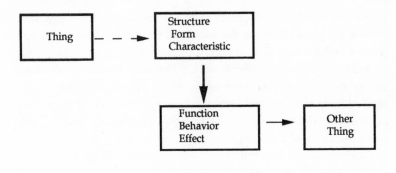

Figure 2–1

Living systems work in the same way as would a washing machine (not yet created by human hands) that is able to wash itself.
Structure and function are in correlation, so the observer can choose
between explaining the function by the structure or the structure
by the function. The distinction between the two seems rather arbitrary and thus dubious. Both are merely different aspects of an
identical process, which finally leads to the external observer perceiving a stable entity distinct from the environment: the cat always
with the same holes where the eyes are.

In the same way, we can consider the origin of a cell membrane,
for example, as the result of cell metabolism. But that metabolism
is possible only because the cell membrane functions as a border
for the environment and so creates the internal space for it (see
Varela 1981). The distinction between system and environment, the
cell unit, is produced and maintained by this circular process.

The process by which living structures receive their form is depicted more adequately in Figure 2–3.

The activities of an organism and the way it works, its operations,
have repercussions on itself. They are self-referential. It is not the
environment or any causes in this environment that ensure that a
living thing preserves its form, but rather the system itself. This
process is called "operational closure"; it can be considered the

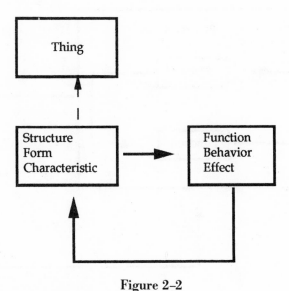

Figure 2–2

distinctive feature of the autonomy of living systems (Varela 1979, von Foerster (1988).

In his works on the ecology of mind, Gregory Bateson (1979) interprets how order originates by self-referential processes that preserve themselves as mind. Not only are life processes organized according to this pattern but also all stable structures. Even the car, which we use as an example of a static structure, can be regarded as the result of such a self-referential, operationally closed process. The only difference is that in inanimate objects, these processes, which allow those objects to preserve their form and structure, occur in a different area of perception, on a different scale: on the molecular level. In order to become aware of them, other methods of observation and examination must be applied. With this extensive understanding of mind as self-referential, Bateson can regard mind and nature as an inseparable unity. The entire universe can then not only be understood as a single, ongoing process of self-organization but also

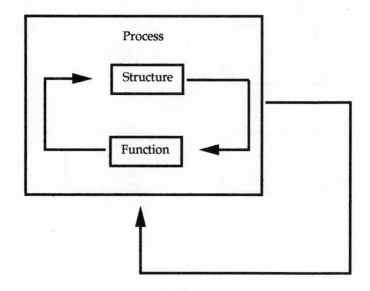

Figure 2–3

as a mental process (see Jantsch 1979). The distinction between mind and matter is superfluous, as material things are the result of mental processes.

One can argue whether such an extensive understanding of mind is meaningful and useful. In any case the features of mental activities—thinking, feeling, acting, and the development and stabilization of psychological structures—also appear in a new light if we see them, as we do all other life processes, as the result of such self-referential sequences that order and stabilize themselves. The mad behavior of a patient cannot be attributed only to a structure that has been disturbed at some time, the psychic trauma, the lump from early childhood, or to a currently disturbed biological function. Instead the process of self-organization of madness as part of the self-organization of all mental processes (in the narrower, traditional sense) must be examined.

THE CYBERNETICS OF CYBERNETICS

The belief in the possibility of objective human cognition, independent of the conditions of the observer, dwindled when cyberneti-
cians began to relate their theories on the self-referential organization of living systems to themselves. In all their statements about
systems, they had tacitly assumed that they were outside these systems and were looking at something from the outside that happened
independent of them and their observation. They were forced to
question this self-certainty. If we look at the larger, overall system—
observer plus system observed by him—we can no longer start from
the outer perspective of observation. The so-called innocent observer
suddenly sees himself as a participating observer who must suspect
himself not only of describing the behavioral patterns of a system
"recognized" by him but also of stabilizing or, even worse, of triggering them in the first place. The neutral and harmless objective
chronicler thus becomes the agent provocateur.

With the observation of observation, the consequent step from
cybernetics to the cybernetics of cybernetics is made, that is, the
application of cybernetic concepts to cybernetics itself.[4] The cybernetics of cybernetics, also called second-order cybernetics, examines
the correlation between the thinking subject and the object of
his cognition. If the observer by observing interferes in the self-
referential process that creates and maintains the structures and
functions of the observed system, it is absolutely possible that he
changes, preserves, or creates what he is observing. The statements
about the object are thus always statements about the observer, his
structures, and behaviors (Figure 2–4).

The fact that human cognition has repercussions on what is being
examined seems at first view to run counter to our everyday understanding of cognition and knowledge. If someone knows that he has
to drive a few hundred yards straight on and then turn right to get
to the train station, this knowledge does not change the location of
the station. The situation is different if he knows which road to take

---

4. This concept was developed by Heinz von Foerster (1974).

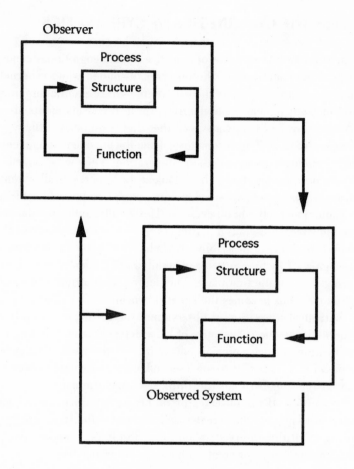

Figure 2–4

to get to a lonely beach. As soon as enough people know about this lonely beach, its position remains the same, but it will not be a lonely beach for very long.

It is a fatal mistake to assume that knowledge is something like a picture, a photo that is put into a drawer and can then cause no harm (or at most be of some use). There are many areas in which the process of cognition has no noteworthy or considerable effect on what has been discerned. To know the course of the stars and be able to predict eclipses of the sun apparently has no very great influence on the sun. In this case the assumption of the external objective perspective seems to be justified. Since Heisenberg's (1989) formulation of the uncertainty principle, it is clear that the assumption that the process of observing an object doesn't change the object does not apply to the field of microphysics, since there the measurement changes what is being measured. Such an influence of the observation on what is being observed is infinitely more clear in our social and cultural life.

From a medical and psychiatric point of view, the cybernetics of cybernetics gains importance as all humans can be regarded as observers, and as observers, they constantly watch other observers observing them. Highly complex self-referential processes result, in the course of which individual and collective structures of cognition, knowledge, and belief ensue—whether rational or irrational.

As clinical epistemology[5] or the science of cognition, cybernetics can thus devote itself to the questions of the connection between bodily processes and mental processes and how they form, change, stabilize each other, and develop together. The special interest of such a clinical science of cognition is how characteristic patterns of belief, knowledge, and behavior raise or lower the danger of developing any bodily or mental symptoms (Dell 1986, Simon 1988).

THE PROCESSIONARY MOTH:
AN EXPERIMENT IN SELF-ORGANIZATION

To carry out this experiment you need quite a number of people who either volunteer to take part or have to participate whether they want to or not. In addition, you require a level surface on which no one can stumble or bump into any objects lying around while playing a sophisticated form of blindman's bluff. Both conditions

---

5. From the Greek *epistéme* meaning knowledge, cognition.

are fulfilled in ballrooms with large dance floors and with all the people willing to follow the instructions of a bandleader or on a barrack square full of soldiers who even obey seemingly senseless commands. But these are not the only places to carry out the experiment. Gymnasiums or school playgrounds are very suitable too. Should you (which is improbable) not be able to recruit so many test subjects, you will have to content yourself with carrying out the experiment in your mind.

So now you have 80 to 200 (or more) persons at your disposal who are willing to do what you tell them. First, you blindfold them one at a time and give each the following instructions:

> "Walk carefully and without any great effort around the room, with outstretched arms, until your hands touch the bar that has been set up somewhere. When you get there you will receive—according to your desire and taste—a glass of beer, wine, spirits, or champagne. The experiment is then over for you, and you may enjoy your reward in peace. [The reward can be varied in accordance with the context.] If your hands touch another person during the search for the bar, do not let that person go. Put your hands on his shoulders and follow him in blind trust, as you will also get your reward when he finds the bar. Should someone put his hands on your shoulders, continue your search unflustered. You are not allowed to go backward."

At the beginning of the experiment you will see a number of people hovering through the universe (the dance floor) as isolated units. But then the close encounter! First contact! An older man has touched a young lady's shoulder. As instructed he puts both hands on her shoulders and follows her like a good boy on the mutual search for promised luck—a new unit has been formed out of two elements. Something similar happens between other persons at different places. How often these collisions and connections come about depends on the number of participants and the size of the dance floor.

After a while you will see that not only have pairs been formed but also longer chains consisting of umpteen elements. Many of the originally independent individuals, pairs, trios, quadruplets, quintuplets, and so on have apparently decided to sacrifice their right to self-determination in favor of a higher community and its higher aims. They seem to have joined a kind of order with a hierarchical—virtually dictatorial—structure. Like lemmings, all follow one leader. A few minutes later you will then see that this subordination is rewarded. All together they reach their destination, and their trust is confirmed ("The best place is always at the bar," as the old German saying goes).

You can also observe the emergence of other structures. As two people put their hands on the shoulders of the same person in front, boughs and branches, treelike specimens are created as the chains grow.

Creatures known in psychology textbooks as "clinched pairs" have also created a quite curious phenomenon, which comes about against all odds when two people unfortunately meet face to face. They then hold one another's shoulders and are immobile from that point on. It is forbidden for either to go backward and neither can go forward; neither reaches the destination of his wishes.

In addition, you may possibly observe a structure whose emergence is also very improbable, yet not impossible: the leading figure of a long chain—blind to his relationship with the other occupants of the dance floor—has connected himself to the end of the chain. The circle is closed, the hierarchy dispersed. There is no leader any more, and each person is absolutely equally involved in the development and preservation of this eternally revolving circle. For the members of the circle, this outcome of the experiment is a failure if their only aim was to obtain their daily champagne. If we judge it according to esthetic categories, the mutually created circle breeds contentment. If we see it from the angle of neither efficacy nor of beauty, we merely determine that this circle is the result of a self-organizational process, a creature without a creator, a design without a designer. The responsibility for the development of the circle cannot be attributed to the abnormal behavior of the person at the front. He followed his instructions quite correctly. The other human chain that is meanwhile dancing merrily round the room to the tune of the "Polonaise" proves that it makes sense to follow these rules. The categories of merit and blame, of doing something right or wrong, provide no explanation for what is happening. They neither tell the participant who wishes to promote the formation of such a circle how he should behave, nor do they give someone who no longer wants to run around in a circle an alternative.

From the perspective of the external observer, however, it is easy to explain that, from the interaction of people who behave individually in accordance with the rules set up in this case, it is logical that inevitably only a limited number of specific social structures can develop.

Our experiment has left open the question as to how the various members of such a chain, tree, circle, or clinched pair describe themselves and the world. If we made it possible, how would you change your behavioral instructions? The participants would probably arrive at quite different descriptions from the external observer, as their eyes are blindfolded and they have no overall view of the new units that are emerging. The idea of questioning their behavior would probably not even occur to the drunken chain links hanging over the bar. But what about the structures of cognition of all those whose thirst can be traced to a lack of circulation disorders? They would probably begin by looking for the culprit. It is only the view from the outer perspective that opens up the chance to break down the self-preserving cycle. This chance is a risk when the problem is to preserve the circle.

The rules of this experiment have not been chosen arbitrarily. There are living beings who seem to follow very similar prescriptive rules: processionary moths. These are night-flying moths whose caterpillars form social systems according to an analogous pattern from which the name for the whole species has been derived. The one with a fellow of the same species in front of it follows it, and the moth with no one in front sets out to search for food.

3

The Role of the Observer

THE SPECTATOR:
AN IMAGINARY EXPERIMENT ON THE
OUTER PERSPECTIVE OF THE OBSERVER

"Did you know that the Alps look awfully sad when you imagine them without mountains?" (Gernhardt et al. 1979)!

This profound and absurd question includes (admittedly in a slightly abbreviated form) literally all the essential problems of epistemology and the theory of science dealt with by philosophers since primeval times. Whenever statements have to be made about the world as a whole, about objects of our perception, us, or natural or unnatural common sense, the question arises as to what we can imagine away (or what we may abstract) without changing the nature of what we are talking about. What is essential for the object under study, and who makes this decision? This is a question not only of philosophical but also of quite practical importance should you, for instance, be the one on whose nature someone philosophizes or the one who has to bear other consequences of such decisions.

Let us turn, then, to the question of what we can imagine away in the case of madness without being punished for it (which does not mean that it is always us who have to pay for imagining something away that ought better not be imagined away). Let us begin with an imaginary experiment to obtain guidance on this task.

These experiments have the advantage of being economical and not time consuming and offering dustless laboratory conditions that cannot be found elsewhere. When the matter is considered seriously, proper experimental research that does justice to all demands expected of it can only be performed in one's mind. For what is essential in such experiments is the fact that the conditions under which these phenomena are observed can be changed in a controlled way. Furthermore, they should not be influenced by this observation, and it must be possible to repeat the entire process. All these conditions can only be fulfilled in one's head, and only in our heads can the annoying marginal conditions that distort so many experiments be excluded, through which nature, completely insensible to the necessities of science, sabotages the most beautiful research projects again and again. One of the great masters in the performance of these experiments was the physicist Georg Christoph Lichtenberg (1742–1799) from Göttingen who perfected this method. It seems that it particularly appeals to people with a profound sense for options, so that they are able to go through what is in actual fact—momentarily—impossible in their minds. Physicists seem particularly inclined to choose this method when focusing either on some faraway galaxies to which they have no direct access or when they have run out of funds for performing proper experiments (see Schöne 1982).

Imagine that you have never ever heard anything about soccer. You do not know that such a game exists, nor do you know the rules, and you have no idea what it is or might be all about. By lucky or unlucky chance you end up one day sitting in the bleachers of a stadium. Twenty-two players, one referee, two linesmen, and a ball are on the field. Apart from you there are another 49,999 more or less enthusiastic spectators in the bleachers.

Now the first experimental change. Imagine that, with the exception of the referee, all participants (including the ball, which is undoubtedly the most swelled-headed of all involved) are wearing magic caps that make them invisible to you, but only to you. The players and the referee can see each other. A match develops, as good or as bad as any other match. The players and spectators cannot see anything different from what occurs on other game days. You are the only one influenced by the magic cap. Imagine, too, that the typical noises of a soccer match (the roars of ecstasy or indignation, whistling, horn blowing, the referee being called to the telephone, and the like) are magically concealed from your perception.

What do you see now? And what do you think about this grown-up, rushing about on the field in his black shorts, occasionally waving a yellow card, blowing a whistle, talking (to himself?), scolding, admonishing, grimacing, and gesticulating violently?

How you judge the behavior of this strange man in black depends on your diagnostic background and fantasy. If you do not believe in magical powers that operate him by remote control, you will probably look for the cause of his hyperactive and incomprehensible behavior within the limits set by his skin. Depending on the preferences of your theoretical model, you will either assume that he has a screw loose, a disordered metabolism, or some mental disorder. In all three attempts at explanation, you limit your field of observation to our test subject. You try to construct a cause-and-effect relationship between the behavior of the referee and some kind of (mechanical, physiological, or psychic) processes going on inside him.

Let us change another variable of our experimental setup. Remove the magic caps from the twenty-two players, the linesmen, and the ball. Now the referee's behavior shows itself in a slightly different light. The whistling and gesticulating with colored cards seem to occur most frequently—you now assume—when one of the gentlemen in a yellow shirt kicks one of the gentlemen in a red jersey in the shin. When you have looked for a while, you will be able to formulate rules (on a trial basis) to describe what is happening on the field. You should be aware, however, that these rules are *descriptive rules*, by which you describe the behavior of the players as you observe it. You cannot know whether our referee and the players are really following such rules (they would then be *prescriptive rules*) or just pretending to do so. In fact, you cannot make any statement about what is happening inside the people involved, about their thoughts and feelings, or about the rules governing their behavior.

At any rate, now that you have extended your field of observation beyond the borders of the individual dressed in black, his behavior seems to be a little more predictable and less absurd. You assume that it is not governed by chance, but is ordered and makes some kind of sense that is hidden somewhere in the rules of the game. In the course of time, with tenacity and imagination, you can construct a set of rules that describe not only what the referee does or does not do but also the entire match (at least what you regard as essential). Logically these rules are without contradiction; the behavior of each player is conclusive as long as it follows the rules you have found or invented. These rules do not predetermine what each player is going to do or when (soccer would be awfully boring and would have died out long ago if that were the case), but they do set up a framework of possible (permitted) and impossible (prohibited) moves.

If, however, still full of the pride of discovery, you realize that this referee, this problem child who has caused you a lot of worry, suddenly awards a penalty to the team wearing the yellow shirts in a situation that, according to what you think you know about soccer, does not call for it, what do you think then? Particularly if this happens not once (which could have been by chance, a mistake), but three times in succession? Now you have to check whether you have overlooked something essential and have to extend your set of rules. If, after careful deliberation, you arrive at the conclusion that the three situations in question had nothing convincing in common and did not differ very much from similar situations on the other side when no penalty was given, you will refrain from formulating a new rule.

However, if you now see all the numerous spectators and realize that the activities of the players are a matter not only of physical training and sports but also of money, you have to ask yourself once again whether you should extend the borders of your field of observation in order to explain these events. If you then hear that the mortgage interest on the nice little home of the referee is due next week and that a substantial amount was paid into his account one day before the match by a firm whose name is printed on the yellow shirts, this information again throws a different light on his behavior: it is no longer mad, but is now understandable, even if it is despicable, corrupt, or reprehensible.

Just as every word obtains its meaning from the sentence, and the sentence obtains its meaning from the (con-)text in which it is set, behavior obtains its meaning as mad or normal only in the interactional frame in which it is set. If we want to explain and understand madness(es), and not only that of alleged referees, we have to ask ourselves in what context we or others can observe them and provide them with a diagnostic label, and which of these context variables we can imagine away.

If we observe madness as something isolated we run the risk of dealing with it like Christian Morgenstern and (his?) knee: "A knee goes through the world alone. It is a knee, nothing else" (1985, p. 27).

THE PLAYER, THE YACHTSMAN, AND THE SHIPWRECKED PERSON: SEVERAL IMAGINARY EXPERIMENTS ON THE INNER PERSPECTIVE OF THE OBSERVER

Let us return to our fantastic soccer match again and compare the outer perspective of the spectator in the bleachers with the inner perspective of the player.

Imagine again that you have never seen a soccer match, let alone participated in one as a player. You have no idea, as in our first experiment, of the aims, purposes, and rules of this game. Now, however, you are not sitting in the bleachers, and nobody is wearing a magic cap. Instead, some unlucky fate has condemned you to participate in the match. For some vague reason, it is important for you to understand how to play this game as quickly as possible (your happiness and life depend on it). For this reason you cannot calmly take a seat in the bleachers and make notes on the conditions under which the referee pulls the red card or coaxes shrill sounds from his whistle. Instead, you are forced to act right from the start. You have to participate right away; in fact, you have to play in such a way that you at least get into no trouble with your teammates, the referee, and the spectators and at best reap their recognition and applause. Every clumsy move will provoke an echo from your teammates that either encourages you to play on as before or to avoid in future the style of play displayed so far. One of your experiences will be that every time you pick the ball up, your teammates react excitedly and signal to you that you are doing something improper. If the ball accidentally bounces off your foot into the opposing team's goal, you will be astonished to discover that the players on the field not only differ in the color of their shirts but also in their reactions to this event. Those who wear the same shirt as you will rush up to you and take your breath away with wild embraces, whereas the sad looks of the others will show their dejection, or their obscene remarks will express their rage. In the course of time you will learn to play soccer by playing soccer. The fact that you are not sent off and the others let you go on playing is proof that you have learned the rules well enough (even if you are not aware of it and answer when asked that you have not the faintest idea of the rules).

Let us now change the scenario: once again you are the test subject in an imaginary experiment. Imagine that you had never sailed, knew nothing about seamanship (not even the meaning of the word), did not know the difference between leeward and windward or between turn and wear, and mistook a shekel for a stable. If you have no idea about these terms, you are the ideal test subject. Now imagine the following terrible scene: after drinking all night you find yourself with gaps in your memory and a dull feeling in your head alone in a yacht on the open sea, with no safe shore in sight. What would you do?

First, you would have to decide whether you want to get out of these dire straits. You could passively accept your fate, be done with life, and give up. You could also—just as passively—trust in the dependability of your guardian angel and calmly await what happens. If you decide to do something yourself (be it with or without trust in your guardian angel), you have to become active and try to stay above water by means of your own strength and by using the available aids. If you finally set the sails, you will just avoid overturning the yacht, nearly run aground on a reef, and avoid other catastrophes by a fraction of an inch. You finally survive this adventure completely soaked through and with a cold—the happy end of the experiment is herewith agreed (one of the liberties pertaining to imaginary experiments). With firm ground under your feet again, you will know something more about wind and waves, boats and sails, about maneuvering and possibly about navigating while drifting too.

You have then—given a long enough apprenticeship—learned to sail while sailing. As in our first experiment your survival (even more clearly, directly, and plausibly) depended on your learning the rules of the game. But can handling a boat, wind, and weather really be compared with playing soccer? What are the connections and differences between rules of nature and social rules?

The difference between the two is immediately clear when we think of the story of the long-haul truck driver and his co-driver in their 4.20-meter-high truck coming to an overpass with the sign "Only for vehicles less than 3.80 meter height." The driver puts on his brakes and says, "We have to find another way, we can't get through here!" His co-driver replies, "Come on, step on it. Nobody's looking."

Let us add a third imaginary experiment: you are shipwrecked, stranded on an unknown island in the South Pacific. To utilize the virtually limitless epistemological possibilities opened up by fantasized catastrophes, we shall change a few of the conditions from the far too simple and obvious situation of proper shipwrecked persons. As a shipwrecked person in our experiment you not only step onto the island for the first time but you also enter your body for the first time. You have the (probably mixed) pleasure of experiencing yourself in your present bodily shape for the first time. In our experiment we are thus taking the division of mind and body seriously: both meet here for the first time.

As an observer with an outer perspective, you will have to deal with several clearly distinguishable areas of reality. Although these areas of reality function according to different rules, they are not absolutely autonomous and independent of each other. To begin with, there is the outer nature, the landscape of the island, the climate, the world of plants and animals. In addition you have to get along with the aborigines of this island, who are notorious cannibals. Whether you survive or are eaten up depends on how you come to terms with the aborigines, whether they cooperate or clash with you (and you with them). And then there is your body, the unknown being.

Your most difficult problem as such a shipwrecked person will probably be that you cannot take the position of the onlooking observer, who can set up a proper and systematic plan for the exploration of the island with its landscape, fauna, and flora. You cannot examine the anatomy and physiology of your body like a scientist. Your situation can possibly be compared best to that of an ethnologist attempting to study the culture of the islanders as a participating observer.

In contrast to the ethnologist, however, after drifting endlessly in the sea you will be hungry, thirsty, and tired. Since you have these feelings for the first time in your life, you do not know what they mean. How should you actually classify these strange new perceptions? Do they belong to you or to your environment? You do not really know who or what is responsible for all these unpleasurable feelings or what to do about them. Who are you anyway? Does your tired body belong to you or to your environment? Has it got a cold or have you? Where do you begin, and where do you end? What put the idea into your head to call that index finger of your left hand your constant companion since you set foot on the island, to call it your own or to see it as part of yourself? How can you identify yourself (you probably don't do that at all) with the reflection of your body, which you saw with narcissistic delight or fright in the still but deep water?

In order to find out all that belongs to you, it is helpful to establish what does *not* belong to you. Is, for instance, the nice aborigine, who supplied you with taro, Coca-Cola, and care ever since your arrival on the island, part of yourself like your thumb? What is the difference between the two? How do you establish the difference between outside and inside? Do your feelings and thoughts belong to you or to the outside? And what about all the dirty desires and fantasies you develop in time regarding your fellow men? Who has to bear the responsibility for them? And how do you know they are dirty? Does this evaluation come from inside or outside? When you hear the voice of a human being, does the voice come from outside the borders of your body, or is it in your head? Once you have brought yourself to set up borders between the areas you regard as belonging to you and those that do not belong to you and have thus constructed a kind of entity (in keeping with psychological tradition we shall call it your self), you have to find out how to guarantee its survival. First of all, this survival concerns the body. Which herbs are digestible and palatable? What can and should you drink? Which animals are harmless, and which are dangerous? And how do you manage to keep that laboriously drawn image of yourself free of the stains continuously aroused by feelings and thoughts, desires and fantasies, which in your view do not fit this self-image. How do you keep all the things outside that you do not want inside?

But is this sequence correct? Would you not starve if you really waited until you had found out where your borders are before eating and drinking? And what influence does the necessity to eat and drink have on setting up these borders, if the already highly praised islander supplies your needs so regularly and sensitively?

How do you communicate with him or her? How do you learn to talk to him or her and all the other people around, how do you come to terms with the others, how do you know whether to fight each other or cooperate, to hate or love?

What kind of relationships, what kind of interactions exist among all these areas: mind, body, thought, feeling, and the social and natural environment? Would you draw such distinctions at all among the different areas of reality from the inner perspective of the laboratory mouse (i.e., the fighting for survival) as is drawn here by the outer perspective of the experimentalist? Have you drawn similar or other distinctions in your own development?

HARDER AND SOFTER REALITIES

In the survival game of our three test subjects, not all the rules are laid down to the same degree; some of them can be influenced by our test subject, whereas others have to be accepted whether he likes it or not. In soccer the test subject has to deal with social rules, which—so it seems from the outer perspective at least—might easily be different. After all, our reluctant player could have gotten caught up in a rugby match or a football game. You are not forced to play ball, and if you do, it need not necessarily be the same game as soccer. For the player in our experiment, the necessity to adapt is a result of the subsidiary circumstance that it is vital for him to find out the rules of the game. It does not result from playing soccer itself. It can rather be compared with relatively arbitrary social conventions and norms that might just as well be different and in fact prescribe different behaviors in different cultures; for example, eating with a knife and fork or with chopsticks. Although it is essential to eat, the worldwide success of American fast food chains proves that this act requires neither proper cutlery nor chopsticks. However, for someone who only gets something to eat if he eats with chopsticks, the adherence to this norm is indirectly vital.

There is a further difference between the necessity to eat and the necessity to use chopsticks. The obligations ensuing from social conventions, norms, and laws are variable and flexible to a larger extent than the obligations resulting from natural laws. Our second test subject, the reluctant yachtsman, had to come to terms with the latter. His chance of influencing wind and weather intentionally was quite small. A soccer player with enough muscle has, at least in theory, a chance of changing the rules of the soccer game by playing soccer. The reality he must adapt to is softer, that is, its rules for survival are more flexible, less rigid and stable. The "things" (his teammates) with whom he has to deal are not autonomous in their behavior and determined by seemingly unchangeable laws to the same extent as those things in the world of the yachtsman—the boat, wind, and weather. The contrast between *harder* and *softer* reality, used here to characterize the difference between the two fields of action (realities), should not be understood pedantically in the sense of a hard and a soft reality, but relatively, in comparison to each other. From the outer perspective the greater or lesser softness or hardness can be explained by the differing influence of the observer on the self-referential processes that preserve the status quo of an area of reality. This differing influence corresponds to the fact that the observer can pretend to a greater or lesser extent to be an objective observer from the outside. Whenever he has to deal with processes that are not influenced by observation, or only to a negligible extent, he can draw an idealized, "objective," picture of the examined object (Figure 3–1).

Drawing such an objective picture is possible in the area described by Newton's classical physics. In this area, the observed phenomena and objects can be regarded as autonomous, and it is possible to imagine the operationally closed feedback cycle that characterizes structures, functions, and processes of such objects without the observer.[1] You can pretend that during the observation of, and interaction with, objects of such a hard reality only the observer changes—he gains insight and knowledge—but the observed object is not altered (see Figure 3–1). Figure 3–1 also makes it clear that in this form of interrelationship between observer and observed system the possibility cannot be ruled out that the status quo of the system is being preserved by the very observation. Only when several observers applying different methods of examination to the object of cognition attain the same results can the notion of imagining the process without the observer be justified. This is what all the methodological rules and regulations of scientific insight try to guarantee.

The opposite situation occurs when the observer's reality is substantially harder than that of the observed system. In our experiment this would have been the case, for instance, if the ignorant soccer player had recognized the game as rugby on entering the field and had in due course managed to bring all his teammates to subject themselves to the rules of rugby. In this case he can only remain unchanged because all the others change (Figure 3–2).

---

1. Heisenberg (1989, p. 115) emphasized that the notion of objective knowledge has also become questionable in natural sciences because of the self-referentiality of knowledge: "What is new about the epistemological situation of quantum theory consisted in the fact that we can only observe what cannot really be separated from us, thus the concept of 'objective' observation seems to become contradictory in itself."

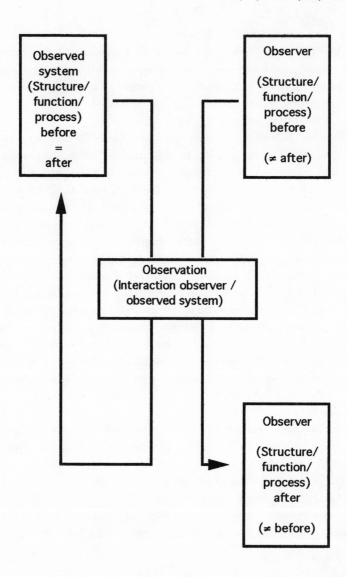

Figure 3–1

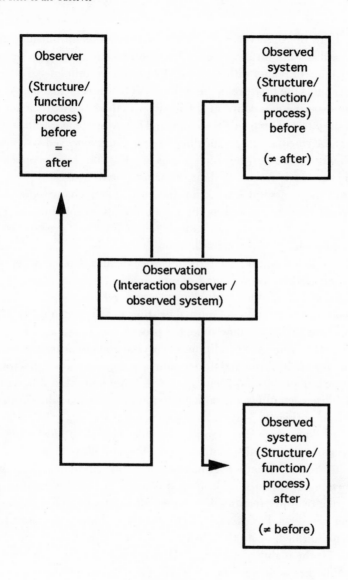

Figure 3–2

Here the observer cannot idealize himself as an outsider and regard his insight as objective because he cannot imagine his description of reality without himself and his own influence. He only ever finds the treasure he hid himself.[2] The shipwrecked person in our experiment is confronted not only with these two extreme forms of the effect of his own observation and behavior but also with countless intermediary stages in which observer and observed system influence each other, in which he has an effect on other people and objects and is subject to their influence (Figure 3–3).

In the course of interaction the participants change—the shipwrecked person as well as the island and all its inhabitants. The one who changes more and adapts to the other to a greater extent decides whose reality is harder.

Humberto Maturana (1976) described the fact that the structures of interacting partners (and observation is a form of interaction) influence each other mutually as "structural coupling," as a process of "conversation" of mutual twisting and turning until both fit together. In this way they undergo a process of development in which each determines the conditions of survival and the criteria of selection for the behavior and the structures of the other. Once this transformation process has been completed, and if both fit together, they stabilize each other and contribute to preserve each other in their structure (Figure 3–4).

The shipwrecked person is faced with the task of attributing all his perceptions and sensations, thoughts, and ideas to a harder or softer reality. Whether he makes use of the different objects and partners of interaction—himself, his body, or social structures—as harder or softer realities determines the influence he has on them, and vice versa. For example, is it sufficient to have desires for them to be fulfilled, or do they have to be accompanied by deeds? How hard is the reality of a thought? Does the body belong to an area of reality that is changed by observation and examination, or do they have no influence on it?

---

2. Karl Kraus accused psychoanalysis of this, although it most certainly applies to other sciences too.

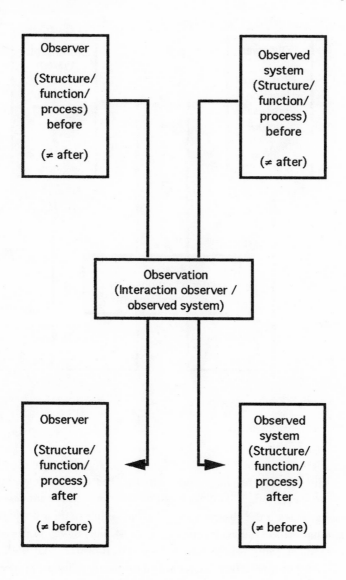

Figure 3–3

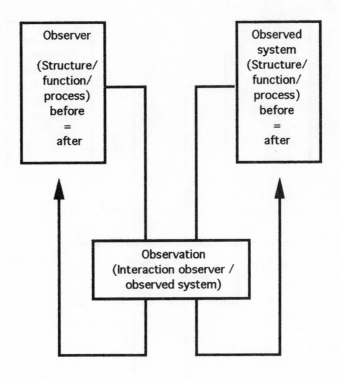

Figure 3–4

The situation becomes complicated when two or more observers observe each other. This is the softer area of reality that can only be hardened if the observers stabilize each other in their world views and patterns of behavior (See Figure 3–4). This model of the development of consensus should not suggest, however, that both participants of interaction are balanced and determine the content of such a consensus to the same extent. Thus the reality of the aborigines of our island might well be harder than that of the shipwrecked person who has to rely on their support and understanding. We can therefore speak of a difference in power, which depends on who needs whom more and who has more opportunities for action at his disposal.[3]

THE CONSENSUS: SEPARATION OF DESCRIPTIVE AND PRESCRIPTIVE RULES

If you want to describe what papaya tastes like to someone who has never eaten it, you will have problems: there are no terms that state unequivocally what you mean. You can help yourself by comparing it to the taste of other food ("sweet, fruity, tastes a bit like honey, like honey melon, like jam, golden yellow, h'm"). But the success of such less-than-ideal solutions is not very convincing. The most simple and probably the only way to communicate adequately what a papaya tastes like is to let the other person taste it and thus give him a similar experience to the one you had yourself when eating papaya. Here, too, the proof of the pudding is in the eating. When he has taken a bite, he will know what the phrase "tastes like papaya" means. G. Spencer-Brown (1969), the English logician, points out that all experimental sciences depend on adhering to such directives: look into a microscope and you will see this or that! Logic and mathematics too are based on the principle of the recipe: do this and you will get that result! If you add three plus three, you get six. Break an egg into a pan with hot fat and (after a few moments of waiting) you will get a fried egg!

The situation of the test subject in our imaginary experiment, as well as that of the newborn baby, can be compared with the situation of the experimental scientist. In order to arrive at a certain description of the world they all have to do something specific. And since one cannot *not behave* (even the proverbial "doing sweet nothing" is a behavior), one will at any rate acquire some kind of taste for it. If something is not done—if you do not bite into the papaya— then you do not arrive at the insight connected with it, you do not

---

3. In this context Helm Stierlin (1959) has spoken of the "reality of the stronger personality."

know what it tastes like. The fact that many people do not recognize various things can be explained by the nonproductive results of their efforts, that is, avoidance. Galileo's ecclesiastical adversaries refused to look through his telescope because they did not want to get into trouble by recognizing something that could not be because it must not be (the Jovian moons).

Now the use of the term "cognition" in this context is somewhat dangerous because it can so easily be understood in the sense of objective knowledge independent of the observer. In order to preclude this misunderstanding, I must once again emphasize that any statement about an object includes a statement about the person making it. Karl Kraus formulated it like this: If you ask someone whether a painting is obscene and he says "yes," then you know a lot about this person, but nothing about the painting (Heinz von Foerster, personal communication, 1985).

Every piece of knowledge is the result of interaction, and interaction is the result of a relationship that is never determined by one of the components alone. If you say that one ball is larger than the other, ascribing the attribute *larger* is valid only in comparison to the smaller one. It is restricted to a special context, to a quite specific constellation of relationships. When we speak of a person recognizing something, this statement can be compared to ascribing the attribute *larger* to one of the two balls. If one keeps in mind that insight is always the result of a characteristic relationship, an unmistakable form of interaction between the observer and what he observes, we can safely go on using this term. The same problem applies to all the other terms that might be used instead. The danger of ascribing reifying attributes and attributes that abstract from the context is inherent in the structure of our (any) language.

Several people can always reach a common view of reality when they manifest similar behaviors that lead to similar experiences and descriptions of reality, and vice versa. To take a further, more consistent and radical step: there is no difference between behavior and insight. Living beings manifesting the same behavior furnish the same description of their environment. This is a view held by the biologist Humberto Maturana (1970), who compares behavior as "first-order description" with linguistic description as "second-order description," that is, as description of the description. Although this use of the term "description" does not comply with our traditions of colloquial speech, the matter at issue is well founded as far as language is concerned. Let us remain with our culinary example: if we see someone biting into a piece of papaya, it seems perfectly reasonable to say that he is thus describing the papaya as edible; his mimicry and gestures describe the papaya as sweet and palatable— the description his drooping features would lend to a lemon would be far more sour. If he eats too much papaya, his long-term behavior, such as repeated visits to the bathroom, would also afford a part of the description of the papaya.

In spite of these good reasons for regarding behavior as description and hence as knowledge, in keeping with colloquial speech, the word "description" will continue to be used here for statements tied to language, unless we speak explicitly of first-order descriptions.

If behavior of the individual is the basis for a consensus on reality, that consensus can best be achieved where all human beings share similar or comparable behaviors. These behaviors are inevitably an experience determined by autonomous bodily functions and processes. They are experienced as elementary needs and their satisfaction: hunger/food, thirst/drink, tiredness/sleep, and the like. But these bodily necessities only dictate relatively few stereotypical behaviors that are valid equally for all people in all cultures. You have to eat, but (thank God) not everybody has to eat the same food, with the same seasonings, the same table manners, equally substantially and often. The mutual experience shared by all humans as a consequence of their bodily structures is rather to be understood in the sense of setting up boundaries, as a minimal requirement for human behavior. *It determines what you **have** to do if you want to survive or avoid unpleasant feelings.*

You must eat, drink, and sleep, but it does not matter how you fulfill these actions with regard to their *content*. Here the body proves itself as an aspect of harder reality that prescribes what has to be done. Occasionally it translates this behavior into action of its own accord, without asking anybody. For example, you simply fall asleep—

this is (self-)description of the first order, unless you hit on the idea of describing yourself as tired, which would be (self-) description of the second order—and go to bed. When people have similar experiences with their bodies, they also arrive at similar descriptions of the body.

The second common boundary for man's behavior and experience options is determined by their collision with the harder reality of the exterior physical environment. *This collision determines what you can do if you want to survive and avoid unpleasant feelings.*

You cannot go at everything headfirst; you cannot touch too hot stove burners without getting burnt. Here too knowledge is the result of bodily changes and experiences combined with certain behavior: the bump on your head, the burnt fingers, and so on.

The rules resulting from these experiences (you have to eat and drink! You cannot go at everything headfirst!) are ambiguous. They can be read as descriptive as well as prescriptive rules. However, the consensus deriving from the relatively hard realities of the bodily and physical world only refers to negative descriptions (first and second order) of (1) the limitation of the scope of human freedom of action by what can on no account be refrained from and what can on no account be done (you cannot refrain from eating, you cannot eat toadstools) and of (2) what is not *real* (man cannot survive without eating, toadstools are not edible).

Thus the basis for interpersonal agreement on reality is rather thin. It is relatively easy to come to an understanding about all that is *not* so and will *not* work. For the mutual adaptation of behavior and the development of a shared view of reality, this only means that the possibilities are somehow limited; it does not, however, dictate how one has to behave and describe reality.

Since man's long-term survival depends on these patterns of behavior and description developed by man (as an individual or as a species), what can be said about the evolution of organismic structures is also true for their development: what survives has adapted (Eigen and Winkler 1975). As in biological evolution, the structures of the organism and its environment determine under what conditions it must die, but not how it must live. Darwin's "survival of the fittest" does not mean that there is only one possibility of surviving.

The relationship of the organism to its environment is characterized by the fact that both mutually *limit* their development options.
They can thus be regarded as a co-evolutionary unity (Bateson 1972).
The development of the organism changes the conditions of the
development of its environment. This reacts as self-referential feedback on the organism and its own development options.

External reality leaves us great scope in which to select our behavior and world views. However, this reality also changes with the
transformation of our views and behavior. The descriptions we
construct about the world have to *fit* this world to survive, that is,
they have to prescribe and allow behavior that is compatible with
life.[4] On the other hand, behavior has to be such that it leaves scope
for a viable image of reality.

The relationship between describing and prescribing rules can
also be understood in the sense of a co-evolutionary entity. Every
behavior leaves scope for the deduction of different descriptions
while definitely excluding specific descriptions, and every description leaves scope for the deduction of different behaviors while
excluding certain behaviors with a large degree of certainty (Figure
3–5). Anyone who has tried to copy birds and fly without aid has
many ways of describing the experience of falling on his nose in
the process. Yet, he is most unlikely to draw the conclusion that he
can really fly like a bird, even though he might tell you that he had
been flying when asked about the scratches on his face.

If you trace the lines of development leading to an interpersonal
consensus on reality (as it is and as it should be), you find that
descriptive and prescriptive rules can be evaluated differently. This
difference in evaluation corresponds to the varying influence of the
observer on his object of observation, the relative hardness or softness of this domain of reality. When the same observer or several
different observers displaying different patterns of behavior always
have the same experiences and reach the same or similar conclusions (descriptive rules), then you can imagine the recipe part of
knowledge away (prescriptive rules) without substantially altering

---

4. The constructivist Ernst von Glasersfeld (1981) has also coined the term *viability* for
this concept of fit.

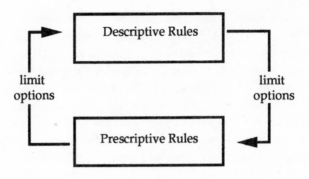

Figure 3–5

the results, the descriptive rules. This is the case where knowledge of harder aspects of reality is concerned. Laws of nature can be regarded as prime examples of such descriptive rules on which it is easy to reach a consensus. Because experience with these natural laws varies little among different people and cultures, it is relatively easy to agree on the characteristics of inanimate nature. When the same observer or several different observers displaying the same kind of behavior always have different experiences and come to different conclusions (descriptive rules), you can then imagine the description part of knowledge away without substantially altering the results, the prescriptive rules. This is the case where knowledge of softer aspects of reality is concerned. All social laws, whether linguistic, moral, ethical, economic, governmental, or political, can be regarded as examples of such prescriptive rules on which it is difficult to reach a consensus. Their range of variation among different people and cultures is too great.

These two situations, in which it is possible to disregard either behavior or description totally, are idealized extreme forms. In a concrete isolated case, the harder and the softer portion of reality have to be evaluated differently. The scope in which something soft can be hardened and something hard softened by the way it is described and treated varies considerably. Reality cannot be organized into two clearly separated realms, a hard, objective one and a soft, subjective one. Since the development of quantum theory, even the hard realm, for which the hard sciences feel responsible, has lost its hardness. Nevertheless, the difference that is also reflected in the difficulties of soft sciences to achieve a consensus on reality should not be denied. In the words of Heinz von Foerster (1972, p. 17), "The 'hard sciences' are successful because they deal with 'soft problems'; 'soft sciences' have to struggle, since they are dealing with 'hard problems.'"

Consequently, there is no universal, human consensus with regard to the softer area of reality, but only islands of agreement in a sea of disagreement and conflict about the truly essential values. These islands of consensus are agreed on consciously or unconsciously via the selection criteria of possible and impossible patterns of behavior and world views. Social entities develop, such as cultures, societies, families, scientific schools and other religious communities, political parties, philatelists, and golf clubs. Their basis is the agreement on certain rules: on a method of hardening a relatively soft reality by making a characteristic selection from the many theoretically possible options and on how to describe reality.

At first glance it seems astonishing that these islands of consensus can develop at all. Here, too, evolution theory provides a plausible explanation. Agreement on a common view of the world and, combined with this, the acceptance of common values for judging what each individual may do or not do provide an opportunity for cooperation. In numerous computer simulations Robert Axelrod, the games theorist, has tested which long-term strategies of interaction are connected with the greatest chances of survival. The result: whenever at least two players decide to cooperate, they have a decisive advantage over those who play against everyone else with everyone for himself (Axelrod 1984). A reassuring and optimistic result, because it shows that ethics require humanity, not the raised index finger and the reference to the higher authority of God-given laws. The sober calculation of the probability calculus reveals that it is economically sensible to look for agreement for individual survival. Even without mathematical justification the necessity of cooperation and finding a consensus ensues from the extremely hard reality of the biological structures of man—once again as an individual and as a species. The survival of every infant depends on somebody looking after it who *understands* what it needs.

LOGICAL THOUGHT: A SOCIAL GAME

Whenever a group of people is in doubt or differs on what is to be regarded as true or false, they will resort to the rules of logic. This is the formal framework for discussion. In the field of science, which has taken up the cause of exploring the truth, only those statements and conclusions are accepted as true that lie within the frame set by logic. These statements are the only ones on which a consensus can be achieved. These laws of logic are of special interest here, because ignoring them is regarded as one of the principal signs of madness. This does not mean that everyone who cannot think logically or logically enough is in danger of being diagnosed as mad. After all, nobody can think logically always, at all times, and in every situation. But when conflicts arise and a reasonable decision has to be made on what is to be regarded as true, the rules of logic form the mutual basis for this decision. These are generally accepted rules for arriving at conclusions, on whose validity a consensus exists long before questions of content are discussed. Since mad thinking and arguing deviate from these rules of logic in a quite specific way, it makes sense to look at their characteristics first.

To think logically is not a law of nature. There are other ways of thinking, and most of the time children do not think logically. Neither do grown-ups all the time. On the one hand, rules of logic are describing rules; on the other hand, they are prescribing rules. They describe how *correct* (i.e., *conclusive*) thinking has to proceed. However, they also provide rules on how to think if you want to think conclusively. In this mixture of describing and prescribing rules the Finnish philosopher Georg Hendrik von Wright (1963) sees the features of game rules[5]:

---

5. From von Wright derives the distinction used here of describing ("descriptive") and prescribing ("prescriptive") rules: As pupil and and administrator of his literary bequest he is strongly influenced by Ludwig Wittgenstein's (1958) concept of "language game."

A game is an activity like thinking or arithmetic. The rules of chess, for instance, determine which moves are permitted and which are not. Sometimes they require a certain move to be made. In a similar sense we might suggest that the rules of logic determine what kind of conclusions and assertions are 'possible' (correct, legitimate, permitted) in thinking. If someone does not play according to the rules of chess, we would say either that he does not play correctly or that he does not play chess at all. If he wanted to follow the rules, but did not know or understand what they required of him, or if he tried to deceive his opponent, we would say the first. If he is not at all interested in following the rules or consciously and consistently played according to different rules, we would say the latter. According to this suggestion we might similarly say that if someone does not draw conclusions in accordance with the rules of logic, he either concludes incorrectly or not at all. We maintain both for more or less the same reasons as in the case of the chess game." [pp. 21–22]

The laws of logic and mathematics determine certain rules of the game that are binding for someone who wants to be accepted as a player. Where this is not the case—as in mad thinking—the question arises as to whether this deviation from the rules of the game means that a different game is being played (a different order of moves is adhered to) or no game at all.

NONSENSE INSTEAD OF CONSENSUS: THE LIMITS OF UNDERSTANDING

Two madmen are playing ludo. One says: "Check!" and receives the excited answer from his opponent: "You idiot, there is no penalty in Halma!"

One should neither over- nor underrate the expressiveness of jokes about madmen. They not only draw a picture of madness and madmen reflecting bias and fear but also reflect experiences connected with the subject of madness in public opinion; occasionally they contain careful observations, and often they are full of everyday explanations for the phenomena described. The Halma-penalty joke, a classic one, records very aptly that madmen do not follow the rules of our social games. And it also provides an explanation for that deviation: the rules of several games are all mixed up. The fact that communication between madmen breaks down in the same way as it does between the mad and the not mad is brilliantly described. One of the madmen calls the other an idiot, because for him his behavior is madness too and remains unpredictable. Both follow very private rules of the game, which allow them to play ludo according to the rules of Halma and to experience the goalkeeper's fear of chess. Such a rule cannot be understood by their fellows.

This is exactly what makes someone who is finally diagnosed as psychotic a madman or lunatic in the eyes of his fellow men. His behavior cannot be understood; sense can neither be read out of nor into it. Patients who have been diagnosed as schizophrenic or manic-depressive can be regarded as exemplary, since they show the extreme forms in the spectrum of behavior, thinking, and feeling patterns that cannot be understood. The schizophrenic patient cannot be understood because he thinks differently; the manic-depressive patient, because he feels differently from the average grown-up citizen (who has also felt and thought before, after all). When the form and content of someone's motives, desires, longings, fears, fantasies, opinions, thoughts, ideas, and conclusions are no longer *understandable* by his fellow men, they are mad. They step beyond the borders of the area within which, at least in principle, consensus is possible.

Although in colloquial language the terms "explaining" and "understanding" are often equated, here understanding is used in a different semantic field. Understanding contains a psychological dimension resulting from the tacit agreement of a similarity between the one that understands and the one that is understood. As a human being, I know from the inner perspective of a human being how humans function; I do not know everybody, but I at least know someone—me. I assume that others think and feel the same as I do. Anyone who wants to understand other humans has to imagine himself in their situation and identify with them in order to comprehend their thoughts and feelings. He can thus use himself as a model: he looks inside himself in order to learn something about the inside of someone else out there. The prerequisite for the successful study of the model is, as in all other studies of all other models, sufficient similarity between the features of the model and those of the object of research. The air resistance of a new car body design can only be studied in the wind tunnel if the model has sufficient similarity with the car body to be tested. The fact that there are bodily and psychological similarities between human beings makes sympathetic understanding possible, makes possible the adoption of the inner perspective of someone who can usually be observed only from the outside.

Lack of similarity, then, is the reason why hardly anybody can understand his washing machine correctly (at least it is doubtful whether the washing machine feels correctly understood). Someone who plays chess with his computer and speculates that he might tire of it in time or, like Bobby Fischer with his opponents, make it nervous and entice it into making careless mistakes will notice that the similarity between him and the computer is limited. The computer does not get tired, but on the other hand a human chess player does not have to be fully charged all the time.

Interhuman understanding is not confined to the collection of data and facts. It is tied to interpretation, to decoding meaning. Human beings and other living beings are able to attribute *meaning* or *sense* to events or incidents going on inside or outside their bodies. Another person can only be understood by someone who is able to attribute similar or identical meaning to similar events or incidents. *Consensus*–the agreement on which meaning is attributed to what–is the prerequisite of understanding.

The behavior of someone who oversteps the limits of this consensus and leaves the area of understanding becomes nonsense to all others. Philosophers pointed out some time ago that madness is characterized above all by the fact that it is not possible to acquire an understanding of it and that it leaves the social consensus. Kant (1789) writes that it is

> Not only disorder and deviation from the rule of using reason, but also positive irrationality, i.e. a different rule, a completely different

point of view into which the soul is transposed, so to speak, and from which it sees all objects in a different way, and finds itself transferred from the sensorio communi necessary for the unity of life (of an animal) to a remote place (hence the word displacement). [p. 531]

Karl Jaspers (1913) sets the criterion of nonunderstanding as a diagnostic standard for the differentiation between psychotic and nonpsychotic phenomena too. He too sets understanding, "the subjective, obvious grasping of mental connections from the inside in so far as they can be grasped in this way" against explaining, which for him is "the objective pointing out of connections, consequences, regularities that cannot be understood and can only be explained by cause and effect" (p. 255). As psychotic phenomena are not understandable for him, they need to be explained. Like generations of psychiatrists after him, he looked for the explanation in pathological bodily processes.

For the explanation of psychoses, however, a far more gripping and much more illuminative question is, How can we explain *how* people understand each other and reach a consensus on what they regard as reality? Once again it is the question of self-evident truths that presents us with the greatest mystery (and possibly helps solve it).

DOUBLE DESCRIPTION:
FREE WILL AND SELF-ORGANIZATION

"Mad or bad?" This is the question that arises when someone leaves the framework of normal rules and ignores the usual laws and taboos. The poker player who pulls the fifth ace out of his sleeve to complete his royal flush obviously knows what he is doing. He is guilty, because he knows the prescriptive rules and yet deliberately oversteps the limits of what is allowed in order to gain an advantage for himself. However, someone who states that there is no penalty in Halma raises doubts as to whether he might have taken leave of his senses or whether he knows what he is saying. Does he actually know the descriptive rules? Does he know what game is being played? Does he see reality in the same way as the people in his environment? Is he capable of guilt? Is he responsible for his deeds?

The distinction between mad and bad has far-reaching consequences. On the level of society it determines the institution responsible for the treatment of the individual violating the rules, namely, prison or hospital. Combined with this distinction, however, is a radical and discontinuous shift of the basic frame of interpretation, which corresponds to the leap from the inner to outer perspective of observation. Our legal system depends on the tacit agreement that the responsible citizen has a free will and has control of his own decisions. His behavior is regarded as an action for which he has to bear the consequences. This is the inner perspective of an observer participating in a softer social reality. The players involved hold themselves and the other players responsible for their individual behavior, for their part in shaping the entire game.

The perspective of sciences, as claimed by medicine as well as psychology, however, is based on the assumption that a harder (here: organic or psychic) reality is being observed from outside. Deviating behavior is regarded as the result of structures, functions, and processes deviating from the biological or psychological norm. It is not evaluated as an action for which the spoilsport who disregards the rules can be blamed and made responsible. In this view he is not the culprit, but the victim of an autonomous bodily or psychological event on which he himself has no significant influence. In this case the human images of psychology and justice are mutually exclusive, thus transforming the question "mad or bad?" into an either/or alternative between power and powerlessness of the individual.

From an evolutionary point of view in regard to the individual as well as to humanity, the perspective of the other player is possibly the older one. Two of our test subjects make us aware that this must be true. Neither the soccer player nor the shipwrecked person ever had the chance to observe events from the perspective of the spectators. If they wanted to influence reality—their fate—they would have to describe themselves as acting subjects and blame themselves for the effects of their behavior. Trial and error[6] was the only way for them to find a standard from which they could select their behavior. But the very term "select" presupposes that they had the freedom to say yes or no. The image of the world they were thus able to draw was egocentric; they themselves stood in the center, and everything revolved inevitably around them. All this applies to the yachtsman too. Like every newborn babe, the soccer player and the shipwrecked person, however, were dealing primarily with other humans. Where they experienced their power as limited, they were confronted with the power of the other players who were similar to them, namely, the referee, the other player, and the cannibal.

They arrived at their descriptive rules by producing—just like other experimental scientists—if/then links between their actions and those of others. When these assumptions and expectations of a connection between one's own behavior and that of others had been confirmed, it was possible to develop from the single if/then description a general whenever/then rule, which could serve in the future as the basis for decisions. Once a collection of such rules had been drawn up, current events could be explained ("As it is forbidden to let attacking players trip over an outstretched leg in the penalty area, the referee gave a penalty") and predictions made for the future ("If I score a goal, my teammates will—probably—hug me").

Hempel (1942) has described this pattern of explanation for the sciences as a "compendium of explanatory laws":

> E is an event of which we know that it occurred in a certain situation and needs an explanation. Why did E happen? To answer this question we refer to certain other events or states $E_1 \ldots E_m$ and to one or more general propositions or laws $L_1 \ldots L_n$, so that the manifestation of E (in the relevant situation) is a logical consequence of these laws and the fact that these other events (states) occurred (exist). [p. 24]

---

6. Ross Ashby (1956) is justified in pointing out that such a form of learning should better be described as "hunt and stick," since in most cases there is more than one correct solution to a problem.

The difference between this scientific explanation and that of our test subjects is that the scientist has to follow a clearly prescribed recipe to arrive at his explanations, whereas our test subjects had the freedom to concoct their knowledge according to their tastes. And in contrast to the scientist, whose ideal of objectivity commends him to place, as best as he can, his object of knowledge in the center, our test subjects place themselves, the observer, in the center. In answer to the question, "Why did E happen?" they refer to their actions $E_1 \ldots E$ ("When I did this, that happened").

Such an explanation tacitly implies that there is a direct cause-and-effect relationship between the consequences of an action and the action itself. It is an idealized description abstracting from all incidental and marginal conditions, or, which is probably a more adequate formulation, one whose attention is not focused on the marginal conditions. The concept of cause and effect, often regarded as a feature of scientific thought, is probably no more than a depersonalization of the other player's inner perspective: for our yachtsman the poetical heaven-born wind becomes the prosaic wind. A thing—the cause and its effect—is put in the place of the guilty person, the culprit and his deed. The linear relationship between both remains unchanged. This is a rather unbecoming simplification in view of the complexity of the network and interrelation of all the events that produce the phenomena of our world.

Proof that the concept of cause and effect is nothing but a projection of social rules onto the rest of the world is provided by the conceptual statements connected with it. Originally the Latin word *causa* had only a legal meaning, and the Greek *aitia*, which can be found in the question of the etiology of phenomena (the explanation of their emergence), can best be translated as guilt. It is most likely that the notions of causality in nature were developed by the ancient Greeks in analogy to their criminal law (Jaeger 1934, Kelsen 1941).

The question arises as to whether the principle of causality is not out of place in science. Bertrand Russell gave the answer three-quarters of a century ago with a clear yes:

All philosophers, of every school, imagine that causation is one of the fundamental axioms or postulates of science, yet, oddly enough, in advanced sciences such as gravitational astronomy, the word "cause" never occurs. . . . The law of causality, I believe, like much that passes muster among philosophers, is a relic of a bygone age, surviving, like the monarchy, only because it is erroneously supposed to do no harm. . . . No doubt the reason why the old "law of causality" has so long continued to pervade the books of philosophers is simply that the idea of a function is unfamiliar to most of them, and therefore they seek an unduly simplified statement. [1912/13, pp. 174, 188]

The Austrian philosopher Ludwig Wittgenstein (1921) suggests similar conclusions when he writes:

In no way can an inference be made from the existence of one state of affairs to the existence of another entirely different from it. There is no causal nexus which justifies such an inference. The events of the future *cannot* be inferred from those of the present. Superstition is the belief in the causal nexus. Freedom of will consists in the fact that future actions cannot be known now. We could only know them if causality were an *inner* necessity, like that of logical deduction.—The connexion of knowledge and what is known is that of logical necessity [§§5.135–5.1362]

What science can provide is descriptions. The functions Russell puts in place of causality are nothing but the if/then links of observed phenomena: if this happens, then that follows. For instance, love grows by the square of the distance ($y = x^2$), i.e., by multiplying value x (the distance from the lover) by itself, you get y (the measure of longing). However, this formula should not be regarded as a universally valid rule to be taken seriously in the field of science just because it might correspond to the personal experience of many a reader. These if/then links are directions to other observers telling them what to do to attain the same descriptive rule as the person formulating it. The ideal of objectivity obliges the scientist to make his descriptions checkable by others. In his reasoning he has to comply with the rules of logic and mathematics, as this is the only way his statements can find a consensus within the scientific community (other communities have different rules for coming to a consensus). He has to state how he arrived at his results, and his suspicious and jealous colleagues have to be able to grasp the same phenomena by this and, still better, other methods and reach the same conclusions by logical reasoning (even if they do not really want to). They should at least be unable to prove that his descriptions and conclusions are false according to the rules of logic or probability. For, as in the case of the everyday knowledge of average people, even scientific methods can never find out what reality is *really* like; they can only say with any certainty what it is *not* like (see Popper's (1972) theory of science and the principle of falsification of hypotheses).

If we apply the concepts of systemic theory, the compendium of explanatory laws changes only insofar as, rather than a straight line between $E_1 \ldots E_m$ and E, the circle is closed, so that E can be regarded as cause and effect. Thus the principle of causality is reduced to absurdity, not, however, the compendium of explanatory laws. Now the self-organizing processes that make a thing or system appear as it appears to us are being examined. The ideal of scientific objectivity requires the observer to account for how far his measures of observation are built into these self-referential cycles. If different observers employing different methods can describe the same phenomena when explaining them, they can pretend they are outside observers of a harder, independent reality, the development and maintenance of which *cannot* be ascribed to them themselves.

It seems doubtful that these conditions are fulfilled by the perspective that examination medicine and psychology confer on madness. Human structures of knowledge, man's patterns of feeling and thinking develop in interaction with other human beings. They can thus be regarded as one of the functions of interhuman communication, as structures and processes that emerge within the framework of communication and are themselves incorporated into the process of structuring social systems. Therefore social systems should be the context within which an explanation of madness is sought. Extracting it from this context not only deprives it of its explicability but also entails the danger of chronicity. If madness is a result of interaction, as is normality, everybody who has anything to do with somebody else's madness is in danger of entering into the very game that brings forth madness. Only his knowledge of the rules of the game, but not his honest motives, can protect him. We have to admit our uncertainty about the correct answer to the question "Mad or bad?" It must probably be evaluated as a component of a specific maddening game in which all involved are uncertain whether they are observing from the inside or the outside, so that they are unsure according to which rules the game should be played.

In attempting to examine the self-organization of madness, the intention is to describe from an outer perspective how normality and madness can be explained as a result (function) of the interaction and communication of the individual with his fellow men.[7] Wittgenstein's reference to the fact that, from the perspective of systemic theory, there is no room for freedom of will becomes the focus of attention. Here the systems examined are abstract. People have no place in them. The events assigned to each other as systems consist of descriptions and patterns of behavior (first- and second-order descriptions) and of interactions. What is examined is the logic of their combination, the order of systems of interaction, knowledge, and communication (Figure 3-6).

In this model all these phenomena described in psychology and colloquial language as an expression of character and personality of the persons involved, their motivation, emotions, perceptions, and actions, can be subsumed under the concept of knowledge, consisting of first- and second-order description, and explained from a new perspective. Since rules are described—logical necessities—there is no room for the arbitrariness of free decisions.

Someone falling from a multistory building cannot change his mind halfway down. His behavior complies with rules of gravity that could not care less about his free will. (It will probably not help

---

7. This is an approach based on the work of the group around Gregory Bateson and was later included and developed further in the therapeutic strategies of systemic therapy used in clinical practice (Bateson 1972, Bateson et al. 1956).

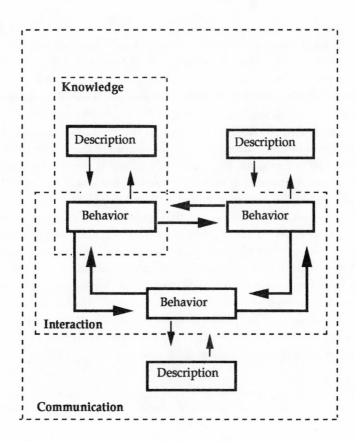

Figure 3-6

much if, as does one of the leading actors in the movie *Atlantic City*, one claims not to believe in gravity.) From the perspective of systems theory a person's unmistakable physical and psychological attributes can be regarded as characteristic features of the environment of knowledge, interaction, and communication systems, which limit their development options. They determine which form of knowledge, interaction, and communication is not possible; not, however, which form becomes reality.

The assumption of freedom of will, the concepts of an acting, self-responsible human being able to feel guilt, may well make sense from the inner view of the other player; the spectator from the outer perspective, however, must not take them for granted if he wishes to arrive at reasonable scientific conclusions.[8] Instead he must ask how to explain the fact that, within the frame of processes of self-organization, people get the idea that they and others have a free will. And he must also explain how, within the frame of such processes, it comes about that somebody arrives at the opinion deviating from the norm that he has no free will, but is remote-controlled and influenced by a transmitter in his tooth.

However, this cannot mean that reality would be grasped more correctly from an outer perspective and with the concept of self-organization than from an inner perspective with the concept of free will. Both have their justification; both include something different. Just as our solid three-dimensional vision results from two two-dimensional pictures seen with two eyes, the double description of the inner and outer view affords the chance of creating a new visual dimension that fulfills the conditions of human existence better than the two views on their own (see Bateson 1979).

---

8. I personally prefer to live in a society and a time in which all these assumptions connected with the notion of free will form the basis of social rules; nor do I believe that we would be able to organize our social institutions better without these assumptions; but this personal opinion and assessment cannot obscure the fact that man's social life can function without the concept of the acting individual, if, for instance, all human behavior is seen as predestined by God.

4

HUMAN COMMUNICATION

THE IMPOSSIBILITY
OF TRANSFERRING INFORMATION

In former times it was the ticking of the clock, or rather its not ticking right, that was used as a model for mental processes; today the brain is regarded as a biological computer by many laymen and specialists alike. Such metaphors seemingly help us grasp and explain complex connections. They are also nice (self-referential) examples of the egocentricity of human cognition.

Man has always used the machines constructed in his era as models for human cognition and concluded with incredible logic that he too functions like clockwork or like the information processor of a computer. As useful as such pictures are to illustrate abstract connections, they are just as fraudulent as the deceptive packaging in which the trusting consumer is sold products that he does not need. The assumptions furnished by such metaphors lead to conclusions that are of little use. They suggest first of all that there has to be an engineer or creator who has created these "things" (this warning is also valid for the metaphor of deceptive packaging, of course). It makes a difference whether we consider reason or irrationality (or deceptive packaging) as something that develops independently or is built in, breathed in, or produced from the outside.

The belief that the structuring of human cognition can be compared to the programming of a computer—as has been held until now[1]—and that human communication runs on the principle of modern telecommunications leads to a dead end. It is tacitly taken for granted that information can be transferred from sender to receiver. External reality is then the sender, the human being is the receiver, and several people communicating with each other are alternately sender and receiver, like telephones. Madness becomes the expression of a disturbance in the processing of information, and the brain of the person behaving madly becomes a computer in which the wires have been soldered wrong or programming mistakes have been made. Or, the brain becomes a television on which films are shown that are not being broadcast. The metaphors used by a patient who thinks he has a transmitter in his tooth, and by a psychiatrist who thinks his patient has a receiver in his head, to explain mad phenomena are terribly similar and obviously come from the same electrical workshop.

Such a (self-)misunderstanding can, as is so often the case, be explained by an unfortunate choice of words. It would be less misleading if we said that in telephones, radios, televisions, and computers signals are transmitted, received, or processed.[2] The difference between signals and information can be sketched as follows. When a siren suddenly goes off in your vicinity, you are subjected to a physical phenomenon. Sound waves reach your eardrums, and you and all around you with similar eardrums hear the dreadful, bloodcurdling sound of the siren. But you do not know whether this sound means anything. Or rather you, like everyone else around you, must decide for yourself what it means for you (whether a nuclear war or lunch break). The vibration of the eardrum is a signal, a change in your bodily state (a difference as opposed to the state of rest) that remains meaningless until you ascribe a meaning to it (something that makes a difference for you). If meaning has been ascribed,

---

1. See Winograd and Flores (1986) for a criticism of present programming methods including the insights of neurobiology reviewed in this section.

2. Heinz von Foerster, the cybernetician, said: "All misfortune began when Shannon called his theory 'information theory'; if he had called it 'signal theory' all would have been well" (personal communication, 1988).

information has emerged. "Information," according to Gregory Bateson (1979), is every "difference that makes a difference."

If you phone home on Mother's Day, you can only hear Mother's warning to make sure you wrap up warm because in Mother's telephone (the sender) sound vibrations are transformed into electrical impulses which, after further conversions and amplifications through wires, cables, satellites, electromagnetic waves, and other conductive media, finally reach a second telephone (the receiver), where they are once again transformed into sound waves. From the inner perspective of the telephone these impulses can be seen as information. If we could ask it, the telephone would probably say, "I have been informed; my brother showed differences in his behavior that made a difference for me too. Through his behavior he has given me clear instructions about how to behave." Fortunately there are few telephones with the necessary amount of self-reference to give an answer like that. Nevertheless it characterizes the content of the technical term "information" quite well: just as the postman delivers his letters and parcels, the telephone exchange delivers electrical impulses (differences) from one place to another. The difference in the behavior of the sender causes the difference in the behavior of the receiver. *Instructive interaction*[3] takes place between the two; that is, a form of interaction in which one of the participants controls (i.e., determines) the behavior of the other. It is the pattern of causal inevitability.

It is no wonder that we meet so few telephones that think about themselves and their behavior. If they did, they would no longer be any good as telephones. Then they too would start thinking about the meaning of the transformations in their insides. They would ask themselves whether it makes sense to react in such a stereotypical way, so obedient and good, and perhaps they would experiment with different kinds of behavior. The result of such attempts at emancipation and insubordination would be anarchistic and un-

---

3. The concept of "instructive interaction" comes from the framework of Humberto Maturana's (1970) biological theory of cognition.

predictable behavior. The external observer phoning his mother would no longer be able to describe fixed rules between the causes in the sender and the effects in the receiver. He would then phone home on Mother's Day, his mother would possibly encourage him to lead a happy, carefree life, and he would still hear: "Think of your bladder, put a warm vest on and those long woollen underpants"! There would no longer be instructive interaction between the two telephones. What Mother says (or means) is something different from what her dear son or daughter hears (or understands). This characterizes the qualitative difference in communication between technical apparatus and living beings, who do not always obey even when they do hear.

THE AUTONOMY OF THE NERVOUS SYSTEM

The advantage of the telephone is that it allows itself no falsifications on its own authority during the transmission of signals. Its working method allows the observer to make a stable and reliable classification of input and output values: whenever/then. The reliability of the transmission of such signals can be established, checked, and measured according to certain standards (high fidelity) by external observers; they can be ascribed to a harder reality. In the frame of human communication, in contrast, no information is transmitted by these signals; they merely create the possibility for information to emerge.

The human brain functions differently from the telephone or computer in that the external observer can describe no fixed input–output rules. These fixed rules do not even apply to the hard data of the perception of physical phenomena, let alone to the reaction of a child to the anxious advice of its parents. The lack of fixed rules is one finding of the experimental research of the neurobiologist Humberto Maturana and his colleagues (1968). They found that the examination of brain activity during the perception of color did not allow recognition of a regular connection between the measurable, hard data in the outer and inner world of the test subject.

No regular association could be found between the wave length of light and measured quantities from which the activity of the brain could be read. Instead, significant correlations were to be found between brain activity and the name used to describe a color. The behavior of the brain could logically be assigned to the names a test subject gives to his perceptions, but not to objective physical phenomena, which until now have been considered the instructive trigger of brain activity. Inside the brain various activities are linked together regularly and arranged in patterns. But the phenomena of the outside world are *not* reflected by characteristic brain activities.

Unfortunately the wording "brain activities are arranged in patterns" is again misleading, for no acting person exists who would bring this order into the processes of brain activity in accordance with a knitting pattern (knit two, purl two). It is the combination of the parts—the activity of single nerve cells—that allows the order of the whole to emerge.[4]

From this and similar neurophysiological experiments Humberto Maturana and Francisco Varela (1984) conclude that the nervous system is *operationally closed* and *autonomous*. The effect of any activity (operation) of the nervous system is in turn an activity of the nervous system. From the outside nothing gets into the nervous system, and no information is absorbed and processed; only inner patterns of activity are varied. When we as outside observers refer to the motor activity of an organism (its behavior) as output and to the sensory stimulus (perception) as input, this differentiation is a characteristic of the description we make as observers and not a feature of the way the nervous system functions. From the inner perspective of the nervous system there is no distinction between inside and outside. The nervous system constantly coordinates sensory and motor activities, as if the nerves that innervate the muscles were directly connected to those of the sense organs (see Maturana

---

4. In his theory of synergetics the physicist Hermann Haken (1981) describes that together the elements of self-organizing systems bring about order parameters who "enslave" the single elements—an ornate use of language that makes nonsense of the simplicity of our everyday ideas of activity and passivity.

and Varela 1984). We can only differentiate between the organism and its environment and say that its interaction with the environment connects the motor output with the sensory input and closes the self-referential loop from the outer perspective.

The nervous system as a whole can be compared to the dancers constantly running around in a circle in our processionary moth experiment. It is made up of an enormous number of single nerve cells (approximately 10^{10}), which can never become active on their own and in isolation. Each change in one of these cells has an influence on all the others; the behavior of each is organized by their combination. Whether they are active or in a state of rest can change the activity pattern of the nervous system, but each cell always remains an element of such a pattern. Every test subject in our experiment behaved as he could and must in accordance with his instructions; the product of the interaction was a chain, a circle, or some other new structure. These entities did not exist for the participants with their inner perspective, who were blind to all greater correlations, feeling only the one in front or behind with their hands. The differentiation between inside and outside the chain or the circle was even more impossible: when no circle can be seen, no part of the circle can be seen. Such a distinction can only be made from the outer perspective.

The nervous system is just such a private party that behaves autonomously toward its environment. The laws according to which the individual party guests behave develop democratically from the grassroots, within the framework of self-organization. From the outside they can be described as a spatial link between the nerve cells and as interplay between the patterns of activity ordered in space and time.

As there can be no instructive interaction between the environment and a self-referential system, Maturana and Varela provide another model for the processes of cognition. Changes in the environment of the living system work as a perturbation of the system. This concept can probably be best translated as disquiet or disturbance and stimulation, because thus the ambiguous character of such a demand for adaptation to the system can best be grasped. It enters a state of crisis and leaves the state of rest. Every such crisis is ambivalent; it can be assessed as either negative or positive. Old structures, behavior patterns, and problem-solving strategies lose their usefulness, which at first seems only negative. These are disturbances of law and order. However, out of the disturbances arises the necessity for further development, and new structures and behavior patterns become necessary and possible. A system that enters a state of crisis has to change itself if it wants to survive. Without crises and perturbations, without disturbances of law and order, there can be no development. But there is always disturbance and stimulus, chance and risk,[5] since the result of this development can be positive or negative.

If we want an example to illustrate such a noninstructive form of interaction between system and environment, we should pick up a kaleidoscope. The patterns we see among the mirrors arise from the relationship of the colored splinters of glass and their manifold reflections and reflections of reflections. These patterns are closed to the environment, as no new splinters of glass come in from the outside. But the figures that appear are not independent of the environment. If we shake the kaleidoscope hard enough (if we subject it to a perturbation), the observable figures change in accordance with the possibilities and necessities that are given, on the one hand, by the form of the glass splinters and their interaction and, on the other hand, by the shaking. Even so, no information penetrates inside from the outside. As an observer, one can link the shaking of the kaleidoscope with the emerging pictures and say that information has been formed in the kaleidoscope: a very kaleidoscopic cognition of human shaking. The difference from the information of the nervous system is that, while the kaleidoscope is shaken, splinters of glass interact mechanically; the possibilities and necessities of mechanical laws limit the combinations of splinters of glass and the emergence of different colored patterns in a way different from the way the laws of self-organization limit the nervous

---

5. For this reason the Chinese sign for "crisis" is made up from the two signs for chance and risk (Capra 1982).

system. When nerve cells interact with each other and are shaken up, only such patterns can emerge that are compatible with the present state of each single nerve cell and the self-referential structure of the nervous system as a whole. This limits chance in a different way from how splinters of glass are limited in the formation of patterns.

COUPLING SYSTEMS

The question remains to be answered: how to explain, in the face of the impossibility of transmitting information between operationally closed systems, the fact that communication between people can succeed. For it is difficult to deny that it looks as though we are able to give each other information. That exchange of information certainly does not correspond to the ambitious ideas often connected with the term "communication," but is surprising enough. For example, we can arrange to meet a colleague at 4:15 P.M. at the station to catch a train, and the colleague not only actually appears at 4:15 P.M., but the train to the desired destination even stops at the platform and, moreover, actually leaves on time.

Technical communication systems are constructed in such a way that, for each distinguishable state produced in the sender, a distinguishable state is produced in the receiver. In order to make the phenomenon of communication possible, a similar correspondence of inner structures and processes has to be created in the communication partners. It is relatively easy to achieve this correspondence where telephones are concerned, as they are put together from the same or similar parts in accordance with the same construction plan. They then have a similar or identical structure and can both manifest corresponding behaviors. Achieving this correspondence is more difficult in the case of the autonomous activity patterns of the human brain. This difficulty can be explained by the structural changes and developments that people undergo in the course of their mutual history.

When living beings live together, they form the environment for each other; each unbalances the other again and again, plunges him into a crisis, and demands adaptation from him to an extent the other never even dreamed of. Both unsettle each other; they disturb and stimulate (as well as irritate) one another. In this way they determine the framework for one another within which each can and must develop his behavioral patterns and structures. Humberto Maturana (1976) calls this process "structural coupling." It is a process of reciprocal adaptation, which comes to rest (at least temporarily) now and then, when neither disturbs nor stimulates (or irritates!) the other anymore. They then understand each other and have found a consensus. Both have developed in such a way that their structures correspond enough so that each can manifest the same behavior. Each knows the behavior displayed by the other from the inner perspective and thus has an idea of its meaning for the other. By their behavior, both then confirm their assumptions. Maturana (1976) writes, "If this process leads to a domain of consensus, it is a case of 'con-versation' in the strict sense, of a mutual twisting and turning in such a way that all concerned experience nontrivial structural changes until behavioral homomorphy is attained and communication can take place."

Accordingly, communication is only possible as the result of a development process in the course of which several people determine the living conditions—the necessary and possible behaviors—for one another. Refusing to do everything possible and being prepared to manifest the behavior stipulated as necessary by the other lead to a restriction of individual scope of behavior and to an increasing behavioral similarity. What is achieved by the uniformity of construction guaranteed by the factory in the case of the telephones is, in the case of living beings, the result of a process of selection, namely, the conformity of behavior. From his knowledge of the internal perspective, each can then ascribe an analogous meaning to the behavior of the other.

In this way understanding becomes possible without the transmission of information, sometimes even without words. This phenomenon can be seen in old married couples whose views, habits, taste, and appearance become more and more similar, just as between master and dog and between horse and rider. However, this phenomenon certainly makes misunderstanding possible too, when the assumption that the other experiences something similar in a similar situation is not true (because the situation is quite different for the other person).

For the reality of a relationship negotiated in this way, the limits between necessity and possibility are set widely. It can—in terms of the scales of softness or hardness of reality proposed here—be the softest of the soft and the hardest of the hard, according to what is agreed on in the wide spectrum between the vagueness and inflexibility of meanings. Observers who observe how other observers observe them and, in addition, observe themselves observing others, who are in turn observing them, self-referentially influence the result of their observation in a way more extreme than can be possible with any other "object" of cognition. Everyone creates his partner during interaction with him, and thereby himself too. Both (or when there are more participants, all) have to actually agree how hard this reality is. To agree does not mean that they sit around the kitchen table and negotiate a contract on whose quirk is an "unchangeable character trait" (harder) or merely a "bad habit" (softer); the agreement refers to all rules of interaction and all descriptions and proves itself in day-to-day behavior.

THE BODY AS ENVIRONMENT

Whoever has followed my line of argument up to this point and read the heading of this section will suspect that in systems theory the body can be considered not only as a system but also as environment. The body (the system of physiological rules), behavior (the system of prescriptive rules), the current world view of a person (the system of descriptive rules), and the social system (the system of interactional rules) can each be seen as self-organizing, operationally closed, autonomous systems that function according to the laws governing the combination of their elements.

In this model we can thus never explain someone's behavior *positively* according to the pattern that *one* (biological, psychic, social, and so on) cause results in *one* particular behavior, but only *negatively*. The behavioral possibilities of an individual person are limited by the various environments (body, world view, system of interaction, physical environment) to such an extent that only few or even only one possibility remains.

There is no hierarchy of these autonomous systems that would enable bodily processes, for example, to stipulate that parents must beat their children or that psychological processes can be the cause of cancer. Instead, a relationship of reciprocity can be seen among them; in the course of their mutual history each system limits the others' scope of survival and development. What happens within these limits cannot be attributed to the effect of the other systems, that is, the various environments. According to the Swiss psychiatrist Luc Ciompi (1988), psyche and body can be regarded as structurally coupled.

An arranged marriage exists between these systems (in this case with absolute certainty, until death do us part) in which the partners were not generally asked beforehand whether they like each other. They have to get along with each other anyhow—divorce is not possible. And they cannot be content to live side by side, but are dependent on one another, whether they love one another or not. One cannot survive without the other. The concept of structural coupling explains how, in this kind of marriage, structures again become more and more alike over time. In each of these systems a selection of structures, functions, and processes that fit the other systems (its environments) takes place.

In a similar way we can also grasp the system-environment relationship between social and bodily processes and analyze, for example, the connection between the health or illness of a person and patterns of family (or other) interaction. The family can never be to blame (the cause) for an illness. It can, however, limit the scope for preserving health. And vice versa—bodily conditions are not the cause of family structures either; they merely limit the range between necessity and possibility. At first glance the distinction between these statements must seem like pure quibbling, but when we look closer we find that each one embodies a different idea about how change comes about.

The somewhat paradoxical-seeming method of overcoming the split between mind and body thus leads first to an even more radical distinction between these areas. The hope associated with this step is that the logic of their interrelationship can be described and an overall picture designed that can overcome the artificial boundaries of these systems. If, for analytical purposes, we direct our attention to the relationship of bodily processes to behavior and the descriptions of individual persons, we then approach the field that psychoanalysis tries to explore, namely, the biology of psychological events and processes.

Some of the central psychoanalytical concepts can be summarized in light of the systemic observations depicted here. This applies in particular to Freud's concept of instinct, which forms the basis of the whole system of theories of classical psychoanalysis. Freud, too, sees the biological and psychic levels as separate and tries to analyze the prerequisites of their relationship:

> We have already alluded to the most important of these postulates; ... it is of a biological nature, and makes use of the concept of "purpose" (or perhaps of expediency) and runs as follows: the nervous system is an apparatus which has the function of getting rid of the stimuli that reach it or of reducing them to the lowest possible level, or which, if it were feasible, would maintain itself in an altogether unstimulated condition. [1915, p. 565]

Freud (1915, p. 566) uses instinct to describe "the demand made upon the mind for work in consequence of its connection with the body."

Using the term "instinct" is by nature connected with the risk of reified ideas. What Freud describes, though, can be understood—a little less materially—as the result of the structural link between bodily and psychological processes. Instinct as a result of the disturbed peace of the nervous system works as a perturbation of the soul, as disturbance, and as the impulse to do something about reestablishing this peace. Even for Freud (1915) the psyche itself is a control system, of which he thinks

that the activity of even the most highly developed mental apparatus is subject to the "pleasure principle," i.e., is automatically regu-
lated by feelings belonging to the pleasure–unpleasure series. The
unpleasurable feelings are connected with an increase and pleasur-
able feelings with a decrease of stimulus. [p. 566]

The effect of the pleasure principle on the satisfaction of these
biologically determined, instinctive needs is thus also a limit, though
not a restriction as regards content. Hunger can be stilled with caviar
just as well as with potato soup, thirst with water or wine, sexual
desires satisfied with a loved partner or in a peep-show. It is regret-
table that Freud (1900) did not stay with his original, much more
appropriate term "unpleasure principle." For the term "pleasure
principle" leads to the assumption that it is not a question of reducing or avoiding disturbances (perturbation), but of aspiring to
concrete aims. The fact that millions of people sit in front of the
television every evening with a bag of chips in their hand proves
well enough that maximization of pleasure is not the most important driving force of human behavior, but rather minimization of
unpleasure. Pleasure is only one of the possible negations of
unpleasure; when we content ourselves with feeling no unpleasure,
this opens up a much wider scope of possible behaviors. We are
dealing here with the difference between active and passive negation, which is discussed more fully in Chapter 8.

The effect of bodily processes on mental ones is not directed to
a concrete positive aim, but to a negative one; it is directed away
from a concrete aim. Bodily need is the famous passenger who gets
into a taxi and says, "I don't know where to, but please drive fast!"
And behavior is the taxi driver who drives off and looks uncertainly
into the rear mirror to see if the passenger is still looking around
excitedly or has fallen into a peaceful sleep. However, on this flight
without direction the driver also has to make sure he does not drive
too fast or overstep other traffic limits, because otherwise the authorities in the form of a policeman will intervene and not allow
poor bodily need to reach his aim ("away from here!") at all.

THE RADIO CENTER AND
THE IGNORANT TAXI DRIVER:
AN ATTEMPT TO MAKE ONESELF
UNDERSTOOD WITH WORDS

You probably know from your own experience how difficult it is to explain what you mean to somebody else. It is particularly difficult when you are limited to the spoken word and have no possibility of feeding your partner papayas or somehow letting him experience what you mean. The reasons for this difficulty ought to become a little clearer in the following game. As you will see at first glance, it is a rather silly bit of childish nonsense, which will not require any great intellectual demands of you as a reader. If you want to go along with it anyway, you need a partner who is prepared to experience the difficulties of verbal communication with you for a few minutes.

The Opening Situation

A temporary taxi driver, who unfortunately does not know his way around the city very well, asks the dispatcher from the taxicab dispatch center to explain the way to the Boardwalk by radio. At the moment he is at Reading Railroad.

Rules of the Game

On the next page you will find a map of the town (Figure 4–1). The Reading Railroad station is marked with a big X that cannot be missed. In addition, several streets and squares—the Boardwalk among others—are marked with numbers. The streets these numbers stand for are explained in the key. This map is in the radio dispatch center and serves to explain the way to the Boardwalk.

At the end of this book you will find a second map (Figure 13–1), on which the names of the streets are not marked. The taxi driver

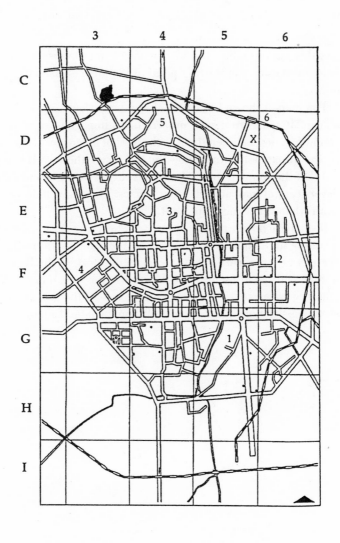

1 Waterworks   4 Park Avenue
2 Mediterranean Ave.   5 Oriental Avenue
3 The Boardwalk   6 Reading Railroad

Figure 4–1

uses this map to follow the instructions from the dispatch center. Only the station, the starting point of the journey, is marked with an X.

The map at the end of the book can be cut out so that the players can sit apart from each other. This is important so as to limit communication between them to the level of language. Since in real life the dispatcher cannot show the taxi driver the way, it is important that the simulation is as true to reality as possible and that the players cannot look at each other's maps. They may, however, talk about whatever seems important.

If you have no one to play with or your heart breaks at the thought of cutting up a book, you can also play the game by yourself. Use a tape recorder to record how you explain the route to the Boardwalk in at least three different ways. Please use three or more different reference systems. You then take on the role of the taxi driver. Follow the instructions you have recorded on the tape. Talk to yourself!

5

Mad Thinking

A KIND OF HOPSCOTCH: ALMOST A CHILDREN'S GAME

You all know the game children play all over the world on sidewalks and roads. You mark out several squares on the surface and throw a stone into one of them. The one whose turn it is then jumps into these squares on one or sometimes on two legs in a sequence unfathomable to the uninitiated. In some of the squares he jumps on one leg; in others he must use both. Sometimes he has to cross his legs, and now and again the stone has to be pushed farther on without landing on a line. When you finally think it's all over, this hopping starts all over again in a different sequence. A similar game is suggested here and should be practiced to attune ourselves to the right mood of mad thinking and feeling. We are not going to jump with our feet, though; we shall use our minds instead. But it is still a matter of squares into and out of which we have to jump.

In preparation the beginner is advised to get a piece of paper and a pen. After a bit of practice the advanced learner will be in a position to do all that is necessary in his head.

You begin with the situation or the room you are in at this moment. Now select something you can perceive right now within this room or situation. It can be an object, a state, an event, a process, or anything else that you see, hear, or feel. Formulate a statement describing what you perceive (example: The coffee is cold!). Write this sentence down, draw a square around it, and give it the number 1 (Figure 5–1). As this sentence stands for things, processes, states, or events *within* the situation or the room—like you—it needs to be made recognizable as a type of sentence we will call the inner

Sentence 1:
The coffee is cold·

Figure 5–1

sentence. For this reason it should be marked with an odd Arabic number. Sentences referring to things, processes, states, or events *outside* this room or this situation (outer sentences) will be made recognizable by even Roman numbers.

The first hopping square is thus completed. You form the second by formulating a sentence describing the whole situation or the whole room in which what you describe in sentence 1 is to be found. For example, the cold coffee is part of a situation in which I am sitting in my study. The study is the room in which all this is going on. Thus my choice for the next sentence is: My study is on the first floor of the house. The situation or rather the room in which the events in sentence 1 take place is now explained from the outside. The study is not a part of the study. Give this sentence the consecutive number II (Roman) and write it down outside the square with sentence 1. Draw a square around sentence II to include sentence 1 (Figure 5–2). You now have drawn the second hopscotch square.

Now you move once more from the outside to the inside and look for something else within the situation or the room described in sentence II (example: There is a picture of Fujiyama on the wall). This sentence gets the consecutive number 3 (Arabic), as it is another inner sentence. Write this sentence within the square for sentence II but outside the square with sentence 1 (Figure 5–3). Again the difference between inside and outside is important. The Fujiyama on the wall can be ascribed to the content of the room, but not to the content of the cold coffee (which might, according to the esthetic criteria of an art critic, also be a rather meaningful classification).

Now you look for a second room or another situation in which what you described in sentence 3 also occurs, and formulate a state-

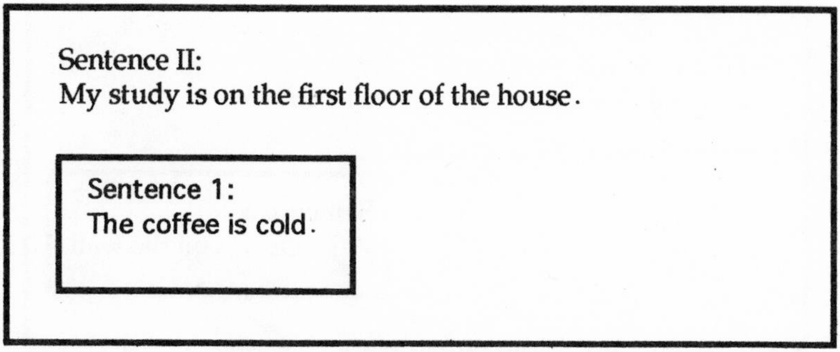

Sentence II:
My study is on the first floor of the house.

Sentence 1:
The coffee is cold.

Figure 5–2

ment that describes this situation or room (example: The souvenir shop is in the Ginza in Tokyo). Give this outside sentence the consecutive number IV (Roman). I must emphasize once again how important it is that the situation or room is described from the outside in these outer sentences. The shop in the Ginza is not inside the shop, but inside the Ginza. Write sentence 3 and its square again and draw a second square with sentence IV and its square around it (Figure 5–4).

The next sentence should again describe a part of what is within the room or situation described in sentence IV (example: The prices

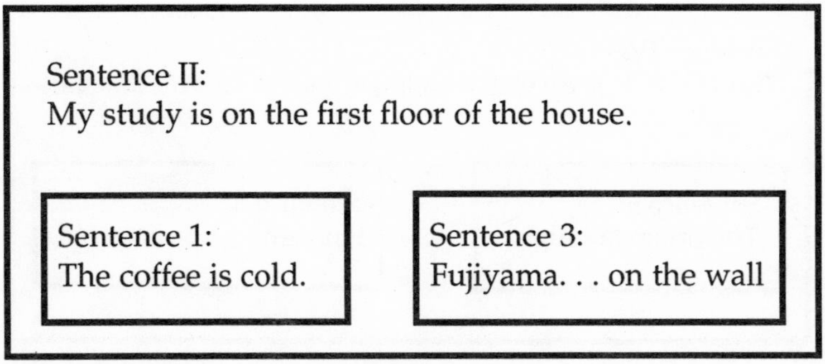

Sentence II:
My study is on the first floor of the house.

Sentence 1:
The coffee is cold.

Sentence 3:
Fujiyama. . . on the wall

Figure 5–3

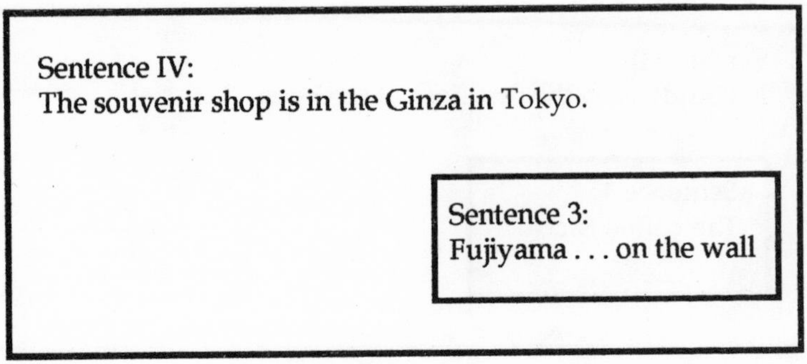

Sentence IV:
The souvenir shop is in the Ginza in Tokyo.

> Sentence 3:
> Fujiyama . . . on the wall

Figure 5-4

are outrageous). In accordance with the now familiar pattern you write this sentence inside the square of sentence IV, but outside the square with sentence 3 (Figure 5-5). This sentence gets the consecutive number 5.

The construction plan for our hopscotch field should now be clear. We always alternate from the inside to the outside and from the outside to the inside, and the same environment or the same content may not be chosen twice. You now choose another situa-

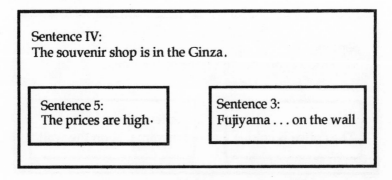

Sentence IV:
The souvenir shop is in the Ginza.

Sentence 5:
The prices are high.

Sentence 3:
Fujiyama . . . on the wall

Figure 5-5

tion or room in which the facts described in sentence 5 fit (example: Tahiti is one of the most expensive places in the world). This sentence gets the consecutive number VI. Then take another inner sentence (The sand is black) and write it down under number 7. Go on producing these squares until you have had enough. Your hopscotch field is now finished. If you want, you can go on to describe your field: on leaving square 3 you enter either square II or IV.

Now to the prescriptive rules that tell you how to hop. Take a coin; on one side is heads, on the other tails. This enables you to decide on which way to go without having to think about the sense or nonsense of your choice. Begin with sentence 1 and write it on a fresh piece of paper. You now toss the coin. Heads means you move to the next sentence with an even, Roman number; tails means you go to the next odd, Arabic number.

Example

Sentence 1:	The coffee is cold!
Coin: Heads	
Sentence II:	My study is on the first floor.
Coin: Heads	
Sentence IV:	The souvenir shop is in the Ginza in Tokyo.
Coin: Tails	
Sentence 5:	The prices are outrageous.
Coin: Tails	
Sentence 7:	The sand is black.

You now have a collection of sentences that are linked (associated) either by a chance exchange of sentences connected by a common (outer or inner) sentence or by exchanging outer and inner sentences. It is a sequence of associations, the regularity of which is unfathomable to anyone but you (in Figure 5–6 you will find a schematic summary).

In a variation of this game, individual terms can be used instead of inner sentences; you then take outer terms instead of outer sentences to describe the context for the meaning of the inner terms. Everything else stays as shown. In that case you get smaller squares but a more sophisticated field.

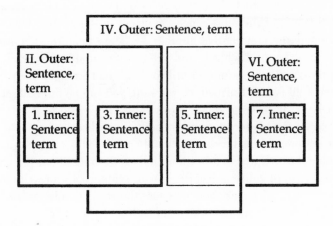

Figure 5–6

This alternate plan is explained in such detail to clarify the inner logic of the rules of the game. It can be made even more complex by ascribing the squares with Roman numbers to the content of a farther outer square (The Ginza is the main shopping street in Tokyo.) This distinction between inside and outside is always relative and always refers to a concrete pair of sentences or terms. When the principle of this exchange has been understood, you can follow this logic (even without squares, paper, and coins) at any time and talk without the risk of anyone understanding you.

You should only do this, however, when you wish to break off communication with your fellow men or want to guarantee your dissociation from them. As a warning, let me add that this way of speaking usually leads to a communication breakdown, even if it is not desired. Anyone who risks this way of speaking over a long period of time in public has a good chance of being put into an institution and diagnosed as mad.

In order to experience the communicative effect of mad speech like this from the inner perspective, this game can be recommended from time to time. It can sometimes give you a certain sense of pleasure to experience how helpless and impotent all the people around you are when they try to understand you in vain. When the others' tongues are hanging out because they are breathlessly trying to keep up with your own associations, always intent on grasping their hidden meaning, you feel the certainty and unassailability of not being understood. But at some stage even the most well-meaning and untiring people in your environment abandon their attempts at interpretation and announce that there is neither sense nor rules nor a system behind such chains of association. Their origin is ascribed to mere chance, a disturbance in the bodily prerequisites for human communication. The rules of the game in this kind of association, in spite of their not being understandable, are usually overlooked.

By the way, the joke about the two madmen playing ludo, when one says "Check" and gets the answer that there is no penalty in Halma, is constructed according to the same scheme or at least can be reconstructed that way (Figure 5–7; start is in Context/Game B, Ludo).

In ludo and in chess the opponent's figures can be threatened and thrown out. The switch from Context/Game B Ludo to Context/Game C Chess makes it possible to use a move from this game, namely check. When the king is checkmated, his situation is similar to that of the goalkeeper when a penalty is given. At any rate, this identification gives rise to the possibility of changing the context to soccer (Game D). The circle is closed by an objection that follows the same logic. The second player takes the other direction, though, from ludo to Halma; both are connected insofar as the same figures are involved. And everyone must admit that a penalty really doesn't fit in Halma.

CONFUSED ASSOCIATIONS

The Swiss psychiatrist Eugen Bleuler (1911, 1916) the inventor of schizophrenia (at least of the term), characterized the difference between schizophrenic thinking and the normal everyday thinking

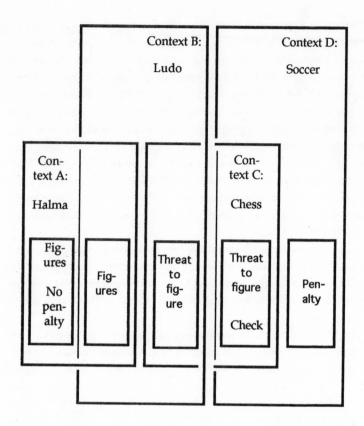

Figure 5–7

of Western adults as a loosening up of associations and as a fragmentation of thought processes. Individual concepts are conceived in a new, unusual, and oblique way; they are "compressed," and one concept is substituted for another. In addition to such "peculiar shifts," affective wishes and aims are interchanged. Due to the lack of focus the train of thought thus loses itself in secondary associations, and there is an inclination to generalization and the transposition of an idea or of a function to other areas (Bleuler 1911, 1916).

The explanation Bleuler gave for this kind of structuring of schizo-phrenic thinking was partly psychological and partly biological. As a psychologist he was strongly influenced by Sigmund Freud and his psychoanalytical ideas; as a psychiatrist worried about his repu-tation he tried to do justice to the biological dogma of orthodox medicine of the time, namely, "Mental illnesses are illnesses of the brain." He assumed that human experience is written down in our brain in some form or another. These engrams should designate certain facts like the words of a language and link them by means of associations. Bleuler considered the links of these engrams to be biologically determined. For this reason they could also get mixed up by biological processes. The effect of such confusion was psy-chological, however: a confusion of associations. Things were linked together that, according to the rules of the normal everyday logic of an adult from central Europe, ought not be linked.

One does not *have* to fall back upon biological mechanisms to explain these phenomena, and there is also much to be said against the reified idea of engrams, that model of little clay blocks in the brain. Regarded psychologically, though, the (dis-)order of schizo-phrenic thinking, feeling, and behavior can be explained quite well by confusion of association. Anyone who relates meanings to each other in a way different from the average man inevitably lives in a reality that is not average.

Concepts, words, signs, and pictures—summarized here and di-verging from the usual specialized definitions (e.g., psychoanalytical) as *symbols*—are usually more than just names for an object or a fact. They are comparable to the cards you take as a Monopoly game player when a throw of the dice takes you to the square of the board marked "Chance." These "Chance" cards tell you where to go next and which is the next step to be taken: Go to jail! Go to Boardwalk! If you alter these associations, you alter the rules of the game.

Something analogous applies to the symbols we use to put our own reality together. They are not only static retainers for some clearly defined meaning but also instructions for a game. They tell us where we *have to go* in a train of thought and where we *must not* go. In schizophrenic thinking a different selection is made. This leads to the player not only giving events a different meaning (when he should go to Boardwalk, he thinks he is to be thrown into jail) but also not keeping to the rules in his behavior (he indignantly insists that Mediterranean Avenue is a part of the Waterworks).

It need not necessarily be a problem that someone uses different symbols or uses symbols in a different way and follows other rules of the game. After all, "up" in English means something quite different than "ab" in German, although both words sound similar. However, schizophrenic thinking is not simply like speaking a different language that can be learned with a little diligence, perseverance, and good will. The difference is that a visitor to a foreign country where an unknown language is spoken can make regular connections between sounds and meanings. For example, someone who ends up in the underground garage for the twentieth time, when he really wanted to go to the top floor of a department store, will realize that in this elevator "up" (= ab) not only does not mean the same as in the elevators at home, but always means the same different thing. A foreign language and different social games can be learned because the behavior of those who speak this language or play such a game repeats itself in an improbable way. It thus seems not to be determined by chance alone. Descriptive rules can be formulated and used as prescriptive rules when speaking the language. This is the essential difference from mad thought, speech, and action, in which the linking of symbols, meanings, and behavior seems coincidental and arbitrary; it does not follow the rules of everyday logic.

TOO MUCH OR TOO LITTLE MEANING

The extremes of schizophrenic speech and thought (we will take speech as an expression of thought for the moment) go in two opposite directions. At one end of the spectrum words and concepts are used in a too narrow and too concrete meaning; at the other end we have the too wide, too general and vague, abstract use of linguistic and other symbols. One aspect of normal thought and normal communication is that we do not take our words or those of others too literally. We always have to add in our minds or imagine away what is not said. At one extreme of schizophrenic thought too much is added; at the other too much is left out.

Two clinical examples may serve to clarify this spectrum of schizophrenic speech. A young man is admitted to a psychiatric hospital on the last day of his end-of-school exams because he has been talking in a confused way that no one understands. A few days later the patient's father makes a couple of photocopies of the school diploma in a department store; in the process he forgets for whatever reason to take the original diploma out of the photocopier. When he realizes what he has done, it is too late, and the certificate is not to be found. The young man comments, "Now my exam is gone!" He identifies the symbol with the symbolized fact, the exam with the piece of paper certifying that he has passed, the menu with the meal. He treats the symbol like a concrete thing: the exam is the certificate. He imagines away an important part of the sphere of meaning normally surrounding this symbol (the certificate) and that says something about itself. He neglects to add this part of the sphere of meaning, namely, that this piece of paper is a symbol, that its value exists not in the quality of the paper but in the social meaning linked with it, and that this meaning remains even though the symbol has been lost.

If you want to be normal there is a whole field (a quantity in the sense of a set theory) of very complex meanings that have to be connected with such a symbol. Over and above this field are a great number of private meanings that every individual connects with a piece of paper like a diploma (have you really passed your end-of-school exams? and so on). And a great number of distinctions are required to connect the correct composition of meanings with the various symbols. In this way loss of a driving license must be evaluated differently from the loss of a $1,000 bill; even the possibility of applying for a photocopy is different. The relationship between appearance and reality is clarified respectively in each concrete case: how much a purchased fifteen-minute swimming test certificate is worth is proved when the owner falls into the water.

The second good example of someone taking colloquial speech too literally is given to us by Dustin Hoffman in his role of a psychiatric patient in the film *Rainman*. He stops in the middle of an intersection when the traffic lights suddenly switch from "Go" to "Don't Go"; neither cajoling nor kicks can persuade him to move on before the traffic lights switch to "Go" again.

You can understand traffic signals only when you draw up a parcel of specific meanings. Our language and our conceptual and symbolic thought function only because the symbols used have more than one meaning. Words, concepts, and signs are practically never names for some clearly defined things or facts (denotation); rather they transport bundles of meanings (connotation). The red traffic light does not simply say "Stop whatever happens!" It says "Stop if you have not stepped into the road yet!" and "Go across quickly if you are in the middle of the road!"

How someone draws together this kind of parcel of meanings shows first and foremost whether he is normal or mad. However, he has the mad opportunity not only to put too little meaning into his parcel, but he can also pack too much into it. In this case the words and concepts are not taken literally enough: anything that sounds, looks, or feels similar is equated, as similarity becomes identity.

This principle of schizophrenic thinking is illustrated by von Domarus (cited in Arieti 1978), the first person to describe it, in the following exemplary case: One of his patients thought "that Jesus, cigar boxes, and sex were identical. Study of this delusion disclosed that the common predicate, which led to the identification, was the state of being encircled. According to the patient, the head of Jesus, as of a saint, is encircled by a halo, the packet of cigars by the tax band, and the woman by the sex glance of the man" (p. 26).

In mad thinking the way from premise to conclusion does not follow the path of sound, everyday logic. In everyday logic you are not allowed to infer the identity of objects from the identity of predicates—the characteristics or behaviors ascribed to these objects. Such a rule of identification follows the pattern: Goethe is a human, Eskimos are humans, therefore Goethe is an Eskimo.

Conversation with someone who gropes his way from one meaning to the other can be rather difficult. There are just too many similarities for one to know or guess which the other has selected. Here is an example of such a (failed) dialogue:

Mr. B. is a philosopher and has been very confused over the past few months. He has been on a psychiatric ward for several weeks and spends most of his time drinking coffee and smoking a large number of cigarettes. When the new ward doctor says that he is smoking rather a lot, he answers, "I've been to Hamburg too." The doctor, now also somewhat confused, tries to clarify the situation by asking, "I don't quite understand. What has Hamburg got to do with it?" The patient answers, "In Lübeck the King of Siam is on." When he concludes, "I've got an account with the building society" and sees the young doctor's despairing frown, the conversation ends. The young doctor retires hurriedly to his room on the ward and, like the patient, smokes one cigarette after the other and drinks several cups of coffee (in the vain hope of clearing his head with the biological effect of nicotine and caffeine). He broods on the connection between smoking and a building society savings account.*

What was so confusing to him and took away the last grain of doubt that he was really in a madhouse was the fact that the patient's thoughts did not follow public paths that, carefully mapped, ensure that there is no chaos on the roads. Instead he struck out across country, taking no notice of signposts, traffic signs, garden fences, and signs with "Trespassers will be prosecuted" on them. These public paths and roads are the channels of logic and causal thinking. They tell us under what conditions we may shift from one meaning to the next: if/then. These roads have a certain width, so that not everyone has to follow exactly the same tracks. However, in the long run it attracts attention when someone frequently or even regularly drives over the curb or through other people's gardens.

The association between smoking and a savings account—or to put it differently, the path from the property with the sign "A lot of

---

*Mr. B. was one of my first patients, and thinking about this savings account not only caused me to give up smoking but it also induced me to write this book (probably).

smoking goes on here" to the property inscribed "I've got a savings account"—was finally reconstructed, even though it took a great deal of effort, with the help of the patient:

Smoking a lot led to a terribly smoky nightclub in Hamburg that the patient had once visited while at university (*I've been to Hamburg too*); it was in a part of the city called *Sankt Pauli*. With Sankt Pauli the patient associated the Boy from Sankt Pauli, the hero of a musical of the same name, played by a singer called *Freddy Quinn*. At the time of the conversation Freddy Quinn was playing the main role in the play *Anna and the King of Siam* in the Town Theater in Lübeck (*In Lübeck the King of Siam is on*). In Lübeck you also find the "Holstentor," not only an impressive and unmistakable piece of architecture but also one of the emblems of Lübeck, and—here comes the association—it is depicted on the *DM 50* note. DM 50 is exactly the amount that the patient paid into his *savings account with the building society* (to be accurate: his mother paid the monthly DM 50).

The principle followed by this train of thought was obviously that in one case *a part was taken for the whole and in the other the whole for a part*. Hamburg was identified with the smoke-filled nightclub, the nightclub with Sankt Pauli, Sankt Pauli with the Boy from Sankt Pauli, the Boy from Sankt Pauli with the actor playing him, the actor with a different role in a different play, the play with the town in which it was being played, the town with its emblem, the emblem with its depiction on a bill, the bill with its value, and the value with the amount paid into the building society.

MAD LOGIC

In a general account of the phenomenon, the American psychiatrist Silvano Arieti (1978) attempts to characterize the logic of schizophrenic cognition. In his opinion it is based on

(1) concretization (or perceptualization) of the concept, (2) identification based upon similarity (the principle of von Domarus), and (3) a changed relationship between connotation and verbalization.

In other words, the usual semantic value of the word is altered and what acquires special value is the word itself, with diminished or ignored relation to its original meaning. [p. 16]

In contrast, in normal thinking in which identity is only assumed on the basis of identical subjects, someone following schizophrenic logic accepts identity on the basis of identical predicates.

In fact it is obvious that the predicate is the most important part of this type of thinking. Since the same subject may have numerous predicates, it is the choice of the predicate in the paleologic premise which will determine the great subjectivity, bizarreness and often unpredictability of autistic thinking. . . . Whereas the healthy person in a weakened state is mainly concerned with the connotation and denotation of a symbol and is capable of shifting his attention from one to another of the two aspects of a symbol, the autistic person is mainly concerned with the denotation and verbalization, and experiences a total or partial impairment of his ability to connote. . . . For the person who thinks paleologically, the verbal symbols cease to be representative of a group or a class, but only refer to the specific object under discussion. [pp. 28 and 31]

Lyman Wynne and Margaret Singer base their characterization of schizophrenic thought on the normal principles of psychological development, described by Werner (1957) as follows: "Wherever development occurs it proceeds from a state of relative globality and lack of differentiation to a state of increasing differentiation, articulation, and hierarchic integration." In their classification of clinically observed schizophrenic disturbances they concentrate on what they consider to be its central aspects:

(a) the capacity to differentiate self from nonself; (b) the capacity to recognize and distinguish different kinds of feeling states, impulses and wishes; (c) the delineation of distinctive, specialized skills—motor, cognitive, expressive, linguistic; (d) the capacity to discriminate different parts of the object world, personal and nonpersonal, and to distinguish abstract and metaphorical representations from their literal and concrete counterparts. [Wynne and Singer 1963, p. 200]

Wynne and Singer distinguish between four different classes of schizophrenic styles of cognition or communication in the patients they examined: an amorphous form, a mixed form, a fragmented form, and a stable, restricted form. These styles are arrayed on a continuum, the two ends of which are amorphous cognition and restricted cognition. At one extreme a patient portrays amorphous thought with wishy-washy and unclearly defined concepts to the extent that he had to come to terms with people and several ideas at the same time and to find a main theme for his ideas. It is notable that he seems unable to find a focus and the right words and does not manage to give his remarks a comprehensive sense. In contrast to amorphous thinking, patients assigned to the mixed form "show islands of perceptual and cognitive clarity, with the ability to make from time to the time surprisingly cogent, clear, and perceptive observations . . ." (p. 204). Patients with fragmented forms of thinking "have relatively clear, differentiated styles of attending, perceiving and communicating" (p. 204). However, they can manifest a serious disorganization in their thoughts when it comes to integrating certain ideas, impulses, and emotions.

> They dissociate and split off disturbing ideas, impulses and affects in an unstable, often chaotic fashion. . . . Thus, these "fragmented" schizophrenic patients are highly vulnerable to emotional stress arising from either inner or external sources. Characteristically, they show abrupt, maladaptive, "unintentional" disruptions of thought processes, "classical" signs of an "over-inclusive" thought disorder. [p. 204]

The fourth group of patients manifested a style of thought that can be described as "stably over-focussed and under-inclusive. . . . Although in one sense they have split off great areas of perception and experience, the splitting has stabilized" (p. 205).

The range of styles of thought—as described by McConaghy (1960)—runs from underinclusive, overorganized and overfocused thought to overinclusive, underorganized and underfocused thought: from making up too extensive, too clearly structured packages of meaning to sending or receiving rather empty, unstructured packages. Normal styles of thought might then be situated midway between these two extremes. In overinclusive thinking and communication the concepts, symbols, and signs are used with a high connotative content, that is, they embrace a broad spectrum of emotionally and situationally associative meanings. In underinclusive thinking and communication concepts, symbols and signs are used as denotatively as possible, that is, they are stripped of associations, of their emotional content that goes beyond the strict designation of an object or fact.

The group around Gregory Bateson, which became known for the formulation of the double-bind hypothesis, attributed the different aspects of schizophrenic thinking and communication (for them these cannot be separated) to the inability to differentiate between logical types. These types are based on Bertrand Russell and Alfred N. Whitehead's "theory of logical classes," according to which concepts can show different grades of abstraction. Thus the concept "man," for example, can stand for one single, concrete person or for the logical class of man, an abstract concept including individual human beings. Anyone who makes the wrong logical classification unavoidably mistakes abstract and concrete, class and element, whole and part. The whole spectrum of symptoms of schizophrenia can in their view be understood as an attempt to escape the paradoxes arising from this form of logical confusion (Bateson et al. 1956).

To sum up, mad thinking is logically organized in a different way from normal thinking. Logical connections between subject and predicate and logical classifications (i.e., differences between abstract and concrete) are made that cannot be understood in the framework of the surrounding language system. This gives rise to a deviation in the connotative and denotative use—the range of meaning of individual concepts and words—of language. Words are either stripped of their connotative content in a concretist way (for example, the feelings connected with them) or identified on the basis of similarities in a way that does not correspond to the social (i.e., colloquial) consensus. This deviation results in the breakdown of communication because the patient's mode of expression is no longer understandable and predictable for the partners with whom he interacts.

As certain similarities exist between this phenomenon and the way a child thinks, it has so far largely been explained in psychoanalytical terms as a regression to old cognitive patterns; thus the term "paleologic." The second approach to an explanation, contemplated as early as Bleuler, sees the structure of this kind of thinking as the more or less random result of specific functional disorders of the brain.

Any attempt to explain this deviation from the accepted norm of cognition and communication will do well to question this apparently self-evident normality and to consider the mechanisms and regularities governing its origin. Why is it that we consider a certain organization of cognition, a certain average scope of a concept's meaning, to be normal, when disorganization is so much more probable?

6

Differences That Make a Difference

MENTAL EXERCISE

What is the difference between dogs and bark? There is no difference. Dogs bark and bark.

What is the difference between a crocodile? It swims in the water and walks on land.

What is the difference between a hippopotamus? There is no difference!

What is the difference between a crocodile and a hippopotamus? As far as the crocodile is concerned, there is a difference, but not as far as the hippopotamus is concerned (Gernhardt et al. 1979, p. 23).

INSIDE OR OUTSIDE

In the course of (Western) intellectual thinking, various attempts have been made to systematize the laws of logic. The problem at stake was always the relationship between concepts and their meanings, their interconnections, the relationship between the content and extent of meaning, and the evaluation of statements as true or false. Different types of logic developed depending on which of these aspects was regarded as fundamental: the *logic of propositions*, dealing with the *truth or falseness* of statements; the *logic of predicates*, considering the *intended content of meaning* (the so-called intention); and *class logic*, considering the *extent of meaning* (the extension) of concepts.

Bertrand Russell (1903) writes: "It has been customary, in works on logic, to distinguish two standpoints, that of extension and that of intension. Philosophers have usually regarded the latter as more fundamental, while Mathematics has been held to deal specially with the former" (p. 56).

These attempts all have in common that they are based on an existing system of concepts and (once again) imagine away the observer. They examine the alleged *actual state* and tacitly take an objective relationship between objects and concepts for granted that is independent of the observer, who views "things" as *entities* clearly separated from their environment, assigns attributes to them, and makes statements on their behavior. Only the static level of the menu is considered, and this is what the academic wrangling of the logicians is all about. Is the statement "This is a wiener schnitzel!" true only if the actual piece of meat on the plate (denotation) is veal, or does the escallop of pork coated with breadcrumbs still belong to the class of "wiener schnitzel" (connotation)?

The idea behind this form of seeking the truth is that it is possible to shape the true relationships of things and circumstances in the static relationships of static concepts (see Wittgenstein 1921). By giving up this static, objectivist perspective and including the observer and the usage of concepts, completely new options of systematizing are revealed. You examine according to which recipes are used to cook the delicacies on the menu and how they came by their more or less appetizing names.

Once again it is a question of examining the relationship between prescriptive and descriptive rules, between first- and second-order descriptions. What does an observer do when he describes objects and their mutual relationships?

In his essay *Laws of Form*, George Spencer-Brown (1969) begins with a similar question. This essay is another, rather unorthodox attempt to bring logic into a comprehensive system. His recipe approach provides an answer that is as simple as it is far reaching. All forms of thinking, hence all forms of logic, can be reduced to the *distinction between inside and outside*. All logical structures can be developed from this single operation, that is, this single (mental or nonmental) process.

The basis of all cognition is drawing a borderline that divides a sphere (of meaning) in such a way that you cannot get from one side of the border—from the inside—to the other side, the outside, without crossing the border. This is true no matter what the content of this space is. A circle on a smooth piece of paper or a hopscotch square on a level sidewalk can serve as an example of this borderline. This borderline divides the space in which the distinction is made (the surface of the piece of paper or the sidewalk) into two completely separate areas, the two sides of the distinction.

The entire space—that is, the entire world that is separated by a distinction—together with the entire content shall be called the "form" of the distinction. In our two examples this means that the entire space of the sidewalk (piece of paper) with its entire content—inside as well as outside of the hopscotch field (circle)—shall be called "form." This understanding of form diverges from its colloquial meaning. If, for instance, we speak of the form of a car, we are giving the car form as an attribute. In Spencer-Brown's definition, however, form is not ascribed to the content differing from the environment (thing, car, system) as a characteristic feature, but to the relationship between the two. When you drive your car into a tree, the border between inside and outside, between the car and the rest of the world, changes, that is, the form, the relationship between system and environment. If you regard form as the attribute of an object, you imagine away one part of the relationship between system and environment. Bathe your finger in hydrochloric acid for a while, and you will no longer doubt that the form of your finger is the result of the interrelationship between the attributes of your finger and its environment. If the distinction between inside and outside dissolves, the form dissolves too (in this barbaric example, your finger).

This relational definition of form can also be used to dissolve the contradiction between the different kinds of logic. In addition to the differences made by the observer, we must also consider the linguistic distinctions. Each of the two sides of a distinction can be named (Figure 6–1). It does not really matter what name you choose for one side or the other. If, for instance, you call the outer side inside and the inner side outside, the linguistic usage and hence the meaning of these concepts change, but in both cases the distinction remains symbolized to the same extent. Mind you, if you then ask your sullen, awkward, uncouth pubescent children to come out of their shell at last instead of looking inward all the time, you would probably get the same answer: "I've tried that already. Nothing doing out there either!"

The label "inside" or "outside" is not a component of the differing content. The name of the wine served with the wiener schnitzel is not a component of the wine. It represents a second distinction in another area of phenomena, in the semantic space of language. The sensory distinction the tipsy drinker makes when he tastes the wine differs from the distinction the buyer makes when reading the label on the bottle. In view of the fact that wine can be doctored and names juggled, that there are people who are not partial to wine and are beer drinkers, you should never assume that the name of a wine could objectively symbolize its taste, the pleasure of drinking it, and the pleasant drunkenness caused by it.

Just as the form is composed of both sides of the distinction, the meaning of the names attributed to these two sides of the distinction always results from the entity of the range of meaning divided by it. Therefore the meaning of a concept can never be grasped in isolation; it depends equally on what is included and on what is excluded by it. The negative meaning determines which meaning is approved of. Thus the content (the intention) of a concept is never

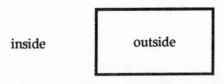

inside   outside

Figure 6–1

determined only positively by the characteristics and patterns of behavior (the predicates) attributed to it alone but also negatively by those that are disputed. To understand what inside means, you have to know what outside means. The same applies to class logic. A concept's extent of meaning (the extension) depends on what is included and excluded by the distinction. An extreme example is the hole. It is only defined by what is outside it (cheese, a sock, and the like), and not by what is inside it (nothing). The context determines the meaning of a concept, its content as well as its extent.

If, finally, one side of the distinction is evaluated as being true and the other as false, you have created a world of binary logic in which all statements can either be true or false. The *dogma of identity*, the *dogma of the excluded contradiction*, and the *dogma of the excluded third party*, which have determined the laws of traditional logic in Western thought since Aristotle, can be explained as the result of distinctions. An observer identifies everything he has localized on the same side of the distinction with each other with regard to the feature of distinction; he is not allowed to attribute the meaning he gives one side to the other side at the same time. If he does so he dissolves the border between the two areas of meaning—he dispenses with a distinction. He has no choice but to affirm or negate each of the two meanings.

All thinkers who have so far tried to systematize logic started from a static system of concepts that already exists and that describes a given and static world. What is new in Spencer-Brown's approach is that he examines the dynamics and development of such a system of concepts, its differentiation and nondifferentiation. This process leads to a completely different understanding of language; words, names, concepts, and other symbols do not primarily have a denotative (i.e., designating) function by which one of these symbols could unambiguously be attributed to one thing or one meaning. They are always ambiguously connected with many different meanings, that is, their connotative content is high. The ambiguity of language requires far less explanation than the relative lack of ambiguity that characterizes our everyday language and our mutual understanding.

If you want to explain mad structures of thought and communication by their distinctions deviating from normality, by their increased or decreased connotative or denotative content, the question arises as to the mechanisms and dynamics of the restriction and expansion of meanings, to the establishment of new and the dissolution of old barriers. What distinguishes the distinction between playing a mad form of hopscotch from playing it normally?

NECESSITY AND POSSIBILITY:
"ALL ARE . . ." AND "THERE IS A . . ."

If you want to comply with the rules of logic when talking, you have to follow clear-cut rules and fulfill certain conditions when attributing meaning to symbols and concepts. These rules determine the limits of the logically correct usage of a word, name, concept, or symbol, that is, the necessities and possibilities that restrict multiple connotative meanings.

Let's take the sentence "All ravens are black" as an example. The formulation "All/are" makes a statement about the claim of validity connected with the assertion that ravens can be given the attribute black. It applies to all ravens. Thus being black is a meaning that must necessarily be connected with raven. Whoever wants to be recognized as a raven should make sure he is seen to be black. If the statement read "Some ravens are black," the limitation would be different.

In the traditional predicate's logic dealing with the relationship between individuals (ravens) and predicates (black), this form of statement is regarded as a numerical limitation of its validity. A symbol referring to *all* individuals (things, objects, and so on) is therefore also called "allquantor." Its opposite is the so-called existence quantor, which states that at least one individual exists to whom this attribute can be ascribed. The validity of the assertion "There is at least one black raven" is far more modest. It describes that it is possible for ravens to be black.

Although when looking at distinctions you cannot assume from the outset that you are dealing with individuals, it is possible to describe the barriers of the logically possible and necessary meanings of a symbol (e.g., of a concept or word) with the statements "All are . . ." and "There is at least one. . . ." The characteristic that distinguishes the space on the inside of the distinction (of the hopscotch field) from the outside must necessarily belong to the meaning ascribed to the symbol for the inside. In addition, the possibility must exist that this characteristic can be ascribed to something. From a logical point of view the distinction black/not black only makes sense if at the same time the conditions "Everything within the distinction is black" and "There is something black" are met. Anyone who wants to end up in this box must fulfill a *necessary* and *possible* condition; it must be possible for an observer to identify him as black. Ravens, hearses, priests, conservative politicians, some cats, black panthers, the beach of Tahiti, black fantasies, the famous black Kulukulu of the South Pacific, and much more make up the content of this box. This does not mean that all ravens or cats or conservative politicians need necessarily be black, but there really must be something or something must be possible that ends up on the inside of the distinction (a raven, a small cat bringing ill luck, or a hearse).

Each system of meaning in which these conditions for the connection of symbols and meanings are fulfilled stays within the scope of logic. However, this does not guarantee that two people who both fulfill these conditions in their use of language associate the same meaning with one single word. Everyone who gives subjective meaning to words or other symbols that do not overstep these two limits remains within the communicative consensus in the form of his thought and language. He does not disturb and stimulate others to change their systems of meaning. He does not trouble (perturb) them and is not perturbed himself, is neither stimulated nor disturbed. And vice versa, where these limits are set for the development of a system of meaning, a kind of thinking develops that is logical enough to end up within the area of consensus. The madness of mad thought can be explained by the fact that meanings do not follow the lines of distinction and limits of normal thought. Formal consensus is abandoned, because linguistic and other symbols are used that have either an increased or decreased connotative content in comparison with the norm, that is, the meaning is either too great or too small. All the characteristics of schizophrenic thought disorder listed here stem from this deviation. They also lead to the hypothesis that mad symbol systems are not subject to the same limits (i.e., the same possibilities and necessities) as those fitting formally into the scope of consensus.

Please note that we are talking here of the formal conditions of consensus. If you abide by them, the question of content still remains, namely, whether the famous black Kulukulu of the South Pacific really exists or might exist. Anyone whose opinion deviates from the sphere of consensus is not usually diagnosed as mad and put into an institution; such a dissident may found his own scientific school, political party, or religious sect. He may fit out expeditions to find the Kulukulu and start enthusiastic missionary activities to help his view of reality to victory. Here we must contradict antipsychiatrists such as David Cooper (1977) who describe schizophrenics as dissidents. Madness is characterized not only by the content but also by the form of departure from the sphere of consensus. Abuse of psychiatry begins where somebody is declared mad because his opinion formally conforms with the consensus, but deviates insofar as content is concerned.

Apparently the self-organization of all systems of meaning (not only those adhering to the rules of logic) follows the same evolutionary principle already described for organisms. Or vice versa. The self-organization of life can be described by the laws of form. The variety of the behavior patterns of a living being are limited in two ways. On the one hand they have to comply with the necessities resulting from their own inner composition; on the other hand they must also comply with the possibilities left open by the environment. The living organism as a *distinction*—its skin separates inside from outside—can only show behavior that matches the inner structures and processes maintaining it as an entity as well as the context of this distinction, its world. By its behavior it gives a description (first order) of the form of this world in which the distinction occurs.

The same applies to the distinctions developing in the domain of systems of symbols, such as language. Symbols and words take the place of organisms; patterns of behavior (first-order descriptions) take the place of meanings (second-order descriptions). The form of the world of an organism, however, does not have to concur with the form of language; the necessities and possibilities of life do not have to concur with those of logic, nor those of cooking and eating with those of developing menus.

THE LANGUAGE OF CHILDREN

The process of progressive inclusion and exclusion of the meaning of symbols can best be studied by examining how children learn to talk. The way they learn their mother tongue differs from the way adults learn a foreign language. Children learn to talk by talking.

In many languages of the world, sounds such as mama, nana, papa, baba, or dada are the child's first words. This mama or papa, however, must not be misunderstood as addressing mother or father personally. In fact these sounds cannot actually be regarded as an expression of language. They are not an attempt at communication, but, in René Spitz's (1954) words, "verbal gestures" expressing subjectively how the child feels, which does not mean that the child *wants* to express how it feels: such a global word represents simply everything the child desires, for instance: "I am hungry," "I want mama," "it hurts," "mama has come into the room," "I am bored," etc.; it can have many meanings. These verbal gestures include much more than one specific thing, they describe a direction, a need and a desire and an atmosphere and the thing or object in question, all at the same time (Spitz 1965). If you compare the child's use of language with how adults or older children use these words, the words of the child have an enormous, almost all-embracing sphere of meaning.

Over a long period, during the so-called one-word phase, all the child's expressions consist of only one word. All these one-word sentences are used with a more comprehensive (overinclusive) meaning than in the language of adults. Several language acquisition researchers therefore describe them as one-word sentences, since they seem to express the idea of an entire sentence (an overview of language acquisition research is given by Szagun [1986]). The child apparently connects a certain word with a certain situation. In the course of time this system of symbols is developed. Without changing the subject, two one-word statements are used within the same context. Both words stand next to each other, in isolation and disconnected, and seem to symbolize different aspects of the same context. The child draws a distinction; it has picked out one of the numerous possible features of the situation and made it into a criterion of distinction.

In this phase of increasing differentiation the child also uses individual words in an "overextended" (Clark 1973) way, compared with their meaning in adult usage of language. This overextension manifests itself when, for instance, a child calls all animals "bow-wows." There are bow-wows with four legs on which you can ride, bow-wows that give milk, and bow-wows that can fly. In the next step the child sometimes distinguishes between the bow-wows that can fly and those that cannot fly. The group of bow-wows that cannot fly acquires a subgroup, the quack-quacks. But the quack-quacks are still bow-wows: "All quack-quacks are bow-wows," but "not all bow-wows are quack-quacks."

This principle of limiting an originally extensive area of meaning is not only to be found in individual language development; traces of it can also be found in the structures of our standard language. We ask someone's height and receive the answer: "He is 1.20 meters tall." Although we would generally assess this height as being rather small for a grown-up man, we use the word "tall." Here the meaning of tall includes an area containing small as well as tall.

If we again illustrate the principle according to which distinctions and distinctions of distinctions are made using hopscotch squares, we get the following picture (Figure 6–2).

The word "tall" stands for two different meanings: first, for the class, which contains two dissociated elements, small and tall, and second, for one of these elements. In the first case it is used in a

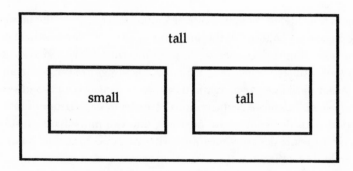

Figure 6–2

more abstract sense. The same applies to the relationship between bow-wow and quack-quack. It would be easy to find a whole series of examples. You sniff a papaya and are asked, "Does it smell?" Of course it has a smell. Only in our use of language, the question "Does it smell?" generally means does it smell bad.

The evolution of the meaning of a word depends on what scope the environment leaves for it. Initially it is mostly the other family members, and later all members of the language community, who have a perturbing (i.e., disturbing and stimulating) effect on the differentiation of the meaning system. By their reaction they signal to the child whether his use of words is appropriate or differs from the norm. If these feedback processes do not question (perturb) the child's criteria of distinction they literally act as an affirmation. In interaction, in this conversation, in mutually twisting and turning it, individual distinctions are synchronized and coordinated. However, the child is generally twisted more than the adult is turned. Yet, we quite frequently observe whole families beginning to use words invented by their children. These are usually mere distortions of proper nouns that are then used generally as pet names. After all, this coinage of new words confirms the principle of the mutuality of twisting and turning.

In conversation the attention of the child is directed to certain elements of a symbol's extent of meaning, which are confirmed socially as belonging to the proper meaning. In this process other meanings are excluded. In the course of language acquisition the private (connotative) content of the meaning of symbols decreases. From the mass of meanings that are lumped together (Clark 1973) in the symbol's subjective extent of meaning, meanings are thrown in and rejected until one's own distinctions are no longer a matter of contention and no more perturbations come from the partner of interaction. This does not mean, however, that two individuals must or could associate the same meanings with the same symbol. It is never merely denotative.

SYMBOLS AS TRADEMARKS: MORE THAN JUST A NAME

The name of a car is no more than the name of a car, or so one would think. If that were really true, however, there would be no such profession as advertising psychologists, patent goods would not have been invented yet, and we would buy a car just like we do a sack of potatoes.

Although potatoes and cars (in spite of being mentioned repeatedly) are not exactly our subject, they and the trademarks under which they are sold, as well as some of the peculiarities of our consumer behavior, can serve as an example of the difference between the connotative and denotative meaning of symbols.

For example, what occurs to you in connection with the following *names* (denotations) of articles or shops in which we buy (or not, as the case may be) Rolls Royce and Tiffany, on the one hand, or Volkswagen and Woolworth, on the other? What characteristics do you attribute to people driving the one car or the other or buying in the one shop or the other? You will realize that you have drawn up a package of meanings long before you were asked this question. You probably not only have a clear idea about how much the respective person has in his wallet, but even of the different traits, political views, circumstances, and experiences of the driver of a Rolls Royce or a Volkswagen. Tell me what car you drive and I'll tell you who you are, at least who I think you are. Of course, buying a car is not a very reliable psychological test. The meanings each individual connects with such a (putative) name are simply too diverse. In addition, the names are variable and usually only valid for a certain time.

There are not many things that cannot become bearers of meaning or symbols. A politician's glasses can thus become an expression of his intelligence, the manager's watch a sign of success, the new washing machine a symbol of a happy marriage. The title of doctor, professor, or of nobility is only used as part of a name, because names are never only just names. In the same way, advertising psychologists try to promote a marketing image to the public in order to sell products. They do this by drawing up bundles of meaning that seduce the buyer by systematically using motives that originally have little to do with the utility value of the commodity.[1] The sexually attractive thighs of beautiful women are associated with the "legs" of cars, so that the lust for these thighs can be shifted to the tires. The pattern on which this transformation of meaning is based corresponds to the (completely mad) pattern of our hopscotch square. The strange thing is that this strategy of identifying things with each other that are not logically related at all actually works; sales of this make of tire increase. This is also proof that we are able to make, more or less, any connections between symbols and meanings—not only logical ones—depending on what our attention is focused on.

The fate of the images of commercial goods proves that these connotative meanings can change. A look at the course of life of the famous crocodile on men's casual shirts shows that the meaning of a symbol can be extended. Obviously the shirts with this animal embroidered on them were of particularly good quality, which, of course, had its price. However, there were enough wealthy people who could afford to buy such expensive products. For them the crocodile became a symbol of good quality. If you were looking for a good shirt you did not have to be an expert in textiles, you only had to look for the crocodile. The complex act of buying a shirt, the difficulty of

1. From the Greek *syn* meaning together and *bállo* meaning I throw (symbol).

choosing, was thus diminished. The price led to a natural selection among shirt buyers. The group of people that could afford them was limited. Henceforth you could draw up a parcel of meanings out of crocodile as being something better. The result was that people who wanted to create the impression of being something special bought shirts with this emblem. The particular quality of the product was at best accepted, although it was not the actual motive for buying it. Finally crocodiles started turning up on the market on garments other than shirts or on cheap imitations. The symbol had become a commodity. This extension in popularity meant that the crocodile lost its original meaning and acquired a new one. It became a symbol for its bearer wanting to seem more than he is. In the meantime buyers interested in the quality of the crocodile shirts have been known to buy the shirts and to take off the crocodile.

Numbers are probably still the best way of narrowing down the connotative content of names. This might be the egalitarian reason why people are always identified by a number when the intention is to render their individual features meaningless. Yet, personal reference numbers can also be charged with meaning during the course of their usage, 007 for example.

DISPLACEMENT AND CONDENSATION: UNCONSCIOUS DISTINCTIONS

Linguistic communication is made possible by the civilized and domesticated meanings of symbols. Two or more people ascribe the same meanings to the same symbol, a word for example. These are the contents of meaning necessary for communication. In addition, each person involved can link several different meanings to the same symbol without necessarily jeopardizing communication. These are possible meanings. It is reflective of the individuality of a single person that he connects unmistakable, subjective meanings with symbols—words, pictures, and signs. They only partially coincide with those of their partners in interaction or the surrounding language system (Figure 6–3).

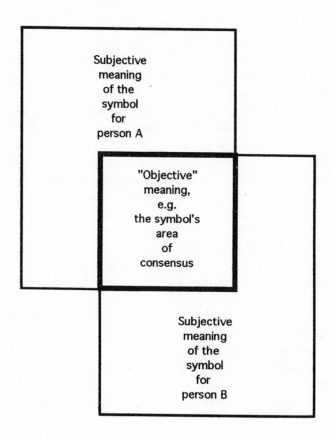

Figure 6–3

Whatever you think about psychoanalysis, one of Sigmund Freud's inestimable contributions is to have demonstrated a way to decode these subjective meanings, namely, free association. It is a simple method enabling everyone to realize which distinctions and equations he makes unconsciously. Simply follow all your ideas on a theme, event, picture, or symbol—if possible without subjecting yourself to inhibitions of thought and feeling. The resulting chain of association does not follow universally valid and socially accepted rules, but private, uncivilized, undomesticated ones.

The interpretation of dreams, which Freud called the "ideal way to the unconscious," gives us further confirmation that the order of this subjective reality follows the principles of a kind of *unconscious set theory* already described during the acquisition of language. Sets of meaning are always divided into subsets or subsets fused with each other to form new entities.

Above all, Freud describes two mechanisms or mechanics by which unconscious structures are transformed into dream structures. *"Dream-displacement* and *dream-condensation* are the two craftsmen to whom we may chiefly ascribe the structure of the dream"* (Freud 1900, p. 264). In his view they characterize not only dream work but also the processes leading to a neurotic formation of symptoms. They are the key for the translation of unconscious meanings into signs, pictures, and behaviors accessible to conscious cognition.

Since there are a great number of elements in such a class and the elements and classes selected can always be subsumed under different class concepts, unconscious meanings are completely veiled by these condensations and displacements. According to psychoanalysis, these obscurations come about when unconscious thoughts and feelings are to be withheld from one's own consciousness (for details see Simon 1984).

Such an explanation turns the unconscious into an active subject, into a culprit looking for camouflage. Motives become understandable and interpretable, even though the logic of the individual, unconscious system of symbols does not follow the rules of consensus of distinctions. If, however, you use the model of self-organization as a basis, you cannot fall back on motives or purposes and intentions, because there is no space for them in this concept. But you can try to explain why you arrive at different selections of meanings in dreams or in the formation of symptoms than when you are consciously awake or free of symptoms (if there is such a thing as freedom of symptoms).

THE FOCUS OF ATTENTION

The building stood out from afar due to its promising neon sign, "Variety Theater." Behind the entrance hall was a big ballroom. He entered without a clear idea of what to expect. Probably various things, if his sparse knowledge of the foreign language did not deceive him. The old ceiling fresco, whose splendor seemed to be slightly outmoded, gave the scene a certain solemnity. The people in the ballroom were in animated conversation. They seemed to have been there quite a while. Some were sipping multicolored cocktails; others were eating. He had the impression that he was not welcome. Self-consciously he sat down at a small marble table. There was nothing more embarrassing for him than to appear at a birthday party without being invited. The waiter brought him something to eat. At first he gobbled it down without recognizing what it was. Then he noticed an unpleasant taste. A passing gentleman in a dark suit stroked his hair. The surface of the table was cold and smooth.

He was confused by the immense variety of what he could hear, see, touch, taste, and smell. He tried to follow the conversations at the table in front and diagonally behind him, but did not quite understand what the people were talking about. Probably everybody was talking about him. Again and again men and women crossed the room, catching his attention by their breathtaking looks.

He no longer knew how or why he had come. But one thing was clear to him: he must not miss anything of importance! But which of the multitude of events and things around him was important? He began to feel uneasy.

Meanwhile the waiter had cleared the table and brought an obviously high-proof, alcoholic drink. His apprehension increased more and more. Something mysterious was going on here he was quite sure, although, or perhaps because, all the other people seemed to be unnaturally relaxed. They probably knew what was going on, had arranged everything among themselves. His heart beat faster; he felt hot. Why was everybody looking at him? He could not get rid of the feeling that disaster was in the air. Something was going to happen; something had to happen. He could not grasp the sense of this strange meeting. His thoughts were jumping to and fro, searching aimlessly. Whatever should he do?

Slowly the lights went off. The conversations stopped. The last exotic-looking individuals took their seats and could be recognized no longer. Everyone moved their chairs so that they could see the stage. He followed their example. When the room was quite dark and nobody could be seen any more, a spotlight was turned on. Its light drew a circle on the stage. A fanfare was sounded. Now he knew where something important was going to happen tonight. He calmed down again.

Admittedly, this story of apprehension has turned out rather theatrical when you consider its banal purpose, its hoped-for effect, namely, to direct the attention of the reader to focus on attention. If the story has not succeeded, it is hoped that the explanation furnished with it will. Because this focusing of attention can be regarded as the decisive factor that influences inclusion and exclusion (i.e., the selection) of meaning.

In communicating with our environment, in particular with the people in it, we are facing an immense variety of impressions and perceptions. It is vital to differentiate between what is important and unimportant, sensible and foolish, meaningful and meaningless. We need to orient ourselves in the world in order to act. To do so, we need some kind of inner map that enables us to give our behavior a conscious direction.

If every one of us were alone in the world, like the yachtsman in our imaginary experiment, we would have to develop this orientation system on our own. We, though, are born into a cultural system in which these maps or sea charts have been charted and handed down from generation to generation. And the meanings culture gives to the world are transmitted to us through interaction, through conversation with other people. But how does this happen, how do we learn our mother tongue, the subtleties of social conventions, in view of the impossibility of instructive interaction, the simple information transfer according to the model of the telephone?

This learning happens by focusing attention during interaction with our environment. If a tourist asks the way to the train station, the local who knows the place well will direct the tourist's attention to the right way, for instance, by pointing in the appropriate direction with his finger while at the same time looking in the same direction and saying, "Go this way." From all the possible streets this tourist might choose, only one is left. The whole behavior of the person who was asked to show the way focuses the tourist's attention like a spotlight and limits the meaning of the sentence, "That is the way to the train station." If the informant had said, "You have to go to the right!" and pointed to the left, the poor tourist would have been rather confused. He would not have been able to orient himself, and the meaning of the sentence, "That is the way to the train station," would have been limited less clearly. If he had wanted to catch a train, he would possibly have panicked and become nervous. Tachycardia, increased blood pressure, and similar symptoms would have been signs of increasing agitation. He would not have been able to take purposeful action and would have responded with stress. Medical tests have revealed that the impossibility of focusing one's attention in such a situation is closely related to bodily stress reactions. If focusing succeeds, the emergency reactions recede.[2]

All environmental factors can expand or limit this focus. Someone who has a toothache will not be able to focus his attention on the brilliant theoretical address of the Nobel Prize winner or the unique opera performance, even with the best will in the world. But there are possibly other exterior events that let this individual forget even his toothache. Whatever manages to captivate the at-

---

2. According to interruption theory, stress develops when organized actions or thought processes are interrupted by internal or external events. All stress is triggered by such an interruption, but not every interruption triggers stress. By interrupting a scheme of action or cognition that is more or less ordered and proceeds in a closed cycle, attention is deviated and has to be focused on new and unexpected requirements. Physical emergency reactions are activated. As soon as attention is focused anew, the signs of bodily stress recede; blood pressure drops again, for instance. Danger recognized is danger averted (Mandler 1982).

tention of a person does not depend on the objective attributes and characteristics of the exterior events alone but also on the given interior structures of the individual, that is, the distinctions he has drawn and the meanings given in the course of his history.

The grammar of the dream and its ambiguous world of images can be explained by the selective function of attention focusing. For the difference between dreaming and waking lies in the very fact that the perception of outer stimuli is canceled out during sleep. Thus the influence of the outer world that focuses attention and limits the meaning of symbols—the necessity to coordinate and adapt the subjective meanings of symbols with those of the partners of interaction—is removed. Although an individual's focus of attention while awake is determined by external and internal events, in dreams the external limitations that secure consensus are removed to a great extent. This condition results in the meaning of symbols being limited by individual attention and determined by subjective valency. Thus the dream becomes an ambiguous image of a private reality. From the view of systems theory there is little to be said for Freud's hypothesis that every dream is the fulfillment of a wish. But even without this assumption the interpretation of our dreams can help us recognize the structure of our inner maps.

Even more extensive screening effects from outside influences are shown by the experiments on so-called sensory deprivation. The test subjects are sent into a *camera silens*,[3] a dark, completely sound-insulated room, so that absolutely nothing can be heard or seen. Not even the individual's own voice produces an echo. Everything is devised in such a way that the test subject in such a room receives as few sensory perceptions and feelings as possible. There is nothing to focus one's attention on; nothing perturbs, irritates, or stimulates. After just a few minutes in a room like this, everyone begins to hallucinate. Without the supporting constraints and limitations of outer reality, we are caught up in the whirlpool of our associations in no time. We embark on a journey into the world of our personal symbolism and thus leave the area of consensus on

---

3. From the Latin *camera* meaning chamber and *silens* meaning silent, quiet.

reality. We hear and see things around us that are not objectively in the room. We cannot distinguish between inside and outside and develop symptoms that can also be observed within the framework of psychotic episodes.

WHITENER: AN EXPERIMENT
TO FOCUS THE ATTENTION

If the effect of focusing attention is not quite clear enough for you, why don't you carry out the following little experiment?

Again you need a test subject. Once you have found a volunteer, look for some white objects in your environment, for example, the ceiling, a piece of paper, or tennis socks. Point to one of these objects and ask your partner, "What color is this?"

He will most likely answer, "White."

Now point to the next object and again ask what color it is. Again the answer will be "white." Repeat your question eight to ten times. Your test subject will give you the same stereotyped answer—"White." Out of the blue you now ask, "What does the cow drink?"

About nine out of ten test subjects will answer: "Milk!"[4]

An explanation for this answer can be found by drawing hopscotch squares for white, milk, cow, and drink (Figure 6–4).

Because of the many questions asking about something white, attention is focused in such a way that everything we are talking about is white. An answer to the next question is now selected from the square with white in it. It must—so the unconscious and not quite rational rule of distinction seems to prescribe—fit into the squares white, what the cow drinks, cow, and drink; it's the milk!

These mechanisms, by which our associations are tied up in knots, are used not only by advertising experts, who always seem determined to associate somehow even the most unerotic articles such as kitchen gadgets and cough medicine with bedroom sagas. Magicians, pickpockets, and politicians also understand how to play with

---

4. My thanks to Andrea Zinser-Schmidt for letting me let the cow drink milk too.

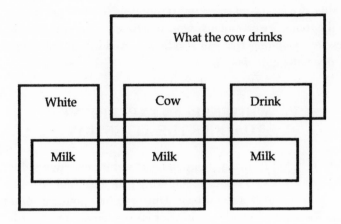

Figure 6–4

the attention of their spectators and victims. However, they often do it the other way round. They shift the focus of attention and direct it to a field where it can rest in peace and do no damage. The magician uses his barely dressed assistant to catch the spectators' eye so that he can carry out his conjuring tricks unobserved, the pickpocket makes sure that his victim is not paying too much attention to his billfold, and the politician avoids the interviewer's irritating question by first expressing his thanks to his voters for their trust and then answering a question that has not been asked at all.

7

Mad Communication

THE PSYCHIATRIST AND HIS PATIENT: AN ACTING GAME

When two people's opinions differ as to whose reality has to be described as delusion and whose delusion as reality, a dangerous, maddening form of communication emerges. In the following game, which is, of course, another experiment, this style of communication can be experienced from the outside or from the inside, depending on whether you take on one of the roles or participate as an outside observer.

You need two test subjects prepared to take on the role of psychiatrist or psychiatric patient. Chance determines which of the two takes on which role (almost like in real life). As in other games of chance, each of the two takes a card; it is marked with either an A or a B. On the back each player finds information about his role and what he has to do.

Both are given these verbal instructions: "Please read which role you are to play and what your task is carefully! Don't talk about or comment on what you read on your card! That would mean the end of the game."

Card A contains the following text: "You are a psychiatrist and are called to a patient you know to be mad. One of his symptoms is that he thinks he is a psychiatrist. Try to convince him to start inpatient treatment of his own free will!"

On card B, on the other hand, is written: "You are a psychiatrist and are called to a patient you know to be mad. One of his symptoms is that he thinks he is a psychiatrist. Try to convince him to start inpatient treatment of his own free will!"[1]

As soon as the game begins, you will be able to observe a style of communication that is characteristic of all systems of interaction in which madness plays an important emotional role for the participants (and in general this means all systems in which it plays any role at all). Such patterns of interaction are mostly to be found in families in which one member has been diagnosed as psychotic or in psychiatric clinics.

To come straight to the point: the blame for the peculiarities you will observe can probably neither be put on the (obviously totally mad) patient in our experiment, nor on the (naturally absolutely mentally healthy) psychiatrist.

Generally the scene begins with the quicker of the actors taking the initiative (we will call him A, as in "active") and asking the patient why he phoned, what is troubling him, what is wrong, what problem is bothering him, and so on. What such questions have in common is that they contain tacit assumptions about the one asking the questions, the one answering them, and the relationship between the two. The relational definition carried covertly (but quite obviously) in these opening questions declares the questioner as psychiatrist; whatever the slower one (we will call him B, or "passive") answers involves the risk of making himself into the patient and submitting to the suggested relationship and role definition. The possibilities of responding to this elegant opening are limited.

In the first possibility, B will try to escape his awkward situation by answering A's questions, which are not really questions, with answers that are not answers. He will seem to avoid any clear statement by shifting the focus of attention, changing the subject, and keeping all his remarks so vague that no kind of agreement with A's secret (scary) offer of a relationship can be deduced from them. The

---

1. The idea for this experiment comes from members of the Palo Alto Group, who referred a psychiatrist and a psychologist, both experienced therapists for schizophrenia, to each other, thereby maintaining to both, the other one's symptom was the delusion (?) of being a schizophrenia specialist (Watzlawick et al. 1967).

erection of a wall of fog is apparently an effective method of protection from attacks on one's own (role) identity. If he has succeeded in confusing A so much that he forgets his question, B then will start a counterattack. He will now attempt to gain the initiative and finally force A to admit that he is mad. However, as A usually is not very enthusiastic about this idea, he will in turn use more or less subtle confusion techniques to avoid the emergence of a clear definition of the relationship that inevitably runs counter to his wishes.

For the external observer this interaction appears to be a fight about reality, in which first one, then the other, plays the obviously more popular role of the psychiatrist without being able to occupy it permanently. And how could he: the psychiatrist can only be played permanently by someone who has the sanction of his patient.

If you carry out this experiment frequently and with different test subjects, you will see small variations in the duration of the phases, but a rhythm will always be preserved in which first one, then the other, is on top (= psychiatrist) or on the bottom (= patient).

As even the most persevering players eventually realize that they cannot win by their own efforts and with their own means, they will start looking for allies to explain that their reality ("I'm the real psychiatrist") is true. In our experiment this is a bit more difficult than in real life, as here there are only two players. However, these limitations of physical reality do not prevent third parties from being used as referees. It is, for example, very popular to have imaginary nurses, doctor's receptionists, and the patient's worried relatives who called the doctor in the first place suddenly come into the room. But mostly third parties are used symbolically as proof of the truth of one's own assertions. Frequently the players resort to examination certificates and diplomas as objective evidence for the right to feel like a psychiatrist. However, when one starts inventing certificates, the other can do the same. As long as no third party interferes in the interaction directly, the question of the winner has to be adjourned. This is a game with no winner or loser, and with no foreseeable end.

In the second possibility, which is the quickest way to bring this game to an end, one of the players decides to accept the role of patient and to undergo inpatient treatment of his own free will. By giving up his identity as an actor, this player has then not fulfilled his task, but at least the argument is over. However, test subjects never actually make use of this option either because they enjoy any kind of competition, and even in this case think they will be able to win in the end, or because they take their task as psychiatrist seriously and want to persuade the poor patient to undergo the necessary treatment (which makes very little difference from the view of the patient).

Sometimes a player submits to the role of patient at first for tactical reasons in order to lure the "real" patient into the institution. There he hopes to find allies who use a straitjacket to make the patient realize who is right. Such maneuvers serve to gain time in order to bring about a majority decision on reality with the help of a third party.

The only way to end the game without the help of others and without accepting the role of loser lies in the conscious agreement that the two players cannot come to an agreement. Only when both accept as their common reality that each is living in his own reality and that it is impossible to clarify whose reality is true can the game described in the first scenario—with no winner or loser and no end— be avoided (and maybe a different game be played instead).

However, that rarely happens, as both players confirm each other (see Figure 7–1).

This experiment is placed at the beginning of the chapter on mad communication because it touches on several important themes for the origin, maintenance, and transformation of madness and normality. First, it demonstrates clearly that the decision on the truth or falsity of the description of reality is a social one. When two argue about it, the third one laughs (or not, as the case may be); in any event he gains the power of defining what really is.

This experiment also illustrates how processes of self-organization are played out in the field of human communication. Two persons have met who both bring their inner structures, their view of the world, their prejudices and values into the interaction. The result is something that oversteps the borders of the participants and their

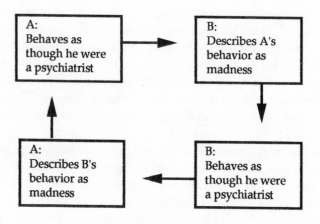

Figure 7-1

individual behavior, namely a game in which descriptive and pre-scriptive rules are developed without one of the participants or any kind of creator or inventor being given the (whole) responsibility, blame, or cause for its emergence.

COMMUNICATION IN THE FAMILY

One of the earliest signs of human existence—3.6 million years old—are the footprints of two adults and a child. Anthropologists inter-pret these tracks as those of two parents leading their child by the hand (Eccles 1989).

The family, in whatever form, can be regarded as the sphere in which the biological conditions of man have always encountered the cultural and social conditions. Without at least one person to care for it, the newborn babe must die. A small child is not autono-mous; it is physically unable to do what is necessary for its survival.

It needs someone who is prepared—for whatever reason—to be built into the child's process of self-preservation. This person is usually the mother. Probability ensures this role since, after all, she is the one whose presence at the birth of a child can be reliably reckoned upon. For this reason she plays the central role in the physical and mental development of the child. However, she does not usually live alone, and she is not the only one to deal with the child and care for it every day. The social system into which the child is born is the family.

In the happy times when there were no psychologists parents could regard their children with fatalistic composure. They were creatures of God, whose fate was fulfilled independent of what the parents did with them. However, the more conscious we became of the influence of social factors on the development of children, the more the focus was directed to the family, in particular to the mother, when it was a question of who really caused the misery of madness and other prominent mental disorders. It was not hard to find who was to blame, namely the parents and in particular the mothers.

This development was probably inevitable. In the late 1940s and 1950s, a few psychiatrists and psychotherapists began to devote themselves to an intensive analysis of patients who were manifesting mad, schizophrenic symptoms. They accompanied their patients on their "journey through insanity." It was an arduous, long, and slow road. They only made small advances and achieved their goal of therapeutic success, a return to normality, in very few cases. However, there were successes. And even where they failed, in the course of many years of therapy the therapists were able to gain insight into the experiences of the patients that had been unknown up until then. These therapists were not satisfied by the simple explanation that their patients had a biochemical screw loose. They would probably not have become involved in such an intricate task as the therapy of psychosis, which demanded everything of them as persons, if they were not of the opinion that there must be social causes for madness that—in the sense of causal therapy—must also be treated socially. As most of these therapists were psychoanalysts,

they started from the assumption that early childhood is the decisive phase for the later fate of man. The causes of what the patient
experienced and did in the here and now were to be sought there
and then. The interaction of the patient with the therapist was merely
a poor imitation, a repetition of his interaction with the persons to
whom the child related most closely in early childhood—Mother or
Father; and the earlier the patient's disorder was established in the
history of his mental development, the more often it was, of course,
the mother who got passed the buck.

This small, rather foreshortened retrospective on the history of
schizophrenic therapy serves as an example of how theoretical assumptions can corroborate themselves. First, there is the direct
scheme of cause and effect, which seeks the reasons for someone
behaving madly today in the past. The "early disorder" is then the
dent in the wing that remains until the therapist comes along to
eliminate it. According to such a view the culprit responsible for
what has happened is the mother or the family—they must take the
blame.

This simple model had various consequences, good as well as bad.
One of the positive consequences is that several researchers began
to study the family more carefully. One of the negative consequences—
still to be lamented even today—is the fact that, as a rule, simple
explanations lead to simple solutions to the problem. The simple
solution for the treatment of patients with schizophrenic symptoms
was for the therapist to try to be a better parent. The patients were
separated from their relatives and visitors were forbidden. Among
other things family therapy models were developed aimed at changing the parents and thus the structure of the family. All these measures were (and are) an expression of the narrow-minded claim of
knowing how good parents should behave.

It was a few years before any opposition developed to this view.
The simple, supposedly therapeutic solution proved to be no solution. The once enthusiastic therapists were forced to accept that
even they, as the better parents, failed. The patients were so un-
grateful as to keep their symptoms. This was obvious to the patients'
relatives too. Many of them would willingly have taken the blame if

doing so would only help. Finally, the knowledge that something was being done wrong opened up the chance of doing it right. However, as the instant solutions that saw salvation in separation from the parents bore no fruit either, the parents no longer needed to bear the blame. They began to put up a fight. In the United States they formed an alliance with the aim not only of improving the intolerable living conditions of the patients within and without the institutions and promoting biological psychiatry but also preventing all research concerned with the connection between family interaction and madness.

This reaction is certainly understandable. Nevertheless it seems rather extreme, as it replaces one too-simple explanation with another, no less simplifying one. Both explanations assume a linear relationship between cause and effect. Neurotransmitters, messengers of the brain, take the place of schizophrenogenic mothers. Once again someone bringing bad news is given the blame for all evil. If one finds biological causes, the acquittal of the family need not merely follow from a lack of evidence of its effect (Dörner et al. 1982). By taking the external perspective of cybernetics and systems theory as the basis, however, any linear explanation in the sense of a straight scheme of cause and effect is equally absurd.

When the family is regarded from the outside as a social, self-organizing system, the possibility presents itself of describing *functional* correlations between the development of madness and the peculiarities of interpersonal communication. After all, the family or the social unit that takes its place gains its social and biological importance from the unique function it plays in the development of the individual, his thinking, feeling, and action. In structural coupling with the other family members, who are emotionally the most important persons for the child for many years, spend most time with him, and make vital decisions for him, the individual makes distinctions that characterize his view of the world. The family is the place where he learns his (mother) tongue and gives meanings to symbols. However, the family is not the only social system that could, should, or must be studied in order to clarify the connection between communication and madness. After all, many people do not become mad until they leave or have left their families. Here the question arises as to the differences between family and the social context in which someone becomes mad. And yet again this is a question of functions, not of cause or blame, even though new options of action (treatment) can evolve from the answers.

DOUBLE-BIND, COMMUNICATION DEVIANCES, AND THE MIXING UP OF CONTEXTS

The development of a cybernetic-systemic view in psychiatric research is closely connected with the work of Gregory Bateson and the publication of the so-called double-bind hypothesis (Bateson 1972, Bateson et al. 1956). Bateson spent many years researching the natives of New Guinea and Bali, and his interest was focused on interactional processes and rules. In the early 1950s he was leading a research project on various problems of communication. He and his study group were strongly influenced by cybernetic ideas that were being developed at this time by such thinkers as Norbert Wiener, John von Neumann, Warren McCulloch, and others who met at the now-legendary cybernetic conferences of the Macy Foundation. The group around Bateson first examined questions that had or seemed to have no strong connection to psychiatric problems. How do animals of the same species who are baring their teeth at each other distinguish whether the other wants to fight or to play? How does a ventriloquist communicate with his doll? What distinguishes a bartender as interlocuter and comforter? How do successful policemen behave when called to intervene in violent family arguments? As the rooms where the research group worked were situated quite close to the psychiatric department of a hospital, they frequently met patients whose behavior was comical and strange. Disturbed and stimulated by these encounters, they decided to examine the phenomenon known as schizophrenia from the standpoint of communication and interaction. At this point a psychiatrist and psychoanalyst with experience in therapy for schizophrenia were consulted.

The result of the study was the formulation of a hypothesis on how the behavior of the patient in the context of family interaction might be explained as meaningful and conclusive. According to this hypothesis the patient is always in a situation in which it is subjectively vital for him to decipher his relatives' messages. However, when he is given two *mutually exclusive messages on different logical levels*, he is unable to determine what sense these messages have. As he always has to behave in some way, he is continually exposed to *paradoxical* demands for action. He always follows them when he is not following them, and he is always not following them when he follows them. As he can neither quit the field nor metacommunicate on family communication—that is, from the external perspective—he is caught up in a logically hopeless situation. Whichever of the two mutually exclusive messages he follows, whichever he considers true and obligatory, he will be punished. He is in a dilemma, a double-bind. According to the Bateson group the various forms of schizophrenic symptoms can be evaluated as an attempt to cope with this continuous dilemma by reacting and not reacting at the same time. Although in the formulation of the double-bind hypothesis a great number of causes and effects were tacitly ascribed to persons (culprits and victims), this study laid the foundation for a new view of psychosis that attempted to explain mad behavior as a result of faulty communication.

One of the first systematic empirical studies on the connection between family communication and schizophrenic thought was carried out by Lyman Wynne and Margaret Singer (1963). In separate sessions they presented patients diagnosed as schizophrenic and their parents with projective tests. The Rorschach test is one example. This test consists of a set of ambiguous and barely structured blobs of ink that the observer must describe. Because their form leaves the observer great scope for interpretation, his interpretation depends on what he reads (projects) into these pictures. To this end he has to mentally structure the entity of one of these blobs of ink, divide it into its parts, and put it back together again. Thus a blob of ink finally turns into a butterfly, the cross-section of the spinal cord, or an obscene depiction of the genitals. Wynne and Singer started from the assumption that the processes of perception and description of these test pictures are analogous to the task facing parents when they try to impart a logically conclusive and adequate view of reality to their children.

From their study they were able to deduce quite specific relationships between the parents' style of communication and the children's thinking. An independent examiner was able to assign correctly the verbatim transcripts of the tests to the individual family members. The examiner was able to do so not only for the patients diagnosed as schizophrenic and their parents but also, and to the same degree, for patients diagnosed as borderline cases (between psychosis and neurosis), neurotic, and even normal and their respective parents. Wynne and Singer came to the conclusion that the disorder of the communication process in the families of schizophrenic patients begins with the lack of agreement on a mutual *focus of attention.* Continuous shifts in focus characterize the communication of family members and inevitably lead to a series of further communication deviances. Communication is ambiguous or without logical meaning. Because it is not clear what is referred to, communication is rendered invalid or contradictory. The assessment of these deviations of communication made it possible to predict which children would later manifest schizophrenic symptoms (Goldstein 1983). Subsequent studies, in which the role of heredity was also included, confirmed a connection between such communication deviances and the development of psychotic symptoms (Tienari et al. 1988).

An example from the everyday life of a family illustrates this form of communication. A newlywed son and his wife visit his parents over the weekend. Tension arises between his mother and his wife, the daughter-in-law. On the surface the practical reason for this tension is that his mother scolds her daughter-in-law, "You're dressed like a whore!" The daughter-in-law's dress really is rather revealing with its plunging neckline and is very short. The mother's statement seems anything but ambiguous; in fact, it is offendingly unambiguous. However, it immediately loses its unambiguity when we consider the whole story—the mother had given her daughter-in-law this dress as a present.

Double-binding communication can be regarded as an extreme case of such ambiguous communication. The messages are not only ambiguous and contradictory but also paradoxical. Paradoxes arise when the logical consequence of a true statement is that it is false, and of a false statement that it is true. Communication in which such evaluations are made provide no lines of inclusion or exclusion for ascribing meaning. It widens the focus of attention to oceanic infinity.

However, in view of the impossibility of instructive interaction, which is the sender/receiver model of information transmission typified by the telephone, it is not the ambiguity of communication that needs explaining, but rather once again the relative clarity with which communication normally seems to succeed. Once again the exception from the rule reveals a glance at the rule; double-binding communication reveals a glance at nondouble-binding communication. For Gregory Bateson one of the most important aspects of the double bind was the unclear marking of different contexts, their being mixed up. It is the failure of metacommunication (i.e., communication about communication) that is the prerequisite for the success of normal communication.

The same does not always mean the same. This is one of the apparent paradoxes of *all* human communication and cognition and applies to symbols as well as to behavior. Their meaning depends on the context in which they appear. The word "ball" means something different in a report on the World Cup than when talking about dancing lessons. A man in short black trousers running up and down the sidewalk on a Saturday morning among the passersby, holding a whistle and colored cards, is judged differently than when he manifests the same behavior on a Saturday afternoon in a stadium.

Adaptation to consensual reality only succeeds when one reacts in different contexts in accordance with different prescriptive rules. Each individual must develop descriptive rules that enable him to distinguish among different contexts. He can only do this if his focus of attention in communication and interaction is directed to the fact that externally identical behaviors do not mean the same when they occur in different situations (contexts). There must be communication about communication through which the contexts of communication are distinguished. This form of communication is generally referred to as context marking.

People who are unable to act accordingly in different social contexts manifest socially deviating behavior, which is unusual and unexpected, in direct interaction, but this behavior is not necessarily mad.

Bateson (1969, 1972) describes the mixing up of contexts, or rather their markings, as a mechanism that not only characterizes communication in the families of patients diagnosed as schizophrenic but is also quite generally a prerequisite for creativity. If a person is exposed to situations in which the context marking is ambiguous, confusing, or even logically contradictory and that leads to paradoxes over a long period, he can choose different possibilities of survival. He can become a clown, a poet, or a schizophrenic or even a combination of these, to name just a few possibilities. It is impossible to predict which of these possibilities will actually come to pass. The effect of context marking is thus not necessarily pathologic; it also forms the basis of such phenonema as humor, jokes, and creativity that make life a little more colorful and more worth living.

Quite generally, the degree of ambiguity of communication and, in connection with this, the greater or lesser hardness or softness of consensual reality depend on how different contexts are marked in interaction. This concept can be illustrated by a few events reported in the newspapers a while ago.

It was reported that in Miami, in full daylight, a shootout took place between two rival gangs of drug dealers. The residents watched unafraid and with interest and called their children to witness this wonderful spectacle. Nobody thought of calling the police because they thought they were watching the filming of an episode of the television series "Miami Vice." Thus, whether an event seems true or untrue, real or feigned, whether it triggers fear or enjoyable curiosity is a question of context marking.

The second example shows that this distinction has wide-ranging practical consequences. A very popular Pakistani actor couple also played a married couple in a film. In the course of the film's plot they were to be divorced. During shooting the husband stood in the market square, as his script prescribed, and spoke the traditional Islamic divorce formula three times. The question that concerned himself, his wife, and above all a number of ecclesiastical dignitaries was whether he was now actually divorced from his (real) wife.

This real situation is another example of reality softening up, as no distinction was made between film and reality. The death sentence imposed on Salman Rushdie by the Ayatollah Khomeini shows that such distinctions can be absolutely vital. The author's comment that the blasphemous thoughts about the prophet Mohammed in his book *Satanic Verses* were merely the dream of one of his characters can only be accepted as an excuse by someone who is prepared to distinguish between the contexts of Salman Rushdie (the person), the book (the story being told), and the character (one of many who appear in the plot).

The psychiatrist working in a hospital is well acquainted with such obscure forms of communication, not only from his dealings with patients—who are champions of ambiguous communication, in particular in shifting attention and mixing contexts—but also from their relatives who are often masters of this art. This does not mean, however, that the inability of family members to communicate clearly should be seen as a deficit. One fact that argues against this deficit notion is that these forms of communication are dependent on themes and situations. Outside the family the family members usually communicate absolutely normally, that is, not oddly. If we see communication deviances such as the shifting of the focus of attention as the expression of a deficit or a handicap, we will be inclined to use a too-simple method of healing. We might prescribe the family members a kind of communication-jogging, a training program; we might send them back to school to learn clear communication skills.

Our experiment with the psychiatrist and the patient implies a different explanation. It is not the *inability to communicate clearly*, but rather the *ability to communicate unclearly* that is used in family interaction; and it is always used when there is a risk of one view of reality being declared as objective reality, one that is not shared commonly and is alarming for one or the other members of the family. Communication deviances are one possibility of preventing a consensus. Where consensus is the prerequisite of a decision on reality, everyone has the right of veto. And where communication takes place in this way, reality is softened.

Even humpback whales who feel threatened create a curtain of bubbles to conceal themselves from their attackers. However, they also produce these bubbles when they attack and do not want to be seen.

PARADOX: DIFFERENCES BETWEEN LIFE AND LOGIC—I

In logic and in communication we try to get rid of it, and in life we are always confronted by it, namely, paradox. It is a good example of the fact that the world of symbols does not always look similar to the real world. However, this difference between (binary) logic and life does not arise from the structures of logic itself, but rather from the way it is used. For its users are of the opinion that, for the sake of order, certain possibilities existing in logic as in life simply should not be. They desire a reality with no ambivalence or contradictions, in which every statement should be "Yes, yes" or "No, no," and the question of truth can be answered definitively.

What has always displeased the Keepers of the Holy Grail, mainly philosophers and mathematicians, about logic is the possibility of *self-reference*. Statements can refer to themselves, and sets can contain themselves. The clear distinction between inside and outside, as required by the distinction between the subject and object of scientific knowledge, is thus abolished. What is embarrassing about self-reference is the fact that we have to ascribe the same meaning to both sides of a distinction, although or rather *because* we follow the rules of logic. We must jump into a hopscotch square with both legs, as it were, and yet stay outside the hopscotch square at the same time. Such commands imply theoretical and practical difficulties, as anyone who has had important meetings in Los Angeles and New York at the same time will know.

The orthodox way to get rid of these unpleasant and contradictory instructions is to declare them invalid and to forbid them from being carried out. However, before we devote ourselves to this kind of solution, here is a rough outline of the problem. As always we begin with normality. The relationship between a symbol and what is symbolized can be explained by a simple example (Figure 7–2).

Figure 7–2 is the formulation of a statement, a sentence that refers to an object, a thing, a distinction in harder reality (whereby nothing is said about the toughness of the schnitzel). A distinction in the realm of language is used to give a name to a distinction in the realm of the material world. The situation is quite different in the next example (Figure 7–3).

In the top box in Figure 7–3 is a sentence that refers to another sentence. A distinction within language is used to ascribe a characteristic (true) to another distinction within language, thus disputing a different characteristic (false), which is logically inconsistent. The descriptive world of symbols thus becomes a described world.

There are two different forms of such linguistic self-reference. Only one of the two, paradox, is a worry to users of logic. Let us begin with the more harmless form, tautology; as it causes no problems and disturbs no one, it is generally treated with contempt and not considered worthy of further discussion (Figure 7–4).

Two sentences make a statement about each other, whereby each confirms the other and thus indirectly confirms itself. It resembles

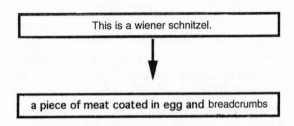

Figure 7–2

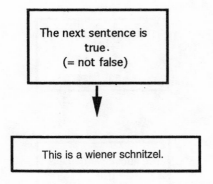

Figure 7–3

a glance in the mirror that merely results in a satisfied nod: "Everything as I expected!" The distinction between true and false and the basic assumptions of binary logic are not questioned by this form of self-reference, but are confirmed. A self-affirming loop has been made. In the case of paradox, on the contrary, a self-negating[2] loop is made (Figure 7–5).

Once again two sentences relate to each other in such a way that each is indirectly related to itself. If the first sentence is true, the second is false. And if the second sentence is false, the first is also false. However, if the first sentence is false, the second sentence is true, in which case the first sentence is also true, and so on. Each sentence is true when it is false and false when it is true. The distinction between true and false has dissolved, and no one knows where it has gone. It is obvious that no consensus can be reached on what should be assessed as true or false when such statements are combined with one another in communication. If the meaning of symbols is not limited, meaning will always be a matter of discretion. If we contravene against the dogma of forbidden contradictions, any meaning is possible, and communication is or becomes impossible.

---

2. In such a case Douglas Hofstadter (1979) speaks of a "strange loop."

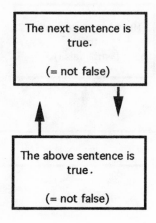

Figure 7–4

Alfred N. Whitehead and Bertrand Russell's (1910–1913) theory of logical classes is exemplary for its ban on the production, circulation, or consumption of self-negating loops. Propositions relating to a class or set are distinguished from statements relating to the elements of the class or set. Even if both have the same external linguistic form, they are nevertheless used in different abstract ways. The term "man" is used in a more abstract way when it refers to man as a species than when it relates to the man sitting at the next table in a café. According to the different levels of abstraction it can be ascribed to a different logical class. Statements about a class or set are thus from a higher logical class than those about the elements of the class or set.

Whitehead and Russell then introduce a kind of apartheid law and declare it impermissible to mix statements of different logical classes. They establish a social class system of concepts and propositions, a hierarchy of varying grades of abstraction that may not be muddled up. Whatever concerns the entity of a class (a hopscotch square) may not be an element of this class (square) at the same time. Statements on language can thus be ascribed to a different logical class than statements about wiener schnitzels.

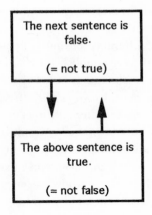

Figure 7–5

In order to explain this difference in use of language, linguists have distinguished between language relating to objects and language relating to language itself. They call the first object language, the second meta-language. The prefix meta- generally signifies that something is being talked *about*.

The laws of form, formulated by Spencer-Brown (1969) about a half-century after the theory of logical classes, indicate that even by the introduction of logical classes an attempt was made to secure the distinction between inside and outside. According to Whitehead and Russell's instructions, what belongs inside (in a class) must be separated from what belongs outside (not in a class). Metaperspective thus is equivalent to the position of the observer we have called external perspective up to this point (and will continue to do so).

The problem, it seems, is solved by a ban. However, as is usual in the case of such laws, not everyone complies with the ban. This is readily understandable, for object language and meta-language are not different languages in the same sense as are English, Hindu, and Tagalog. Neither vocabulary nor grammar distinguishes object language from meta-language. A naive speaker would never dream that he was speaking in meta-language when telling a linguist that meta-language is a ridiculous term. However, the introduction of such an imaginary difference obviously helps those who consider this distinction real to re-establish the distinction between inside and outside and to rescue the disputed system of binary logic.

The solution Spencer-Brown (1969) offers for the problem of paradox points in a quite different direction. He introduces *time*. All the difficulties caused by paradox result from the tacit assumption that we must describe a static world in which a sentence remains true or false once it has been recognized as true or false. In traditional binary logic, time is always imagined away. If we add time to binary logic in our minds, paradox disappears. The two sentences from Figure 7–5 then change their truth or falseness in time. They *oscillate* between both values of truth.

It has been known for a long time that such a logical pattern can be useful in technology, and we have probably all profited from the way it functions at some time. This pattern has been realized in a doorbell of the type found in private homes. Pressing the button closes the electrical circuit. Electricity flows through a coil that surrounds an iron core. The core is magnetized by the flow of electricity. The now-active magnet attracts a metal plate to which a clapper is fixed, and the clapper hits the bell: "Ting-a-ling!" The fact that the metal plate is attracted causes the circuit to be interrupted. No more electricity flows through the coil, the magnet becomes inactive, and the metal plate with the clapper is pulled back to its original position by a spring. When the button is pressed, this closes the circuit again, and the cycle starts from the beginning. This results in a continuous oscillation between electricity on and off, magnet on and off, clapper on the bell, and clapper at rest.

If we imagine away the factor of time, the possibility of things happening one after the other, we can find no sense in this construction; it seems to be an annoying waste of wire, metal, and other raw materials that ought to be forbidden straight away.

The inclusion of time renders it unnecessary to limit the possibilities within the structures of logic by external bans. These bans were only necessary as long as logic was needed to establish a consensus on a *static* world in which it was necessary to be able to distinguish clearly between mind and nature, the subject and object of cognition. When we want to describe a dynamic, changing world of self-organizing structures, processes, and things, we need a logic in which there is a possibility of self-reference. The tautology in which the logic of a static world was absolutely superfluous now proves to be the logical pattern of self-organization, of operational closure, of the autonomy and autopoiesis of living systems (Bateson 1979). It is the pattern of the closed circle between "a membrane is formed" and "cell metabolism takes place."

The tautological form of self-affirmative loops is not the only organizational principle of the living world, however. We sleep in order to wake again and are awake in order to go to sleep again; we breathe in and out and in and out. Many living processes can best be described by the self-negating pattern of paradox, as an oscillation between two mutually exclusive conditions. It is the *pulse* of these rhythms and the length of the phases that distinguish between heart flutter and a regular pulse, between well-being and suffering, between health and sickness.

The individual feels this principle of organization from his inner perspective as the wish and need to breathe in after breathing out deeply and to breathe out after breathing in deeply, and of course in thousands of other ambivalences, such as the wish for contact when he feels lonely and the wish to be alone when he feels closeness.

This pattern is only a paradox for someone who believes he always has to be the same, to feel, think, and do the same, independent of time.

IMAGINARY SPACES:
TIME, DELUSION, AND HALLUCINATION

Time is created by paradox. *Time has to be invented for the sake of the consistency of logic.* This statement seems rather radical in view of the fact that we are used to moving in a seemingly objective time, meeting at stations at a scheduled time, trusting timetables and appointments, and speculating about the past and the future. However, even time does not exist independent of observers; what seems to be objectivity is the result of agreement between people, the expression of consensus.

In contrast to events taking place in space (in us or around us), we cannot perceive time with our senses. Man can only experience current events for himself. The nervous system always has only one current pattern of activity. Each nerve cell is either firing or not; it knows nothing about yesterday and tomorrow, but knows only the present. The effects of the past and the shadow of the future always affect the present. "Time is creation or it is nothing at all" (Bergson 1988, p. 276).

The developmental psychologist Jean Piaget, who has researched the origin and development of human cognition from infancy to adulthood more carefully than anyone, sees the construction of all concepts and categories linked with the behavior of the observer. He experiences the repercussions of his own actual or mental behavior (operations) on himself and so orders them. Time also provides the opportunity to bring order into events: "[T]he succession of psychological phenomena can only be grasped by an observer who goes beyond them and so resurrects a physical time that is no longer" (Piaget 1955, p. 277).

In this description Piaget tacitly presupposes the identity of the observer. In order to render time necessary the assumption is required that in two distinct situations (e.g., yesterday and today) the observer stays the same. If we look at such a situation from the external perspective of the observer of the observer, the observer in this situation has four different possibilities to order the events of yesterday and today: (1) He can describe himself as well as the environment as the same today and yesterday. (2) He can describe the environment today as the same as yesterday, but himself as changed. (3) He can describe himself today as the same as yesterday, but the environment as changed. (4) He can describe both as different.

If we accept Spencer-Brown's definition that every form is composed of the space or content lying on both sides of the distinction, the form of the world of the observer who regards himself and his environment from the internal perspective is unchanged only in the first case. Yesterday's truth is today's truth. The fourth possibility brings no logical problems either, as it represents two different forms of world that are not connected, two distinguishable circles on two different pieces of paper. In the second and third case there is a paradox, namely, when the inside of the distinction today (the observer) is identified with the inside of the distinction yesterday (the observer), the outside of the distinction today and yesterday must consequently be the same too. The same applies when the outside of the distinction today is identified with that for yesterday. Together they make up the form: if one side of the distinction changes, the whole form changes, and if one side of the distinction remains the same, the whole form is unchanged. This is a classical paradox: the circle on the piece of paper stays the same and is different. The form changes, yet is still identical. Yesterday's truth is false today, yet remains true.

The consistency of logic, and thus the possibility of establishing a consensus on truth and falsehood, can be saved if the two-placeness (either true or false) of logic is supplemented by a third value. A third, *imaginary* space must be added to the space on both sides of the distinction.

The form of the world is extended by a new distinction coming into place next to the inside–outside distinction, namely, the before–after distinction. In space, events are distinguished as simultaneous (synchronic). With the invention of time they can be localized in an imaginary space—past or future—and be distinguished as not simultaneous (diachronic).

In the introduction to the first American edition of his *Laws of Form* Spencer-Brown (1969) illustrates the effect of imaginary value by a simple mathematical example. In addition to the concepts "true" or "false," which can result in paradox (see Figure 7–5), we need the category "meaningless" as well; only this gives us the possibility to deny a sentence any meaning.

Analogous to these categories, we may start from the assumption that a number can be *positive*, *negative*, or *zero*. If we consider the equation

$$x^2 + 1 = 0$$

it can be converted to

$$x^2 = -1$$

If we divide both sides by x we get

$$x = \frac{-1}{x}$$

It is easy to see that this equation is self-referential and that x appears on both sides of the equal sign. In order to fulfill the equation numerically, x must be some kind of unit. If we assume just two forms of unit, +1 and –1, the result when we take x = +1 is

$$+1 = \frac{-1}{+1} = -1$$

which is obviously a paradox. If we take x = –1 we get

$$-1 = \frac{-1}{-1} = +1$$

which is no less paradoxical.

In mathematics the problem is solved by introducing a fourth class of numbers, the *imaginary* numbers. In this way we can find the square roots: x is the root of –1, called i. A huge field of mathematical and practical technical problems would be insoluble without the use of these imaginary numbers and if the stop signs that say "Attention! You are leaving the sector of (not imaginary) reality" were taken all too seriously.

As a consequence of the mathematical solution to the problem of paradox and self-reference, Spencer-Brown (1969) demands that in the case of logic, too, meaningful argument cannot consist of only two classes of statements, but three: true, false, and imaginary. He also proposes time as a possible imaginary space. In this view of time he joins philosophers and other researchers who have examined the development of the concept of time in children and adults (Elias 1984, Piaget 1955).

It is apparently so easy to reach a consensus on time as imaginary space that we completely lose our consciousness of its imaginary character or never develop it in the first place. Anyone who uses time to remove paradox remains within the necessities and possibilities of normality.

The meaning of time is that it makes the question as to whether something *is* true or not *undecidable*. The continuous necessity to make a decision about the truth of statements about static *being* is abolished. Instead the possibility of a changing, dynamic identity is introduced.

However, the invention of time is only one of the possibilities of using an imaginary space to rescue logical structures from the threat of paradox. Other imaginations, other creative oversteppings of borders that lead to a new reality resolving old contradictions have a similar effect as time. Ludwig Wittgenstein provides the fairy tale of the clever farmer's daughter as an example. The King had had the girl's father thrown into prison. If she wants to free him she must appear before the King "neither naked nor clothed." The daughter's solution is to appear enveloped in a fishing net, naked but covered. The King, who has the power to decide whether the riddle is solved, lets the father go and marries the daughter. And then they lived happily ever after, but still confronted by seemingly insoluble tasks (Fischer and Simon 1988).

The girl in the fairy tale succeeded in finding a solution to the contradiction within the consensus. Delusion and hallucination, though, are individual realities in which contradictions are solved. From a logical point of view their effect can be compared with that of time. The production of hallucinations and the construction of systems of delusion are other ways to keep the question as to the truth of statements undecidable.

In general, however, the effects of hallucinations and systems of delusion are not compared to those of time, because time is a form of imagination legitimized by general consensus and therefore belongs to normality. However, delusion and hallucinations also render it impossible to decide which of the two statements of a paradoxical, self-negating loop is true.

The hallucinatory voice that warns a patient that the people in his environment are all part of a worldwide conspiracy to declare him mad cannot be proved wrong. When a psychiatrist explains to his patient that the voice is a symptom of illness, he thus confirms what the voices are saying. If the voice's statement is true, the psychiatrist's statement is false. If the psychiatrist's statement is true, the voice's statement is false. This is a classical paradox if we take both statements equally seriously. The same applies to systems of delusion, the falseness of which cannot be proved either. They start from imaginary assumptions and come—quite logically—to imaginary conclusions. Systems of delusion are operationally closed as well, that is, their assumptions are confirmed by the conclusions. A man who walks along clapping his hands to shoo the elephants away starts from such imaginary assumptions, and the success of his cautionary measures confirms them.

Let us take another look at the four ways that the observer caught up in a situation can order the changes from yesterday to today in his view of reality. In the first case, in which he describes himself and his environment as unchanged, his well-being will depend in the long term on whether the environment matches its picture. If at the age of 20 he describes himself and his environment the same way as he did at the age of 2, he needs a really loving and infinitely patient mother in order to be able to survive. In the second case, in which he regards the environment as unchanged but himself as different, he will experience a severe identity crisis, possibly even a personality split. The continuity of his description of himself has been interrupted. However, if he sees himself as unchanged and the environment as transformed, he loses his reality from one moment to the next. Here, too, he loses continuity of experience, the historical aspect of his own existence. In the fourth case, in which he experiences both himself and his environment as changed, he enjoys living in respectively logically consistent worlds, but the outside observer probably concludes that he is dealing with a severe case of multiple personality—Dr. Jekyll and Mr. Hyde.

The paradox of human cognition that makes it possible to explain practically all psychotic symptoms is that the Aristotelian dogma of identity can only be maintained in the long run if identity can change—which is a contradiction of the dogma of identity, namely, "two things, x and y, are identical when any characteristic P applying to x also applies to y and vice versa" (Hilbert cited in Klaus 1964).

It is, however, well known that you cannot fall into the same river twice—in the same way as a river cannot wash around the same person twice. Our language and the binary logic connected with it seduce us again and again into regarding the whole world (ourselves included) as a static, unchanging formation, a point of view that inevitably leads to paradox. And if the hypothesis that madness can be put into any kind of functional correlation with paradox should prove meaningful and useful, the result is a further paradox, namely, *only someone who thinks logically (binarily) can become mad.*

8

The Order of Feelings

"What is this illness called? It has a name, I guess?"
"Amour." "A pretty word. Tell me some things
To know it by—the symptoms, more or less."
"You get such pains the ecstasy of kings
Is dull and boring in comparison
With this condition.
You quite forget yourself—you could
Be happy, solitary in a wood.
You lean and look into a stream:
You don't see you, you only see this
dream
Which recurs everywhere and endlessly.
Except for that, you have no eyes to see.
There is a shepherd, where you're from,
The sight or voice of whom,
Even the name, can make you blush.
You think of him, your breath comes in a rush:
You sigh; you don' t know why;
And yet you sigh,
Afraid you'll see him, though you long to
see him."
—From Jean de la Fontaine (1621–1695),
Thyrsis and Amaranta (Fables, VIII, 13).

LOVE AND HATE: THE EVOLUTION
AND DISSOLUTION OF SOCIAL (SURVIVAL) UNITS

Feeling is prelinguistic. This quality renders any attempt to trans-
late the experience of one's own feelings into words into a balanc-

ing act where one runs the risk of falling into banality, on the one hand, and of falling just as far into sentimental drivel, on the other hand. When describing feelings, the denotative value of words is even smaller than when describing the taste of a papaya that has never been tried before. What does somebody actually mean when he says, "I love you?" Many of the conflicts that make living with someone hell develop because everybody thinks he or she knows the objective meaning of a statement such as this one, namely, exactly what it means for him or her subjectively.

You cannot really talk about feelings. However, you need not keep your mouth shut either. You always have the possibility of using the overtone of words, the connotative aspect of language. Literature and poetry attain their significance from this use of language. They set the tone, create an atmosphere; whoever listens will feel the echo inside him, as a kind of resonance develops.

Without judging their artistic value, the texts of pop songs can be regarded as an exemplary attempt to express feelings with words. The weekly sales charts are the thermometer that measures how warm or frigid a nation's feelings are; they are the result of the popular votes of record buyers. The number one song's combination of text and music goes down so well that thousands and sometimes even millions of people are prepared to spend their money on it. Even though the text may not be the decisive factor, it has to fit the music so as not to obliterate its emotional effect. Consider that it is rather difficult to sing, "I can't get no satisfaction," to the tune of "Jingle Bells."

Love and being in love, the feelings that are sung about most often, are presented in pop songs as invariably dealing with intense bodily sensations, in every sense of the word. Love is always a matter of extreme contradictions: fire and ice, on top of the world one minute and down in the dumps the next. Everyone can find enough examples by just turning on the radio, so they are not listed here in detail. In general we can establish that in most cases we are dealing with an altered perception of the body accompanied—in physical and chemical terms—by an increase in body temperature, a change in the specific gravity and physical condition of whoever is experiencing these

changes and is suffering deliciously. First comes the excitement, hot
flushes, feeling lighter, elation, and floating on air, which finally
culminate in the selflessness of a total fusion with one's lover. The
lovers' outlines dissolve, and the external difference between the two
makes no difference any more. Two become one; both identify with
each other, one heart and one soul. We shall never separate, without
you I am nothing, I cannot live without you. . . .

The difference between the image of love and being in love in
these texts and the analyses provided by philosophers is not very
great (if we disregard the fact that philosophers do not normally
publish texts that sell a comparable number of copies in such a short
period).

Plato has provided a classical example of this kind of philosophical interpretation. In the *Symposium* he lets Aristophanes give the
following mythical explanation for the phenomenon of being in love:

> The sexes were not two as they are now, but originally three in num-
> ber; there was man, woman, and the union of the two, having a name
> corresponding to this double nature, which had once a real exist-
> ence, but is now lost, and the word "Androgynous" is only preserved
> as a term of reproach. In the second place, the primeval man was
> round, his back and sides forming a circle; and he had four hands
> and four feet, one head with two faces, looking opposite ways, set on
> a round neck and precisely alike; also four ears, two privy members,
> and the remainder to correspond. . . . Terrible was their might and
> strength, and the thoughts of their hearts were great, and they made
> an attack up on the gods. [Plato 1984b, 89e]

This attack of course, could not work, because the gods do not like
anyone disputing them. After long consideration Zeus advised cutting the humans in two halves. They would have to stop their "madness" then. Cut in two they would not only be weaker, but also more
in number and therefore more useful. "If they continue insolent
and will not be quiet, I will split them again and they shall hop
about on a single leg. He spoke and cut men in two, like a sorb-apple
which is halved for pickling, or as you might divide an egg with a
hair" (Plato 1984b, 190a). He ordered Apollo to turn their necks

around so that man might always see where he had been disjoined. Above the belly the skin was pulled up and fastened in a knot; the navel was complete as "a memorial of the primeval state" (190b). Now, however, "after the division the two parts of man, each desiring his other half, came together and throwing their arms about one another, entwined in mutual embraces, longing to grow into one, they were on the point of dying from hunger and self-neglect, because they did not like to do anything apart" (190c). By making some minor changes to the private parts—moving them to the front— Zeus created the possibility of combining business with pleasure

> in order that by the mutual embraces of man and woman they might breed, and the race might continue; or if man came to man they might be satisfied, and rest, and go their ways to the business of life: so ancient is the desire of one another which is implanted in us, reuniting our original nature, making one of two, and healing the state of man. [Plato 1984b, 190d]

If we abstain from seeking these causal explanations and content ourselves once more, in all modesty, with relating observations from the perspective of the external observer to those of an observer from an inner perspective, we are able to describe some of the interactional and social effects of feelings, even though we still do not know what feelings, these strange things, really are.

Prosaically one might say that being in love and love itself obviously have the effect—just as Aristophanes depicts it—of enabling the development of new social entities that exceed the framework of the organic entity of the individual. Love enables individuals to unite and do together what they cannot do alone.

Being acutely in love, with all its sexual desires, can be regarded as a specific perturbation of the system of the individual living being, as a stimulation, agitation, and arousal disturbing natural daily routines and behavior patterns. The focus of attention of the poor or unhappy victims of such confusion is extremely limited. They can only think of one thing. As it is put so nicely, they "lose their heads," which means nothing more or less than that their usual standards of thought and action seem to be in force no longer. Their current interest revolves around a certain person who seems to radiate a magic attraction. If these feelings are mutual, both seek the company of the other. First they approach each other, and then they rush at each other. They find peace again if there takes place a quite characteristic form of structural coupling: sexual intercourse, a term well chosen for a concept whose mechanically sensuous meaning is immediately comprehensible. Feelings are the greatest matchmakers; they lead—not only sexually—to cooperation and communication (admittedly a rather sober choice of words). They may have a number of other effects, but they certainly fulfill this purpose too.

If the mutual attraction of two people is preserved beyond the moment of being in love, a relationship develops between them. If they can do as they wish, both spend more time with one another than they would normally in accordance with the rules of probability. They have more opportunities for direct interaction, for perturbing and comforting each other again. They inevitably experience a mutual process of development and live through a common history. They come to a consensus about the reality of their relationship, about the meaning of behavior, words, and gestures. They create their own unmistakable mutual culture. This effect can also be achieved without emotional enmeshment; arranged marriages are one example. One of the possible consequences of such feelings that have more than a momentary effect, as characterized by the concept of love, is the development of communication systems and the formation of couples and of families.

Let us emphasize once more: feelings cannot be explained by the description of a few of their effects. These phenomena have merely been presented on the level of behavior and ascribed to the level of experience. Notably, behavior described as an effect of love corresponds to what behaviorists call a bond:

> Attraction induces an individual to follow a partner when he moves on and to stay for his sake when he remains where he is, or even to search for him actively should he disappear. For this bond (as Lorenz

called it) no characteristic movement mode is required, but rather a
certain condition or situation in which a movement mode occurs. . . .
Thus we use the word bond to designate what makes free individuals
stay together or in certain places. [Wickler and Seibt 1977, pp. 306–
307]

Scientists who wish to examine the behavior of animals only have
access to behavior patterns that can be observed directly from the
outside. They cannot ask gray geese how they feel, what they think
and mean, and why they do this or that. However, this disadvantage is compensated for by the fact that there is far less risk of mixing
up observations from the inner and outer perspective. *Bond* can
then be defined quite coarsely as follows:

One ought to demand quite generally that social bonds be described
in the form of preferences, that is behaviors defined which are preferably or exclusively directed to certain objects, locations or individuals. The individual to whom such behavior is preferably directed is
then the partner per definition. . . . When individuals develop preferences among themselves the result is that social interaction does
not occur by chance, but is ordered in some way. We call this order
(who copulates with whom, who raises whose young, which individuals
hunt together etc.) social structure. [Wickler and Seibt, p. 313]

Bonds and the social structures deriving from them obviously
have a biological basis. If we find the description of evolving social
structures satisfactory, we can find great similarities between man
and some animals. Because we as human beings have the advantage of being able to observe human beings both from the outside
and from the inside, it is natural to regard the development of social
bonds in man as well as in animals as one of the functions of feeling. The very aspect of human behavior that, according to common
sense, characterizes humanity might well be part of our animal
heritage. Consequently crocodiles and horses seem rather human.
This family resemblance probably has its roots in the peculiar piece-
meal structure of our brain.

The brain scientist MacLean (1962) describes this similarity as follows:

> Man is in the dilemma that in principle nature has provided him with three brains that have to function together in spite of major structural distinctions. The oldest of these brains originates basically from the reptilian period. The second he inherited from the early mammals, and the third developed over the period of the mammals; it reaches its culmination point in the primates and has made man into what he is today.
>
> Speaking allegorically about these three brains in one brain, you could say: when a psychiatrist asks his patient to lie down on the couch, he is forcing him to lie next to a horse and a crocodile. The crocodile may be willing to shed a few tears. and the horse may neigh loudly or quietly, but when they are asked to put their problems into words it soon becomes clear that they are unable to. [p. 289]

Speaking and thinking are connected with the phylogenetically younger parts of the human brain. The descriptions of the world given by horses, crocodiles, and dung beetles are necessarily different from those given by humans. The descriptions given by animals cannot be influenced by cultural and linguistic structures. Yet, crocodiles do describe their world; they do behave and make differences in it. However, they are less able than man to learn from experience. They are not able to invent an imaginary space in which they can indulge in fantasies about themselves and their environment and in which they can test different options for action in an imaginary experiment to the same extent as can man. Their bodily heritage enables them, however, to make the necessary distinctions in a given situation and to behave accordingly.

When the phylogenetically older parts of the human brain and their functions are examined, they prove to be closely connected with the area of feeling and the so-called instinctive behavior of hunger, sex, struggle, and flight. In evolution these parts of the brain have been able to prove their fitness successfully. As the brain always functions as an operationally closed system, each part influences the other. As in a thin-walled tenant building, each part has the de facto right to determine whether the neighbor will have a quiet or a restless night. If the patterns do not go together, organizational problems can develop from this lack of building appropriate boundaries between subsystems. Or, in an analogy related to the level of descriptions, if the thoughts do not match the feelings, there can be organizational problems.

The conflicts resulting from this lack of fit are primarily related to the area of interpersonal relations, because our feelings determine our behavior toward other people to a great extent.

Affects have social effects. They either link individuals to larger social units or dissolve these links and bonds. Being in love, sympathy, and love on one side of the spectrum correspond to aversion, antipathy, and hate on the other. As the term *aversion* indicates, we are dealing here with a behavioral direction of movement, the striving for distance. The consequence is that direct interaction is less likely, and there is less mutual stimulation, agitation, arousal, and soothing; less communication; less need to develop a consensus; and a smaller chance to develop a consensus on reality.

Man's spiteful desire and attempt to kill the other are nothing but extreme cases of attempted dissociation. A hostile neighbor lying slain in a ditch can no longer perturb me in direct interaction. Killing him simplifies the complexity of the world. Out of sight, out of mind. The more dead a potential troublemaker is, the less trouble he can make: the phrase "The only good Indian is a dead Indian" is a terrible simplification of this concept.

Let us turn again to the inner perspective of someone who feels. Feelings, too, can be understood as descriptions of the world that have a characteristic, prescribing influence on the behavior of the individual. If one draws conclusions from these effects, love and hate establish a distinction between inside and outside, between what can be attributed to one's own unit of survival and what can be attributed to an environment threatening the survival of this unit.

The effect of feelings lies in dissociation, in the definition of a living system with regard to its environment. The self, which is defined as a unit of survival, can be an individual, a couple, a family, or even some abstract entity, such as an idea, for example, the fatherland, world revolution, or the truth. Thus the effect of love is to cause the distinction between someone who loves and his beloved object to disappear. The goals and motives of individual actions exceed individual boundaries. One's own survival is equated with the survival of the loved one.

In the course of evolution, feeling has proved its ability to survive. Without feelings mankind would have died out. Even if a human being were fathered accidentally or babies were procreated gemmiparously or by layering, like living room rubber trees or other ornamental plants, they would still require—since they are the way they are—at least *one* caring person to warm them when they are cold, give them food and drink when they are hungry and thirsty, talk to them, touch and caress them, and reflect their existence.

Up to now, feeling has proved its evolutionary significance for the survival of humanity as a whole—not for that of the individual—under the condition of direct interaction between people confronting one another face to face. If under the impulse of the moment somebody had his skull bashed in by mistake, this would have no appreciable statistical bearing on the survival of mankind. However, conditions have changed in our age with its means of mass extermination. When you press the release button of an H-bomb, people are killed with whom you have nothing to do directly, have not met personally, do not see or know. Because the consequences of aggressive actions are no longer limited to a very small number of directly interacting people, risks are magnified, to the disadvantage of the survival of mankind. However, this need not only be a cause for pessimism, for in cases where the consequences of an aggressive act cannot be limited to the enemy, a self-referential or, to be more precise, a self-denying circle is inevitably created. Aggression becomes autoaggression. This increases the chances that the power of feelings can perhaps be utilized for a larger unit of survival, namely, for mankind.

QUICK SIMPLIFICATIONS: GOOD AND BAD, STRONG AND WEAK, ACTIVE AND PASSIVE

A great danger of reification is connected with the naming of feelings. A bucket full of love, a quarter of a pound of hate, two pieces of tenderness, and a pinch of melancholy. An emotion is great or small, sincere or insincere, new or old, more or less. Here, too, the menu is not the meal, the map not the territory. If you mistake the characteristics of the map for those of the territory, mountains appear to be flat, oceans dry, the Sahara to consist of paper, and the earth to be rectangular. The same can happen when talking about feelings if the characteristics of language are mistaken for those of feelings. Dissociations and relations between different concepts (individual feelings) can then be confused with what you feel when feeling. It should not be taken for granted that the dynamics of feeling correspond to language's principles of order. However, you cannot help using words and talking about feelings when dealing with other people or perhaps even tackling the phenomenon of feeling scientifically. After all, feeling is a very private matter; talking about one's own feelings always involves crossing a border (opening–closing), the opening up of an area of perception not directly accessible to an outsider. And yet it is not feeling itself, but a description (second order) of feeling.

It is much easier for two people to talk about a third subject located outside themselves, such as the weather, the neighbors, an unruly child, or an arbitrary object. In this objective area that is equally accessible to the perception of all concerned, it is relatively easy to come to terms about reality, about the meaning of phenomena, and the appropriate use of language. You can point to a board resting horizontally on some legs with your finger and call it a "table." And if you do that somebody else can grasp not only the object pointed out but also the meaning of the word "table." It is much more difficult to talk about feelings in a fitting manner. The possibilities of objectifying, of including and excluding meanings, are limited.

The distinction between pointing something out and the object pointed out is far less possible in the sphere of feeling than in the sphere of objects. Other people can only perceive people's behavior from the outside, not what they feel. One is blushing with shame, another's teeth are chattering with fright, and a third is weeping with sadness or rage. This close connection between feelings and characteristic patterns of behavior finds its expression in the ambiguity of linguistic formulations referring to feelings. Nobody actually knows exactly what somebody else means when this person tells us excitedly that Mr. Miller and Ms. Smith "love each other." He might be saying something about their feelings, describing a certain form of relationship, or even talking about an act they are performing right at this moment observed by a voyeur through the keyhole. In this case the statement about their feelings cannot be separated from that about their behavior and their relationship.

This close connection between feeling, relationship definition, and behavior is confirmed by the research of the psycholinguist Osgood and his colleagues (1975). In order to be able to comprehend the subjective meaning of feelings, they have developed a process that enables them to record the common meanings of affectively loaded concepts in twenty-two different languages. They found out that wherever feelings are involved, distinctions are made in three independent dimensions of meaning, namely, between *strong* and *weak*, *active* and *passive*, and *good* and *bad*.

Judgments in these three dimensions of meaning suffice to enable those involved in this great game of life (survival) to make decisions. One of the decisive distinctions between the inner and outer observer of such a game is that the co-player has no time to think. In situations of danger he has to do one thing or the other quickly or forget it. He thus requires quite simple schemes to be able to orient himself here and now without a long period of contemplation. Anyone who tries to be discriminating in his judgment is threatened by the immense complexity of the world with an inability to act. If he always tries to weigh all the facts, include all possible perspectives, and mentally anticipate any conceivable complication, he would inevitably have to stay in bed paralyzed and avoid any movement, which could also have fatal consequences.

Feelings enable an obviously *egocentric* analysis of a world that is sufficiently simple and sufficiently differentiated to enable quick action. You can even ask yourself whether feeling cannot be regarded as a part or a preliminary stage of this action. After all, what is experienced from the inner perspective as feeling is often connected with bodily (alarm) reactions that create the physical prerequisites for certain patterns of behavior, for example, flight and fight. At any rate the step from feeling to behavior and/or to change in behavior is not very great. Certain feelings increase or decrease the probability of certain patterns of behavior in the individual.

Like Stone Age man, we obviously trust in our feelings to distinguish whether a person, animal, plant, thing, or action is active or passive, strong or weak, good or bad in relation to us and/or the unit of survival with which we identify. Of course we do not know whether he, she, or it is really like that, but when trusting our feelings we act as if that were the case.

Everything interesting for human emotions occurs in the space of meaning composed of these three dimensions. The dramatic pattern of world literature, the cliches of sentimental movies in idealized settings, the Wild West and Rambo movies, but also the rules of video games or political campaigns follow the dividing lines of these patterns. There is always a battle between the powers of evil and the threatened virtues of what is good. Poor, unprotected widows and orphans (= weak, passive, good) are at the mercy of rich and powerful oppressors (= strong, active, bad). The avenger of the disinherited and underprivileged enters (= strong, active, good) and reestablishes law and order. The possibilities of combining these three attributes are limited. However, they are completely sufficient to construct the characters of the main actors.

Thus the world, if we believe our feelings, is filled with objects and persons that can be reduced—inevitably, according to mathematics—to a few distinctive categories. These categories provide the material from which positively or negatively idealized heroes and their actions can be constructed, in which a clear division is made between good and bad, in which the principle of all or nothing rules, a clear either–or, black or white.

The number and form of relationships in such an emotional world are also limited. The obligation to act as a result of these descriptions seems to be of suggestive inevitability: the bad must be kept weak and passive, the good has to be activated and strengthened, and so on.

In the course of individual and collective mental development, the idealizing and simplifying inner perspective of feeling is differentiated, questioned, and commented on by a quasi-outer perspective of thought. How this pattern of active–passive, strong–weak, and good–bad is filled with content determines the unmistakable values and world views not only of the individual but also of social systems, cultures, industrial organizations, institutions, clubs, parties and—above all—families.

THE BALANCE OF OPPOSING TENDENCIES: DIFFERENCES BETWEEN LIFE AND LOGIC–II

With our feelings we value what is happening in us and around us, what we and others do and do not do. If we did not think at the same time, the world as we feel it would be ordered without contradictions according to simple opposites, black or white. However, since we hardly ever manage *just* to feel, the world loses its beautiful and terrible simplicity.

Our feeling is tied to the moment; it does not know time, no yesterday and no tomorrow. It induces us to act, to take flight, to fight, or to accept despondently a fate we cannot change. It manifests the necessarily limited view of the player involved in the events.

Thinking, in contrast, opens up a wide range of new perspectives. We can imagine taking up the imaginary positions of outside spectators watching from the right, left, front, back, up, down, before, or after. Thus our picture becomes more differentiated, a dull black-and-white snapshot turns into a play whose principal actors wear shimmering costumes and are prepared to rehearse different plots.

Our thinking gives us access to an imaginary world that grants us the right to exchange our decisions. We act on a trial basis and experience—without obligation, on approval—the matching feelings. However, this possibility makes life more complicated. It is agonizing to have to choose.

Whatever was good from the restricted perspective of the moment now suddenly seems bad, strong becomes weak, and active is transformed into passive. Whosoever permits himself to think inevitably gets into conflicts. He loses the ability to live without ambivalence. Blessed are probably only those who are really poor in spirit. For whatever we do or do not do, whatever happens, has good and bad consequences. Observed from the outside and over a longer period, one can always find contradictory aspects that can or must be evaluated contrarily.

It is a paradox that the phenomenon of ambivalence results from the interplay between consistent feeling and logical thought that demands consistency. As long as we feel only in the here and now, the world is without contradiction. When time is introduced and alternatives can be considered, contradictory feelings can be experienced simultaneously—and ambivalently.

Probably best known, because it wanders through many psychological textbooks like a ghost out of touch with real life, is the example of the ambivalence you can experience toward an apple. You can keep the apple, and then you have it later on in times of need when your hunger is greatest. The price you have to pay is abstaining from the pleasure of eating it in the here and now. If you eat it straight away because you feel like it right now, you will not have it later on. This example of the apple is probably so popular because it incites a broad spectrum of associations by way of displacement or condensation, for example, Eve's dilemma in paradise. Ambivalence is the price you have to pay for eating the forbidden fruit from the tree of knowledge.

In linguistic descriptions, and thus in our language-bound thinking, a relatively high degree of unambiguity can be achieved; behavior is always more ambiguous. The conflict between the first- and second-order descriptions that we give of ourselves and the world is preprogrammed. Our language suggests that we have only the choice of either jumping into the hopscotch square labeled "good" or into the one labeled "bad" (into the one with the label "hero" or "villain," "culprit" or "victim," and so on.) Linguistic descriptions are ordered by binary distinctions. Everything within the border of such distinctions negates everything outside it.

If we consider the level of behavior, it becomes clear that negation does not equal negation. We can distinguish between two forms of negation, active and passive negation. The philosopher Jon Elster (1979, p. 178), who has coined these concepts following one of Kant's ideas, gives the following three propositions as an example:

I. Person A believes statement p to be true [abbreviated: A believes p].

II. It is not the case that A believes p [abbreviated: Not (A believes p)].

III. A believes the contrary of p [abbreviated: A believes not-p].

Proposition II is the passive negation of proposition I; proposition III its active negation.

The sentence "I do not love you" is the passive negation of the sentence "I love you"; the sentence "I hate you" is its active negation. The assertion "There is no God" is an active negation of God; the sentence "I do not know whether there is a God" is the passive negation. Anyone who was not for the Nazis negated them passively; those who joined the resistance negated them actively.

If a certain behavior is *refrained* from, we are dealing with the passive negation of this behavior (you do not agree with the person you are talking to; you are neither economical nor stingy with your money; you are not depressive; you do not hold left-wing political views). If, however, you *do* something that has an opposite meaning, we are dealing with active negation (you not only do not agree with the person you are talking to, but you contradict him; you behave not only uneconomically, but extravagantly; you are not only not depressive, but are euphoric and manic; you hold not only no left-wing political views but right-wing views). The possibility of passive negation changes a meaning system in which there was only either–or into one with neither–nor as well. However, this does not exhaust the possibilities. Contradictory, logically exclusive meanings can and often must be ascribed to the behavior patterns of a living organism. Here a conflict with Aristotelian logic arises: "[C]ontradictory statements are not at the same time true," and "[T]he same attribute cannot at the same time belong to the same subject and in the same respect" (Aristotle 1984). For this dogma of excluded contradiction is connected with the blinker perspective, in which we regard the same thing at the same time only in one *respect* and refrain from drawing up different perspectives at different points in time. This sentence is only valid if we imagine dynamics and change out of the world.

Life deals with contradictions differently than logic. It overcomes logic by joining it to something new and thereby preserves it, not allowing it to be lost (Hegel 1807). Living systems must always balance contradictory tendencies. The constancy of their structures depends on their flexibility. The tree that cannot bend in the wind snaps. It is a "systemic antagonism" (Morin 1977) characterizing the processes of life, a tightrope act in which a loss of balance is constantly imminent. The artist on the tightrope has to move continuously and perform small swinging motions in order to fall neither to the right nor to the left. He has to move in opposite directions, *both* to the right *and* to the left.

Thus a world view in which it should be possible to describe ambivalent patterns of behavior whose meaning is contradictory requires a *both–and* hopscotch square. The original either–or field changes into a tetralemma field with four distinct meanings.

Let us take the tightrope performer as an example, as his balancing act reveals the necessities and possibilities of lifesaving balancing processes. Four options are open to him (Figure 8–1). He can move to either the right or to the left, both to the right and to the left, and neither to the left, nor to the right.

If he moves only to the right or to the left, he is going to fall from the wire. He therefore has only two possibilities of keeping his balance. He either refrains from any movement to the right or left, that is, he tries to negate falling down to the right or the left

	Do	Don't do
Do	**either** left	**both** left **and** right
Don't do	**neither** left **nor** right	**or** right

Figure 8–1

passively. Or he moves both to the right and the left, that is, he actively negates falling down to the right and the left. As anybody who has ever tried to perform on the tightrope knows, the static balance resulting from refraining from any movement is rather unsafe. The slightest gust of wind can lead to disaster, the slightest exterior change to a fall. The area of survival is extremely limited, namely, to one single spot. In contrast, oscillating around this center of gravity can balance out many disturbances and perturbations. The area of survival is wider and the dynamic balance more stable.

Let us look at this tightrope performer's apprentice years. What kind of instructions for action is he given by his environment, the tightrope, or in its place, his parents, who have balanced for years and know how to handle the wire? They must inevitably give him the following contradictory message: move to the right *and* to the left! A double bind? The criteria seem to be fulfilled. A vital relationship (between artist and rope), logically exclusive directions (whoever is on the right or moves to the right cannot be on the left or move to the left at the same time), the field (rope) cannot be quitted, and metacommunication is not possible (it is difficult to imagine anything more mute than a rope). Nevertheless the tightrope performer does not become mad. He moves to the right and left consecutively and neutralizes the supposed contradiction of the two partial movements in a new superior entity, oscillation. He moves not only in space but also in time. Time offers him the possibility of resolving the contradiction. This seems so self-evident that it is almost embarrassing to mention it here. Such a contradictory instruction only becomes a double bind when time is not available as imaginary (flight) space.

This is the case when a statement is made about a person's being. As long as behavior is talked about, processes are described in time. When you talk about how somebody *is*, behavior is translated into *characteristics*. *Constancy* is presupposed, and the fact that the world is changeable is neglected. We abstract from the passage of time. A double bind can only develop when a person is given contradictory instructions about how he should *be*, for example, a good person, loyal and dependable, strong and beautiful. As are all paradoxes, double binds too always develop from the features of a concept that presuppose something static, from mistaking the menu with the meal. We should prohibit not only—as is occasionally demanded—nouns but also the auxiliary verb "to be." For nothing in the world *is*; everything is in process of *growth* and *decay*.

9

Mad Feeling

FOR AND/OR AGAINST: A GAME OF DICE

Are you in doubt about whether you should go on reading this book (or whether you should leave your husband/wife/children/job) or not? Up until now you have been faithful and reliable and have stuck it out, but is it really worthwhile to stay involved in this venture? This is a question that applies not only to the relationship of a reader to his book, even though it is usually answered without being posed. In order to come to a decision please complete the questionnaire below. It has two categories: for and against. Try to find six arguments that support each of the two possibilities. For each of these reasons write a word to symbolize it under the relevant heading.

For	*Against*
1.	1.
2.	2.
3.	3.
4.	4.
5.	5.
6.	6.

You now have six good, consecutively numbered reasons why it is meaningful or meaningless to carry on as before. Take a white and a black die. With the white die, decide which of the arguments for and with the black die which of the arguments against you are going to think about, that is, on which you are going to focus your attention. Please note how you feel when you consider each argument. You are free to decide for yourself how much time you leave be-

tween each throw of the dice. However, you should try to determine whether varying time patterns result from the different variations of the game.

Variation 1: You throw both dice simultaneously and try to make
both arguments the basis of your decision at the same time. Do this
twelve times in a row! Try to behave in accordance with the decision thus made!

Variation 2: First you throw the white die twelve times and then
the black one. Try again to behave in accordance with the decision
thus made!

Variation 3: Throw the dice 24 times, but this time alternately,
first the white die and then the black one. And again try to do what
each die advises!

Variation 4: Refrain from throwing the dice 24 times in a row!
Think of further variations yourself!

BOTH–AND OR NEITHER–NOR:
THE CONTEMPORANEOUSNESS
OF CONFLICTING TENDENCIES

The terms "ambivalence" and "schizophrenia"[1] have both been
influenced by Eugen Bleuler, who considered them closely related.
Ambivalence is a symptom of schizophrenia. Sigmund Freud later
used the term in his psychoanalytical observations to describe conflicting feelings, not only in psychotic experience. Today newspa-
per reporters speculate on the ambivalences of politicians, popes,
or pop stars. The term is a part of everyday language. It is obvious
that it names a phenomenon that cannot be specific to madness.

"Two souls dwell in my breast," laments Faust, who inimitably
commented on so many important subjects. However, his words serve

---

1. Ambivalence, from the Latin *ambo* meaning both and *valeo* meaning I am worth, mean,
am for. Schizophrenia, from the Greek *schizo* meaning I split, divide, tear apart, and *phren*
meaning diaphragm, mind, consciousness. This equation of diaphragm with mind comes
from its being long considered the location of human consciousness because it is the organ
strained most by laughing, and laughing was considered a characteristic of the human mind.

to veil the drama of the situation. When people share an apartment, their relationships to each other determine whether and what problems arise. If one is the main tenant, it is obvious who asserts himself in case of conflict. Yet, the relationship between the inhabitants of Faust's breast seems to be equal; both are equally strong, which is what makes everything so difficult.

Ambivalence is an old subject and comes up again and again in literature. Plato speaks of two conflicting halves of the soul and compares them to a team of two horses—one is handsome and good and the other base, one strives towards heaven and the other pulls with all his might toward earth, and one is the location of the better passions and the other that of all sensual lusts (Plato 1984a).

If ambivalence is something so trivial, so well known to everyone since ages past, the question arises as to what distinguishes the ambivalence of madness from normal ambivalence. The Platonic image of the team of horses or the two souls in Faust's breast can both be used quite well to describe this distinction. In normal everyday ambivalence, we are always dealing with three main actors: the two inhabitants of the breast and the one who claims that it is his breast. The one who claims that it is his breast observes these two contradictory characters with the critical view and detachment of the external perspective. He *is* neither the one nor the other, that is, he does not identify himself with one feeling or the other. Nor does he spontaneously follow the contradictory impulses to action connected with his feelings. Torn this way and that, he allows the conflict in order to finally take the side of one or the other—at the latest point when external events no longer permit him to avoid making a decision. Or he resolves this ambivalence and ambitendency creatively by proposing a solution that reconciles the contradictions: for example, the landlord who follows his tenants' argument and makes a decision by either intervening and providing an acceptable compromise or by throwing one of the tenants out; the driver of the team of horses who either manages to drive both in the same direction or drives on with one horse.

In the case of mad ambivalence the external third party, who might intervene or come to a decision, is missing. Anyone who experiences this kind of ambivalence is definitely comparable to the horse, who feels the pull either to the right *or* to the left. Two mutually exclusive views and experiences from the inner perspective alternate rapidly. The impulse to action is followed—now farther, now less far—depending on the speed of the change from left to right. In this kind of ambivalence the contradiction is not conscious; the outer perspective is necessary for it to become conscious. In this way an action is begun only to change into its (active or passive) negation. Someone lifts a spoon to his mouth, but pours the soup back into the bowl instead of eating it; he lifts the spoon to his mouth and pours the soup back into the bowl; and so on. Laughing turns to crying turns to laughing turns to crying; love turns into hate turns into love turns into hate.

Strangely enough, someone who feels and acts in this way does not call himself ambivalent at all. He has matters quite straightened out in himself, and he loves and hates with absolutely no conflict—he simply alternates rapidly. His fellow beings, particularly the psychiatrists among them, who observe these contradictory actions and emotional expressions from the outside, tacitly assume that someone's personality, desires, and impulses cannot change from one minute to the next. They interpret such conflicting behavior (certainly not unjustly) as an expression of ambivalence. However, such conflicting behavior *is* normal. What is not normal is how it is ordered and split into two independent, respectively logically conclusive areas following the dogma of forbidden contradiction. If this person were a couple, both partners would be able to go their own way separately, according to their different wishes. The entity of the human body, however, sets up natural limits.

It is one of the characteristics of schizophrenic ambivalence that the freedom of current subjective experience (inner perspective) from contradiction seems from the outside (outer perspective) to be an expression of extreme contradiction. The patient or rather his mind seems to be split into two irreconcilable parts standing next to each other, to be "schizophrenic." Even his mimicry and gestures seem divided—his eyes can cry while his mouth is laughing.

This contradiction can manifest itself in two different patterns of behavior, namely, the both–and pattern or the neither–nor pattern. In the first case behaviors are combined that mutually negate each other actively, and in the second case these combined actions mutually negate each other passively.

Let us begin with the both–and pattern. From the outside it seems as though the conflicting tendencies are transformed into behavior *contemporaneously*, as ambivalent feelings are lived out. The tightrope is set swinging violently; it swings as far as possible to right and left. The sense of the behavior and linguistic expression cannot be understood by the observer, as their meaning dissolves as measured against the consensus.

Anyone who keeps his balance in this way tends toward stark activity and emotional outbursts of all kinds. Tenderness can turn into rage, megalomania into feelings of smallness, elation into profound self-doubt. Chaotically he is always busy doing one thing without forgetting the other, the opposite. He is unbearable to the people around him; eventually he is diagnosed as an acute psychotic and taken to a doctor or clinic for calming down, which triggers both relief and indignation in the patient. How could it be otherwise!

The picture is quite different in the neither–nor pattern. Here balance is kept by avoiding any behavior that could be ascribed a meaning in either direction. Anyone who behaves this way seems to an observer to be frozen in a playing-dead reflex. He is passive and shows neither willingness nor desire to do anything. He is often satisfied with lying in bed for long periods, sleeping a lot, and watching television. He seems neither to feel nor to think anything in particular. What is going on inside him is nobody's business. We can only assume what and how he feels, probably neither–nor. Diagnostically this behavior is usually classified as minus symptoms, which seem to be characterized more by the lack of elementary drive and motive or rather by what seems to the observer to express this lack. Somehow he seems to be beyond good or bad, neither fish nor fowl.

This same person may oscillate between these patterns of behavior, following first one and then the other. However, the both–and pattern is very tiring, so that in the long term it is more chronically economical to live out the neither–nor pattern. In both cases the balance between the conflicting tendencies is maintained by living them *contemporaneously*.[2] The ambivalence is not decided, so logically all possibilities are always kept open.

For the average human being, neither of these patterns of feeling is understandable. Even when the phenomenon of ambivalence is known to everyone, most people manage temporarily and for a certain time to decide on their ambivalences or—with open eyes—to bear them.

Another afterthought: such examples as the landlord or the driver of a team of horses should not be misunderstood as an explanation. They serve merely to illustrate the arising (dis)order of feeling. In psychoanalytical theory one would call the landlord the "ego" and the tenant's notice to quit the "defense." However, even these weighty technical terms serve only to describe an organizational process. The danger of all personalizing comparisons is that we look for personalizing explanations as well; for example, the landlord's noble motive of bringing about peace. We ought really look for concepts that do justice not only to our opinions but also to the theoretical concepts of self-organization; just as the landlord wants peace and quiet, so the system of thinking, feeling, and action must come to terms with perturbations and adapt to them.

EITHER–OR: THE NONCONTEMPORANEOUSNESS OF CONFLICTING TENDENCIES

The opposite metaphor to the ambivalence of schizophrenic feeling is manic-depressive feeling. Anyone who feels in this way seems to the observer to be mad because he appears to be absolutely without ambivalence.[3] He would never laugh with one eye while crying with the other; rather he would be either wholly or not at all, all or nothing, laughing or crying, black or white, fish or fowl. This lack

---

2. One might speak here of "synchronic dissociation" (Simon et al. 1989).
3. In textbooks this condition is referred to as "intolerance of ambiguity" (Kraus 1989).

of ambivalence causes him to leave the spectrum of culturally accepted feeling and behavior. The diagnosis of major affective disorders is made because being in a very good or very bad mood for weeks and months on end—fully disregarding the nice or terrible things going on in the world—is not in accordance with normal experience (the consensus).

Let us begin with the more pleasant side of this pattern, namely, mania. However, this aspect is only more pleasant for the person who manifests manic behavior. In fact, his close relatives get along better with him when he is depressive. Yet, there is obviously a great difference between the reaction of relatives and that of other people who have contact with a manic. To strangers he appears to be very attractive, funny, and full of ideas and initiative. A party where a manic is present is hardly likely to be a flop. He can carry all the others along with him, hits it off marvelously with others, and has a great number of contacts; even sexually he manifests himself as "one for the ladies" and is ready for any adventure. However, you ought not rely on the party being a success, as the combination of fewer inhibitions and overactivity can sometimes result in the shameless disregard of social conventions. When you get into an argument with a manic person, his outbursts of aggression may be just as catching as his wit was before, and his quickwittedness can suddenly change shape. When overactivity turns into fits of rage, manics no longer seem to be such lovable and amusing companions.

However, manics always see themselves—without any self-doubt at all—as strong and good and active and behave accordingly. Their capability seems inexhaustible and begins with physical resilience. They need no sleep, tiredness has vanished forever, and pain is a phenomenon from a faraway, incomprehensible world. Even intellectually and socially undreamed-of capacities are activated. Some patients declare retrospectively that they owe their whole career to the ability to react manically. Their bosses were never more satisfied with them; they were never more creative, never got on so well with their colleagues, and were never able to work so much as during these periods. Even the absences during subsequent hospitalization were more than offset by their manic creativity and productivity.

This increased activity is not only used productively, however. It frequently results in the person's overestimating his own strength, above all his financial strength. Yet, strength is, of course, not a concept that can be ascribed a meaning independent of the social framework. It was thus certainly mad of the retired widow living in a 60-square-foot one-room apartment to buy 76 yards of curtain material for her kitchen. And when a 22-year-old office messenger boy suddenly buys a Porsche without having inherited funds or won the lottery, one doubts whether he has summoned up the normal ambivalence regarding this purchase. It is not surprising that relatives and acquaintances conclude that such a person is not in a position to take personal responsibility for his decisions. From the outside it seems obvious that he has lost the ability to control his impulses. The consequence is that mother or father, wife or husband try to take over responsibility for the manic person, and not only for keeping a bank account. However, anyone who feels so great does not see himself as a patient in need of care or control—after all, he feels better than ever. Conflict with all who try to check him is inevitable.

The price for the euphoria of mania has to be paid back in times of depression. Then nothing is left of the radiant self-confidence. Self-doubt, delusions of inferiority, and impoverishment take the place of megalomania, again quite without ambivalence. Nothing remains of the effusive cheerfulness either. It becomes the opposite—inconsolable sadness.

Such patients see themselves as patients and often feel physically ill and restricted. Their bodies no longer function as usual. This disturbance in health begins with the digestion, which has lost its nice and relieving regularity; their appetite also leaves a great deal to be desired, as nothing tastes good any more. Some women do not get their menstrual period, and in some men there can be no more talk of potency. Yet, they hardly feel like becoming involved in any great sexual adventures anyway. Constant tiredness that finds no relief in sleep, absolute exhaustion, and a general feeling of listlessness are other symptoms. Nothing is doing any more.

These patients consider themselves punished by God and the world for a life of sin, as they are bad and weak. Their thoughts circle around the same ideas again and again. They doubt the sense of life, and it is often only their passivity that prevents them from committing suicide. Manic and depressive behavior belong together and form a pattern. The same person can be depressive for a few weeks or months and then be manic, interrupted by a shorter or longer pause, which can sometimes last for years. However, there are also patients who live out only one side, mostly the depressive one.

We limit ourselves to examining those who live out both their depression and their mania. As in schizophrenic patterns their experience and behavior are both subjectively free of ambivalence. However, seen from the outside there is a lack of the contemporaneousness of conflicting tendencies so characteristic of the schizophrenic order. Rather, the tendencies are *noncontemporaneous*, are consecutive. The contradictions are dissolved in that either the one or the other is done. Both stand irreconcilably next to each other. The patients are either above the line or below the line, as female and male nurses in psychiatric clinics usually diagnose their manic-depressive customers.[4]

Those concerned seem to have only one soul dwelling in their breasts and only one of the horses seems to be pulling Socrates' cart. If we assume that human life is always marked by antagonistic tendencies and must be ambivalent, the question arises—to keep to the metaphor—as to what happens to the second inhabitant of the breast or to the second horse of the team in the meantime. The fact that they are not dead and buried is obvious from the experience that they can prove very lively after a while. They seem then to have been temporarily withdrawn from circulation in order to be able to expose themselves later, with renewed strength, to the struggle with their antagonist. However, there is no struggle, as now the antagonist has disappeared. Anyone who lives according to a

---

4. Thus we can speak here of "diachronic dissociation" (Simon et al. 1989).

manic-depressive pattern behaves like the driver who always un-hitches one horse, drugs it, and puts it on the back of the cart. After a while, when the working horse has been trotting long enough in the direction it wanted and has gradually lost strength, the second horse, in a state of suspended animation, awakes. It is lifted down from the cart and hitched up. Now this horse may determine the direction. This way there can be no conflict between the two parts of the team, and the driver has peace. He can let both go as they wish; after a while he reaches the place he started out from with his team. Again the ambivalence does not have to be decided on.

For manic-depressive individuals, two directions of behavior that mutually negate each other actively are combined, so that over a longer period something similar to a balance is achieved. However, this is very costly. It is as though a tightrope performer let himself fall to the left into the abyss in order to climb back onto the wire after a long period of recovery in hospital, balance normally for a few yards, only to fall into the abyss on the right, and so on.

HOW LONG IS NOW?: FAST AND SLOW RHYTHMS

In the words of Bertold Brecht (1967, p. 383), "A man who had not seen Mr. K. for a long time greeted him with the words, 'You haven't changed at all.' 'Oh!' said Mr. K. and turned pale." An incorrect reading of the above quote: "A man who had not seen Mr. K. for five minutes greeted him with the words, 'You've changed a lot.' 'Oh!' said Mr. K. and turned pale."

The world changes—as do we in it. And yet we usually pretend that it remains stable, in the here and now. We only expect change over long periods of time. Our passports and identity cards are only valid for a few years, as the similarity between the passport photo and the owner fades more and more with the passage of time. Now, it seems, the world *is* stable; only later will it be different.

When after several years we see the children of relatives who live far away, we are shocked to find how much they have grown and how old we ourselves have become. For our own children we need marks on the kitchen door to check whether they have grown enough for their ages. The changes in people, in their growth and development, generally occur continuously, gradually, and hardly visibly. In larger intervals—when observation is discontinuous—the many small differences that make no difference for the constant observer amount to a difference that makes a difference.

Now everything stays as it is—later everything will be different. How long does this Now, for which the constancy of our world is important, last? After what interval do we pale in the face of change, after which in the face of lacking change? The answer to this question is decisive for the understanding of the mad order of feeling and thinking that deviates from the consensus. If we characterize the schizophrenic split of ambivalent feeling as contemporaneous and the manic-depressive as noncontemporaneous, we base the present—the here and now—on the interval in which we think we observe both souls in one breast.

The contemporaneousness described in the metaphor of the two souls or of the two horses pulling in different directions at the same time assumes a different, spatial kind of interval. We organize the events we experience and observe in time and space. When we use the term "ambivalence," we are on the level of linguistic description, and as always we must check whether we are not mistaking the attributes of description with those of what is being described. Is there ambivalence? Can people have several feelings at the same time, in the same way that we can write with one hand and scratch ourselves with the other simultaneously?

In the perception of our external world we can perceive various events with our five senses at the same time. We can listen to the news on the radio, watch a soap opera on television, smell the roast cooking in the kitchen, feel the coolness of the glass in our hand, and taste the beer with which we wash down some crackers. We can do and perceive all this *simultaneously* with no trouble. Even changes can be registered quickly. When the beer glass is empty and the roast smells burnt, we are quickly perturbed and can hurriedly take emergency and countermeasures. Such sudden reactions are possible because a part of our nervous system transmits its signals through fast-working conduction lines (in this case in the same sense as the telephone). The perception of the so-called diacritical system[5] is outlined by and follows from the sensory organs. The connections to the cerebral cortex, to conscious thinking, and the horizontally striped skeletal muscles of the limbs, the performing organs of our actions, are very close.

In the so-called kinesthetic system,[6] in contrast, which is closely connected to the brainstem and our feelings, hormones are also used as transmitters of signals. Their effect is slower and more unspecific than the quick telephone wires of the diacritical system. This system gives no clearly defined perception, but rather dull, vague sensations. We register a change in our physical body, in our stomach, in our bowels, around our heart. Such sensations cannot be ascribed to specific sense organs, as the body reacts as a whole and alters its readiness to act, for example, prepares for fight or flight. This integral functioning of the body does not allow us to have two feelings simultaneously. Even the tightrope performer can only oscillate *either* to the right *or* to the left at one moment.

So apparently our feelings—as in schizophrenic and manic-depressive patterns—normally oscillate between contradictory tendencies too. The fact that we can nevertheless experience ourselves as ambivalent can only be explained by the fact that we pretend to stay the same, although our feelings and actions change. Even when we call another person ambivalent, we assume that he remains identical over time, even though he is loving one moment and aggressive the next. This assumption is a case of reducing two observations to one and constructing a personal identity independent of time. We also say that the tightrope performer oscillates to and fro, although at one moment in time he only oscillates to or fro. We combine these two momentary, partial movements to a new, larger entity. In the same way we unify the good Dr. Jekyll and the bad Mr. Hyde into the ambivalent Dr. Jydell, who outlasts time the same as most synthetic products.

---

5. From the Greek *dia* meaning through and *krino* meaning I divide, distinguish, judge.
6. From the Greek *koinos* meaning joint and *aisthesis* meaning perception, knowledge.

Several differences between normality and madness(es) now manifest themselves.

It seems to be a characteristic sign of madness that in every moment one or the other behavioral tendency, one feeling or the other, is dominant, quite without ambivalence. This lack of ambivalence can be seen as an expression of the dissolution of personal identity. When the self-description no longer unifies the self-image of yesterday, today, and tomorrow into a multidimensional picture that outlasts time, the contradictory character of Dr. Jydell dissolves into Dr. Jekyll and Mr. Hyde, who both experience their days and nights free of such contradictions.

There is a difference between the intervals in which the oscillation between both sides of the ambivalence, between Dr. Jekyll's day and Mr. Hyde's night, takes place.

In schizophrenic patterns the alternation occurs quicker than the standards of the consensus on reality allow. Anyone who changes himself and his behavior so rapidly oversteps the limits of comprehensibility. In this case the rhythms are too rapid, the times of constancy too short. Anyone who observes the periodical flipping to and fro of such persons with a longer sense of *now*, and expects constancy of mood for hours or days, will come to the conclusion that this person is living both sides of his ambivalence at the same time.

In the manic-depressive pattern the sphere of comprehensibility is left since the interval after which change occurs is longer than usual. If the external observer once again bases his standard on a *now* lasting hours or days, he will describe an either–or pattern in which ambivalence is experienced noncontemporaneously.

It seems as though Dr. Jekyll's day and Mr. Hyde's night alternate very quickly in schizophrenic patterns. The earth turns so fast that day and night only last minutes or even seconds, and it is difficult to come to terms with this rapid change. You have just gotten up in the morning and it is time to go to bed again; you have just gone to bed and closed your eyes and it is getting light again. In contrast, in the manic-depressive rhythm the earth revolves slower than usual. It is as though it takes a year (sometimes more, sometimes less) for one revolution instead of twenty-four hours. Half a year for Dr. Jekyll's day, half a year for Mr. Hyde's night.

Such varying rhythms make a difference not only between normality and madness but also between the different forms of madness.

10

The Process of Individuation

TRANSFORMATIONS: AN INCREDIBLE STORY AND ANOTHER IMAGINARY EXPERIMENT

When he woke up one morning after a night of troubled dreams, he felt upset. Something was wrong. He had spent the night in the bathroom as usual. He felt most comfortable there. Soapsuds held a strange attraction for him. Whenever he could, he looked for a wet and slippery spot, where he could feel the moisture and splash around in it to his heart's content. But today something was different than other days. At dawn, before half-past six, he wanted to fly from the fearful stare of the other inhabitants and their furious attempts to kill him. When he tried to run away, his legs no longer obeyed him. His strongest leg in particular, the one on the left, simply went numb. He tried to feel it without success. He could not reach it. He did not do any better with the right one. Instead he managed to bend his head so far forward that he could see his belly. Paralyzed with terror, he saw an arched, fleshy surface. It was not a dream. The proportions were not right. He became quite calm and sober; nothing remained of the slight intoxication always caused by sniffing soapsuds. He managed to bend his head down farther than usual. He now saw a strange leg. When he wriggled his own tiny hind legs, the strange leg moved. Nothing happened when he tried to move his front limbs. He saw nothing and felt nothing. He felt a sharp pain in his back, at a spot where he had never felt anything before. He tried to turn his head to look at his back, but without success. Without the help of his front legs he crawled to a puddle to see his reflection. Two of his legs were missing, his feelers were nowhere to be seen, and his hard protective shell had disappeared. Instead he was covered all over with the same soft, vulnerable skin. Underneath his shoulder blade he had a new wound. He did not know how he had come by it. "What has happened to me?" he thought. He looked into the mirror and saw neither Mother nor Father nor any other relatives. He had been transformed into an enormous vermin. He had changed from a proud dung beetle into one of those horrible, repulsive humans. . . . It remains to be mentioned that in later years he took on the position of a traveling salesman for dry goods.

There are living beings whose bodily shape changes radically, sometimes gradually and sometimes from one moment to the next. Humble caterpillars turn into beautiful butterflies, ugly ducklings into white swans, the croaking frog into Prince Charming. In man such transformations generally happen little by little and are thus, with the exception of the adolescent boy whose voice is breaking, hardly perceptible. Crying babies turn into talking schoolchildren, adolescents into adults, people in their most productive years into old people. The market woman in the fairy tale does not let her son into the house anymore because a wicked witch has changed him—his appearance—into a dwarf with a long nose. Bodily changes such as these that occur overnight are usually painful exceptions to the rule, the result of accidents and personal catastrophes that interrupt normal development, such as the amputation of a leg after a car crash, or the burning of the face of racing driver Niki Lauda.

However, even in these cases the transformation is never as radical as in the fictional plots of American soap operas. Television viewers cannot recognize Miss Ellie, mother of the Ewing family in Dallas, whom everyone loved, from one episode to the next. Without suspicion the members of her family pretend she is still the same when she is clearly not. Apparently difficulties arose between the producers and the actress playing the part of Miss Ellie during fee negotiations. She was replaced by another actress who did not resemble her one bit. Television viewers in the non-English-speaking world are only reminded of the old, true, "real" Miss Ellie by the familiar voice of the synchronizer. When the new Miss Ellie (or should we now say actress?) gets sick and dies, the old one returns, and with her the unmistakable love of a true mother who understands and forgives everything. Could Ellie's substitute, who had a different build, different mimicry and gestures, but thanks to the same scriptwriters kept her same character and same patterns of behavior, remain the same Miss Ellie? It is a question of the role of the characteristics of body and mind during the development and preservation of one's personal identity.

The question confronts the pretty young girl who has been surrounded by many adorers for years and suddenly realizes that she is approaching age 70 and has changed somewhat in the course of time. Is she still the same—in her eyes and in the eyes of the others? When a 20-year-old daughter tells her parents she wants to have an operation because she has actually been a man all the time and only an unhappy fault of nature had resulted in her birth in the body of a woman, is the young man who returns from the hospital still their daughter? And when a 45-year-old husband tells his wife and his 14- and 12-year-old children that he wants to be remodeled as a woman, as this is the only way to do justice to his enduring feeling of being a woman "in reality," should the children still call her "Papa" after the operation?

I present here another imaginary experiment in order to examine in greater detail the maddening logical traps that may result from preserving one's personal identity in a changing world.

Imagine that the life of a person has been filmed. From the moment the umbilical cord was cut, a picture has been shot of him every second. Today this person is celebrating his fortieth birthday. On the film there are sixty shots per minute, 3,600 per hour, and 86,400 per day. If we reckon with ten leap years in forty years, our film consists of 1,265,304,000 shots. The picture shot when the umbilical cord was cut shows a small child, a person who is *not* able to live independently and act on his own authority. The last picture of the fortieth birthday, however, shows an adult, a person who is able to act independently and on his own authority.

The logical result of these postulates is that our film must contain a picture of a person *not* acting on his own authority followed by a picture with a person acting on his own authority.

> The validity of this argument results from the application of the proposition of the smallest number, a theorem of mathematical logic that lays down 1 through n for any random series: If 1 has a definite predicate or defining characteristics and n does not, then there must be a "smallest number" (within the amount of numbers the series consists of) which does not have this predicate. [Falletta 1983, p. 21]

From the 1,265,304,000 pictures of the film, find the two that capture the difference between being an adult and not yet being an adult from one second to the next! Imagine that your life had been captured on film like that. When was the decisive second? On your eighteenth birthday?

If you have the impression that something is wrong with this task or argument, what is it? It is not the logic that is incorrect.

What seems ridiculous in the light of experience may be logically correct. The *proposition of the smallest number*, on which this "proof" of the change from child to adult within seconds is based, is founded on the assumption that the characteristics examined can be distinguished clearly and unambiguously. If you could recognize the ability of your fellow men to live independently and act on their own authority by the fact that they wear a top hat, it would not be difficult to find two shots of a film in which the hat is still hovering a few millimeters above the head at one moment, and is actually on the head in the next second. Bang! Logical and linguistic structures are all based on distinctions. In the same way as a hopscotch square is drawn on a level surface, these structures construct entities dissociated from the environment. A continuum is divided into two areas. By drawing such a border the dimension of space is divided into interior and exterior, the dimension of time into before and after. Thus two concepts are presupposed in the proposition of the smallest number: (1) we are talking about features and characteristics of spatial entities (objects, things, individuals) and (2) the transformation of these features occurs in stages, that is, discontinuously. In each case the being of the object of observation is being examined, so you have to jump from one moment of being to the next.

Wherever such conditions are fulfilled, it is relatively easy to come to a consensus on reality. When they are not fulfilled, conflicts about the features of such distinctions may arise. This is why it is so easy to establish the winner of a 100-meter race and so difficult in figure skating. When counting peas or flies' legs you are dealing with harder features of distinction, with preset entities largely independent of observation that you need only count. When assessing the quality of a movie you must establish first of all what conditions have to be met for the movie to be rated "commendable." These esthetic features of distinction are softer; it is difficult to establish whether they are based more on the peculiarities of the observer or on what he observes.

Logical problems such as the filmed leap into maturity develop when such concepts as "adult," "independent viability," or "responsible," the meanings of which are fraying at the edges and are wishy-washy, are employed in accordance with the rules of logic that presuppose unambiguous definitions. Only a sloppy and barely exact use of language can protect us from these logical traps; this alone is adequate when dealing with the area of softer reality.

SELF-DESCRIPTIONS

Indistinctness and ambiguity begin with the question of where to draw the borders around the individual in relation to his environment; for example, in relation to other people. Who or what can be regarded as an independent entity? The idea of the individual acting on his own authority is one of the foundations of our Western consensus on reality. Our legal system is based on it, our moral attitude is shaped by it, and our rules of mutual respect and disrespect are founded on it. When we describe ourselves, this idea becomes the basis of our self-description, our self-esteem, or our feeling of unworthiness.

It seems reasonable to equate an individual's boundaries with his bodily boundaries, but even this seeming clarity is deceptive. From an outer perspective the organism of an individual can undoubtedly be described as an entity dissociated from his environment. However, a description of an individual as autonomous and viable is not adequate in every case. Babies and toddlers, for instance, cannot survive without the care of other people who take on the role of parents. If people from their environment described them as autonomous and independent, their error would prove itself rather quickly, since the smaller children would die. Different standards are valid when dealing with children; the younger they are, the less responsibility is expected from them. In the course of the history of man from infant to adult, the expectations of him and his independence change. His self-description has to change too.

In our Western system of language and thought, the concept of the individual is central and defines its structure. The languages of Indo-Europeans are all organized around the core of three or more pronominal categories of persons, which are in turn hinged on one category which we refer to as first person singular (Whorf 1942). It is decisive for an individual's development, behavior, and mental normality or madness which meaning he connects with the concept "I." How does he relate it to concepts standing for other or several people: you, he, it, we, you (plural), and they? How and when do these concepts and their relationships to each other change for him?

In order to behave in accordance with these prescriptive rules of the interaction system, a self-description is necessary that matches these rules. Their development, preservation, and transformation—the process of individuation—refer to three central areas of meaning:

1. *The distinction between before and after* when describing oneself and someone else: Is continuity of the world or rather change and development experienced? Are there breaks in the line of development? How much change can be coped with in which period of time without a resulting feeling of estrangement, depersonalization, or derealization, that is, the incomprehensible loss of exterior or interior reality developing?

2. *The distinction between inside and outside*, between the individual (his self[1]) and his environment, for example, other people: What does he define consciously or unconsciously as the smallest unit of survival, the preservation of which he equates with his own survival? How does he dissociate himself from others? Which boundaries does he dissolve, that is, with whom or what does he identify himself? For the survival and well-being of which other person or institution, which ideal or material values does he hold himself responsible? Which characteristics and features form, in his opinion, the distinguishing marks of his personal identity?

3. *The distinction between guilt and innocence* of the explanation of transformation: How does he know whether to hold himself or the environment responsible for an event? For instance, are his or somebody else's behavior patterns and their consequences the result of autonomous processes that occur independent of his own desires and decisions or of his own actions for which he has to accept responsibility? How powerful or powerless is he? What about his own maturity and culpability? How does he distinguish between action and behavior?

If you draw distinctions and boundaries in these three areas that divert too far and for too long from the dividing lines of the consensus on reality, you think and feel in a mad way. If you behave according to such feelings and thoughts, you violate the generally practiced rules of direct interaction and have a good chance of being finally diagnosed as mad.

CONSISTENCY: DIFFERENCES THAT MAKE NO DIFFERENCE

How can we explain our impression that we live in the world as stable and dissociated units? Identity is not so much an attribute of the observed object as of description. This impression emerges when

---

1. As a rule this concept is used in psychological and sociopsychological literature for the sum of ascriptions directed toward one's own person. Synonymously one speaks also of the identity of a human being (Simon 1984).

an observer cannot establish any differences between two observations separate in time (before and after) either because they are beyond his perception or because he imagines them away.

Small differences can be disregarded easily, so that frequent glimpses lead to the impression that things stay as they were. Continuity of observation conveys the impression of consistency of what is observed. This is the reason why other people's children make us realize how old we are getting much more than do our own. Discontinuity of observation gives the impression that what is observed has changed. This time-lapse effect can also be experienced when looking at old family photos.

We can and must observe nothing as regularly and constantly, without major intervals, as our own bodies. Our bodies grow and age very gradually; yet we still recognize ourselves when we look in the mirror in the morning. Although we are shocked at how we look, the characteristic distinguishing marks still predominate: the unmistakable sad eyes, the voice, the unique form of the mouth. We simply imagine away our greasy hair and the rings under our eyes or imagine ourselves with the usual cheerful, beaming smile and typical blow-dried curls. Although an unattractive mirror image impairs most people's view of themselves, they are nevertheless able to preserve the feeling of being the same person as the night before. If the sight is all too unbearable we can resort to countermeasures, such as putting on cream to cover the spots and taking a trip to the hairdresser.

Our self-description remains true to itself either because we do not see how different we look or, if we see it, we make sure that others do not notice it so much. However, even our own view of ourselves changes in small steps too, so that we do not realize how much it changes over time. If it did not change, we would inevitably begin to doubt our personal identity and would experience estrangement.

We deal with the people in our everyday environment similarly and imagine differences in them away. A husband shaves off his beard, his wife dyes her blond hair red, and both receive this answer to the self-conscious question, "How do I look?" "As always!

Why do you ask? Don't say you've bought another new pair of shoes?" Such small changes are of no consequence.

We are able to develop a stable picture of ourselves and others because the processes preserving our bodies are largely autonomous and ensure that its structures appear stable to us as observers. The individual appearance of our bodies guarantees that we will not be mistaken for somebody else. If you know what someone looks like, you do not actually know him, but you recognize him when you meet him in the street or in front of the mirror. Doubles are rare. Thus the body is the core of every self-description and self-identity.

Bodily reality, however, is not equally hard in all spheres: it can change as a result of observation. Someone who is not satisfied with his looks can make changes within certain limits. Famous bank robbers turn to famous cosmetic surgeons to make them unrecognizable. A transsexual's wish to have the sex of his body changed is an attempt to render the reality of his own self-description harder than that of organic structures.

The importance of the bodily features mentioned here for the development of personal identity, however, does not result from the biological peculiarities of the body alone. Imagine once again that you live in South Africa. One morning you notice that your "wonderful," fashionably sun-tanned skin has suddenly turned black, and your "perm" into Negroid curls. Or vice versa. From the inside black skin probably feels no different from white skin; it is a difference that makes no difference. From the outer perspective, however, it is a difference that makes a bigger and different difference in South Africa than in Melanesia or Germany.

Looks, beauty, ugliness, an athletic body, and red hair are not features of the body in itself, but of the cultural context, of the system of descriptions. When we talk about the body we are always talking about social phenomena, whether we want to or not. We make social evaluations with our choice of words. And vice versa, when talking about a social system, we are also talking about the body, the necessities dictated by it, and the used and missed possibilities of its use. Here we are automatically moving on a level of economical, political, moral, ethical, or esthetic evaluations.

Thus bodily characteristics are only one of many components of personal identity that all develop in communication with others. Bodily and social necessities and possibilities cannot be distinguished clearly. Together they make up the common borders within which many different self-descriptions can develop and fit.

WHAT DOES "I" MEAN?
THE DEPENDENCE OF RELATIONSHIPS

Bodily necessities and possibilities are what force us into relationships with other people and render communication with them a prerequisite of survival. However, it would probably be more apt to say that it is bodily impossibilities that make us socially dependent.

This process begins in the cradle and ends on the bier, and is interrupted by times of limited independence. Contrary to many other animals who start supporting themselves as soon as they are born, the newborn human being cannot live independently. Have you ever heard of a baby who picked up its briefcase right after its first cry to make its way to the office? It cannot even obtain milk on its own. Man's incompleteness leaves the individual many developmental options. Man is not born with fixed patterns of behavior and can thus adapt to many different social environments, to their descriptive and prescriptive rules. The mother who happens to be available determines the mother tongue in which the child will later think.

In addition to bodily necessities and (im-)possibilities, social constraints form the second kind of protective barriers confining our freedom of movement on the way to development. Thus the possibilities of self-description are limited by our bodies and by society.

Unfortunately babies cannot tell us much about their prenatal life in the womb and the time immediately after birth, and consequently we have no access to the inner perspective of observation. (The authenticity of adults' memories of their own births as occasionally reported seems rather doubtful, since they remind us far too concretely of the well-known nightmares about being squeezed down the drain into the cold from a warm bathtub.) We thus have no choice but to reconstruct man's first distinctions on the basis of observations from the outer perspective.

During intrauterine life the physical necessities for the survival and growth of the unborn are met automatically. The infant organism is embedded in the processes that keep the organism of the mother in equilibrium. It does not have to think or act to maintain its physiological balance. At birth at the latest, this automatism is dissolved; the environment of the infant organism has changed radically. From an organic point of view, child and mother are now independent systems.

The separation throws the child's bodily needs and their satisfaction off balance. It leads to an immense perturbation. To use a neutral term, the content of which is not too biased by the qualities of experience of adult life, we should really say, "In the beginning was perturbation." If we use such terms as "fear," "panic," or "horror," which we use to describe similar adult perturbations, to describe the birth experience, we would be tacitly assuming an adult's ability, acquired in the course of history, to observe himself and his situation (in his imagination) from the outside and make comparisons with similar situations. Sigmund Freud (1926) stated succinctly that psychological concepts are not appropriate in this case:

> In the act of birth there is a real danger to life. We know what this means objectively; but what it means in a psychological sense we have no idea. The danger of birth has as yet no mental content for the subject. One cannot possibly suppose that the foetus has any sort of knowledge that its life is in danger of being destroyed. . . . The situation, then, that it regards as a *danger* and against which it wants to be safe-guarded is one of non-gratification, of a *growing tension due to need*, against which it is helpless. [p. 135]

It is the loss of its physiological equilibrium that stimulates the child to change its inner structures and develop something akin to mental processes. In order to overcome perturbations, interaction with other people (in most cases the mother) replaces physiological control mechanisms.

These cycles of perturbation and negation of perturbation are repeated. From an outer perspective they can be described as follows: the child is *perturbed* and *behaves* accordingly; it cries, for instance. Its mother hears its cries and is *perturbed* in turn. She is stimulated by the child and actively begins to *do* something; she gives the child her breast or a bottle. The child *behaves* appropriately; it sucks and drinks. After awhile it is no longer *perturbed*, which can be seen from the fact that it now *behaves* differently—the famous beam of a contented baby. The mother is *calm* again too.[2]

This description of interaction between mother (and/or other people) and child from the outer perspective presupposes, in accordance with the rules of consensus and our language system, the distinction among different individuals (mother, child), their inner condition (distress/calmness), and their exterior patterns of behavior (crying, feeding). In this presentation the people are treated as consistent and invariable, remaining identical with themselves. In a way they are the "things" unchanged in the course of time to which characteristics and patterns of behavior are ascribed. All this and much more as well belong to the connotations and assumptions conveyed in a simple description of interaction between mother and child.

On the road from infancy to adulthood the child has to comprehend many such distinctions and nondistinctions when trying to learn (and sometimes change) social rules as a player.

In the course of development bodily distinctions between inside and outside may well cause the least problems. Since there are far more nerve connections within the body than to the outside world, anatomy itself ensures a distinction into two different spheres of perception: "As there are only a few 100 million sensory receptors and about 10,000 billion synapses in our nervous system, we are 100,000 times more sensitive to changes in our inner environment than to changes in our outer environment" (von Foerster 1973, p. 35).

---

2. John Bowlby (1969) has thoroughly studied and described the seduction of a mother by her baby.

To describe oneself as a bodily entity or one's body as a thing does not mean regarding oneself as a self-reliant and independent viable being. After all, you can regard your left eye as a living entity without believing it to be viable without the rest of the body and without believing that it is blinking roguishly because it wants to convey that everything is not really the way it looks itself and of its own accord.

If this eye could talk, it would certainly never enter its mind to utter the Gestalt prayer of Fritz Perls to the other organs of the body:

> I live my life and you live yours,
> I am not in the world to fulfill your expectations, and you
> are not here to be guided by my wishes.
> You are yourself and I am myself.
> It would be nice if we met—
> if not, there's nothing we can do about it. [cited in Petzold and Paula 1976, p. 47]

This "I" would not remain "I" if it did not encounter the rest of the body.

The situation of the child can be compared with that of the eye. The child is not viable on its own. It can only maintain its entity in the context of (mostly family) interaction. For the child the smallest unit of survival is not the individual (I), but the relationship with those who care for it (we). To describe itself as a separate individual or even an acting subject not only would not be apt but would also be self-destructive. Its behavior and its descriptions must aim to maintain the identity of the relationship or relationship patterns.

This aim might explain children's special sensibility to the quality of relationships. It is an area on which they have to focus their attention; within it they can train their sensitivity every day. The maxim, "children and fools tell the truth," is true about relationships. However, this ability is not rewarded in the course of attaining an adult view of the world. In our Western language, thought, and social systems, the main task of individuation is learning to describe oneself, in whatever context, in a reified way. Successful individuation means a successful split between subject and object—

known as differentiation of self and object in the specialist language of psychologists and psychotherapists. The aim is to maintain the feeling of remaining identical with oneself even in changing physical environments and in different kinds of relationships to different people: "I am I, you are you, and the world is as it is."

In this case too, the suggestion of a personal identity or personality detached from the context is conveyed—like all reified assumptions about the world—by language and the concept of being, which have probably not developed in this way by accident.

Some Eastern languages prove that other language structures exist in which "I" is not used free of context in the same way as in Indo-European languages. For example, Erich Wulff (1972) reports that the Vietnamese language has no word for "I." Instead of the personal pronoun, a term is used that characterizes the relationship with the person with whom one is conversing: "'I' am either 'slave,' 'child,' 'body,' 'little brother,' 'big sister,' 'master,' etc., i.e., how I characterize myself, but also what I am called by other people, depends on the kind of relationship I have with the person I am talking to" (Wulff 1972, p. 74).

The notion of a completely autonomous self-being independent of relationships to others is, of course, absurd. It should not really be necessary to prove this absurdity by logical arguments. After all, everyone has experienced that he is a different person when he is with somebody he likes than when he is in the society of a person he abhors, particularly if this encounter takes place in the bedroom. Even the president of the board is a different person during a board meeting than in the company of his mother, the clergyman in the pulpit is a different person when he preaches to his children than when he preaches to his congregation, the senior consultant is a different person on his business rounds than when he is stopped by a policeman for speeding, and the policeman too is a different person when giving a ticket than when he is on his surgeon's operating table. The logical absurdity of an "I" independent of the context and of imagining away the frame of relationships becomes clear when we recall Spencer-Brown's (1969) laws of form. The meaning of a sign or symbol always depends on what is included *and* excluded by a distinction. In different spatial, temporal, or social contexts, completely different meanings of "I" are carved out of the totality of the situation by the distinction I = inside and the rest of the world = outside. Our language does not offer prefabricated East Asian patterns to record our nonidentity in different contexts. We always say "I" and mean something different every time. The unavoidable contextual and relationship aspect of the meaning of "I" leaves its mark on the relevant alternating connotation. This aspect is carried along hidden away like a stowaway, but secretly it is the captain.

On their way into adult normality, children and adolescents must learn to consider the supposed objective—that is, independent of context—characteristics of humans and things as important and focus their attention on them. They have to drop their sensibility to relationships or at least pretend to do so.

ACTION OR EVENT? THE INVENTION OF PERPETRATOR AND VICTIM

During a visit to an island in the South Pacific, a 6-year-old child who grew up in Europe discovers that "the sun goes round the other way here"—from right to left. When asked how she explains this phenomenon, the child answers, "That's the way things are done here!" Different countries have different customs; after all, they eat taros on that island instead of potatoes.

At first glance this seems to be a typically childlike, maybe even childish explanation. However, on closer examination this presumptuous certainty of its childlike quality should dwindle. For centuries adults all over the world believed that the course of the sun depended on personal decisions, although not on their own. An eclipse of the sun occurred because the gods had switched off the light and had to be bribed by sacrifices to turn it on again. Even the excessive behavior of the sun could be influenced indirectly and was thus subject to various local customs and traditions.

It is not easy to distinguish between phenomena we can change and those against which we are helpless. Here too the cultural consensus determines the dividing lines—and they change during the course of history. Along their development you can distinguish between power and impotence, between fate and free will, between control and loss of control. For instance, is washing your hands for several hours a day a sign of particular cleanliness, a bad habit, or the symptom of an obsessional neurosis? Does someone who pours several bottles of alcoholic drink down his throat every day raise the glass of whiskey to his lips himself, or is addiction (a woman?) controlling him?

The way we deal with those manifesting such behavior depends on how we answer these questions. The issue is whether we see them (or us) as *acting subjects* who are able to decide on their (our) behavior autonomously and take the blame for it. If the person who drinks alcohol in the question above is seen as an acting subject, we are dealing with an "unrestrained, depraved drunkard." If he is seen has someone who cannot control his actions, he is "ill" and in need of help.

This is not a philosophical question dissociated from the problems of everyday life, but the basis of interaction with ourselves and others. Whether we describe our situation with the words "I can't do anything about it," or "I must do something about it," whether we describe an event or state as "it just happened" or "it was caused deliberately" has far-reaching consequences in the interplay of describing and prescribing rules. Almost all rules of interaction with all variations of possible relationship formations depend on how we describe our world.

Every player—whether yachtsman, shipwrecked person, or infant—who wants to deduce instructions for his actions from his description of the world must distinguish between events (or states) that he can bring about and those that come over him out of the blue without any chance of his intervening in them. To do so he has to make a distinction between inside and outside when allocating blame. Are perceived events and states to be understood as an effect of your own behavior or not? Are your own patterns of behavior to be attributed to some inner or outer, controllable or uncontrollable processes? This distinction is connected with a pattern for explanations, namely, the *perpetrator–victim pattern*. Reifying individuals, severing them from the context of relationships, makes the perpetrator the cause and them the victim. The effect of allocating blame in this way can be compared with a stop sign: Stop, no more why-questions from here on!

To pretend that you yourself create some kind of effect with your behavior is a form of self-description that opens up space for the notion of man's free will. Regarded from the outside, this is a gross simplification imagining away hundreds of thousands of (self-evident) influential quantities, but it is obviously a very practical and useful simplification matching our patterns of feeling. It is the prerequisite for the development of several social institutions, for instance our legal system.

Let us use our infant in interaction with its mother as an example. As an observer from the inner perspective, at first the infant can only notice the overwhelming perturbation of its lost physiological balance, in an integral kinesthetic manner. Perturbation and relief alternate more or less regularly. After a few weeks the infant's ability to distinguish details of its environment increases with the development of diacritical perception. Several events occur contemporaneously, namely the holistic perception of its own state and some external events. They are thus connected, whether by accident or not. Some connections repeat themselves; others do not. The regular coincidence of internal and external events leads to a transformation of the child's inner structure. Its own patterns of behavior and states coincide with external events.

If something like the memory of earlier events is maintained, noncontemporaneous events can be connected with each other too. We can draw hopscotch squares containing contemporaneous and non-contemporaneous events. And we can draw multitemporal hopscotch squares and construct if/then rules: if this event happens now, then this will happen. However, in order to preclude misunderstandings we ought really to say, of course: hopscotch squares can draw themselves and construct if/then rules. Once again it is a question of a process of self-organization that develops from the coincidence of inner and outer events.

What the child (and also the adult) knows consists in and develops from these connections (associations). The child turns out the way he does as a result of the infinitely complicated and incomprehensible interrelations between the events of the world. Completely

different events might coincide, and different associations and hopscotch squares ensue. However, not only must all those events be
imaginable but they also must be possible.[3] During the process of
evolution from infant to adult, the hopscotch squares that do not
fit in man's environment—his body, inanimate nature, and social
conditions—become extinct. They are not viable.

To illustrate the principle of gaining knowledge and the role
chance plays in it, the scientific sociologist Robert Merton quotes
the columnist, café-goer, and city idler of seventeenth-century London, John Aubrey, who narrates the following pleasant episode: "A
woman (I think in Italy) endeavored to poyson her husband (who
was a Dropsicall Man) by boyling a toade in his Potage; which cured
him: this was the occasion of finding out the Medicine" (Merton
1965, p. 14). The boiled toad obviously had a soothing effect on
the husband's water balance. After eating this soup he ought to have
been gratefully convinced of his wife's love, provided he equated
the toad's effect with his wife's intention. If, however, he was convinced that she wanted to kill him, he probably handed her over to
the police for attempted murder. No matter how and from what
motives it was accomplished, the knowledge of the effect of toad
stock could and still can be used. If nobody had paid any attention
to the husband's bodily reactions after consuming the soup, its phar-
macological effect would not have been realized, and nobody would
eat this so-beneficial toad soup today.

If the responsibility for an event and its consequences is attributed to an individual, it has become an "action" or its effect. We
have thus drawn a distinction between those events, states, and
processes that can be influenced and those that cannot. If you blink
your left eyelid by accident one day and find that you are regarded
as a charming and humorous person as a result, you might want to
cultivate this blink to a wink. An observer who knows this blinker
as a humorous and roguish person will regard this blinking as a
wink from the start. Someone who sees him for the first time will
possibly consider the blinking of the eyelid to be a symptom of great

---

3. In the language of philosophy a coincidence of events is called a "contingency."

nervousness and not call it winking but a tic. Although it cannot be distinguished physiologically (objectively), this brief blinking is an action (an act) in the first case and an event in the second. "The logical distinction between acts and events is a distinction between 'activity' and 'passivity.' An act requires an actor" (von Wright 1971, p. 48). The responsibility or blame for the occurrence of an action is attributed to a person, to a culprit, but not so for events.

In times or areas in which the world is considered as pervaded by souls, all events are attributed to the despotism of some culprit, namely, the struggle between the gods or the influence of ghosts. With the depersonalization of the world, which has been accompanied by a split between mind and nature, nonpersonal culprits are conceivable: they become causes. Thus actions turn into events. This distinction, the perfection of which took centuries in cultural history, must also be accomplished by each individual on his way to achieving the consensus of Western thought. Small children curse "bad doors" into which they have bumped and thus blame the door (its furtive deed) for their bump, and not the fact that they stumbled. And thunder and lightning are signs that the gods are angry, not scientifically explainable events.

However, the concept of action must be subdivided even further. First, the concept of activity has to be distinguished from that of action. Sleeping, for instance, is an activity that cannot be rated as an action. Going to bed, however, is an action. The distinctive feature is the assumption of a conscious decision. Once we are asleep we make no more decisions, but we still behave. "We cannot not behave" (Watzlawick et al. 1967), but obviously we can "not act." For whether we do something or not is an aspect of softer reality. It is decided by the observer's interpretation of behavior.[4]

It is particularly difficult to distinguish between nonaction and refraining from action. "If, for instance, in a certain situation a

4. The philosopher Gilbert Ryle has coined the concept of *thick description* to express that when describing human behavior we are never dealing with data free of interpretation. They are always "thick," i.e., loaded with interpretations and connotations; and the anthropologist Clifford Geertz (1973) defines thick description as the basis of the methods of anthropology.

certain window is closed, then we do not close it in this situation—but we do not refrain from closing it, either. Further, we do not do things that surpass our human abilities (such as changing the weather)—which does not mean, however, that we refrain from doing it" (von Wright 1971, p. 56). This results in the following definition of abstention: in a given situation an acting person refrains from doing something particular when he could do it, but does not. But who decides what is possible?

It is thus not easy to establish whether a 20-year-old, who has stayed in bed until noon every morning for months and shows no sign of supporting himself, is performing an action or is the victim of events for which he is not responsible. Does he refrain from getting up, or does he actually stay in bed actively? Is he too lazy to get up and work, or can't he do so? Does he even stay in bed to annoy his father, who leaves the house as dependably as a civil servant every morning to get to the office punctually? The parents—and he himself too—are in an undecidable situation. Their son's behavior does not allow a decisive answer to the question "mad or bad?" The answer to this question tells us in which context we are and which rules of interaction are to be applied. If these contexts are mixed up, all concerned are subject to contradictory requests for action or treatment. Someone who acts is treated differently from someone who does not act—he is treated.

BEWARE OF STEPS: CHANGES IN CONTEXT

Some of these tribes regard the novice as dead during the entire novice period. The novitiate lasts for a relatively long period and aims at a physical and spiritual impairment of the person to be initiated, no doubt so that he loses all memory of his childhood. Then comes the positive part of the initiation ceremony; the introduction into tribal law and step-by-step instruction by performing totemistic ceremonies and reciting myths etc. in front of the novice. The final act ... constitutes a religious ceremony and especially a particular mutilation (extraction of a tooth, for example, circumcision etc.) which varies from tribe to tribe and identifies the novice with the adults of his tribe for ever. [van Gennep 1909, p. 79]

With these words Arnold van Gennep describes the rites of south and southeast Australian tribes that are performed to transform a child into an adult. There are or were cultures in which it is no problem to shoot a film about the life of a person and to photograph the precise shots, the second in which he stops being a child and starts being an adult. In the same way, in our culture we could find the two shots—photographed at intervals of a second—of a wedding film in which the couple consists first of two legally still independent, unmarried persons and in the next moment of two spouses burdened with their respective marital rights and duties. A ceremony, a rite, has changed (several) personal attributes and characteristics of both from one moment to the next.

In his classic book *Rites of Passage*, van Gennep describes a multitude of rites through which spatial and temporal transitions are symbolized and accomplished. All these rites deal with the question of changing and transforming a part of the consensus on reality, and thus rendering it binding.

Initiation rites that make a child into an adult are only an example of how erratic changes occur in the description of an individual. The physical development from child to adult is gradual, a slow process of petering out; in the tribes that van Gennep referred to as "half civilized," in contrast, social development takes its course by degrees (discontinuously). Passage from one stage to the next is connected with rites by means of which the community changes the *personality* and the status of the person to be initiated step by step.

Man's biological development provides us with only a few *harder* standards that enable us to reach a consensus, without any great difficulty, on whether someone is mature or not. Except for the first menstruation, none of these transformations can be established definitely, or at least doing so is very difficult. However, since it is important for interaction between human beings to determine whether adults are dealing with adults, adults with children, or children with children, rites of transition ensure clarity of status.

Thus the life of a human being consists of a series of stages whose ends and beginnings are similar, namely, birth, social puberty, parenthood, rise into a higher class, specializing. Each of these events has ceremonies with identical goals, that is to lead the individual from one defined situation into another defined just as specifically. [van Gennep 1909, p. 15]

Characteristically, these rites have three components. *Separation rites* provide for parting and detachment from the old identity, that is, from the social group to which the person belonged. *Liminal* or *transformation rites* characterize the in-between stage when the individual is floating between two worlds, and *joining rites* provide for the official acceptance in the new identity. Rites of passage are almost always connected with an operation that leaves indelible traces. People are tattooed and circumcised, teeth are pulled out, end joints of the little finger are chopped off, and similarly loving carving work is performed; the human body is treated "like a simple piece of wood," as whatever protrudes is cut off, walls are pierced, and smooth surfaces are carved (van Gennep 1909, p. 21).

The magical effect of these rites of transition consists in the fact that they are able to change the reality, the being of an individual. They change the description given of him, the attribution of characteristics to him, and, as a consequence, his behavior. This changed attribution of characteristics is really an aspect of *softer* reality; however, by connecting it with physical operations, such as tatoos and mutilations, it becomes an irreversible component of harder, physical reality. At first glance the adult can now be identified by his physical characteristics. What nature unfortunately neglected has now been made up for socially.

To sum up, all rites of transition serve the purpose of determining unambiguously a change of context in communication. They follow an either–or pattern of the distinction between inside and outside social characteristics. You either belong inside (the hopscotch square) or outside. Either the end joint of the little finger is missing (you are dealing with an adult) or is still there (you are dealing with a child). Thus various contexts in which different rules of play and interpretation are in force are separated clearly. There can be little or no misunderstanding about who is what.

Thus two directions of attributing meaning are combined. Either distinctions are made socially where none exist biologically, or where distinctions evolve biologically none are made socially. Physical changes emerging over the years are only acknowledged socially when the ritual has been performed, and when the ritual has been performed the individual has changed, even though biologically little change can be seen from one moment to the next. The human paradox that man must change although he wants to remain the same and that he has to remain the same although he wants to change is organized in the sense of an either–or pattern and an irreversible temporal sequence. Change can be imagined away for a while, then ritualized change is added in one's imagination, then imagined away for a while again, and so on.

From the point of view of communication theory, these rites are very useful, since they render a mixing up of contexts less probable. They mark a change not only in the role and status of the individual but also and above all in his relationships to others.

The more civilized a society becomes, the less important these rites are. They still exist, but are no longer obligatory; externally their symbols are less visible and easier to change. Couples still get married, but now people can live together without a marriage certificate and wedding ring. Even wedding rings can be taken off and left in restrooms (by accident). You cannot tell at first glance to which professional group somebody belongs from his clothes; not even all priests wear a cassock anymore. Furthermore, the initiation rites that still exist—in the form of examinations, for example—are no longer connected with physical cruelty, but rather with mental cruelty and humiliation.

However, the less ritualized and public these transitions are made, the more difficult they are for the individual and the people directly connected with him. The identity and self-description of an individual are the result of communication with his environment. If, for instance, neither he himself nor his family has clear standards for whether a young person is to be regarded as an adult and autonomous or as personally irresponsible, ambiguous, contradictory communication is frequently the result. The transformation phase in transition rites has clearly defined limits and sometimes only lasts a few days during which the novice is excluded from the rest of the community (and is socially considered dead, for example). However, without these rites the transition phase can take years. The more individualized the contextual changes are, the more individualized are the personal identity crises.[5]

The transition from youth to adult is one of the steps that entails the most consequences. Almost all relationships change radically as this step is taken. In place of parental care comes the necessity to provide for one's own livelihood. A relationship based on inequality (adult–child) becomes one based on equality (adult–adult). You can no longer expect strangers to make allowances when judging your behavior. You become capable of guilt and have to bear the consequences of your own behavior.

Similar grave transitions ensue if you become involved in a partner relationship that is experienced as enduring and obligatory (till death do us part) or bring children into the world. These are all changes in context connected with a profound change in an individual's self-description. Yet, these developmental steps are not established so clearly and inevitably as to be recognized by everybody. As in the case of other steps, the height of which cannot be seen clearly, it is easy to stumble and fall upward or downward.

Sometimes, however, even this unritualized transition phase goes on and on. During the course of so-called psychotic lives hovering between worlds, temporary social death, sitting on a fence, oscillating between inside and outside can last for many years.

MAD INDIVIDUATION

All madnesses can be understood and explained as a *form* of individuation deviating from the rules of consensus. The player describes himself in a way that does not correspond with the description that other players give of him.

---

5. See in particular Erik H. Erikson (1959) and his concept of successive crises of identity in the course of individual development.

If you compare these two descriptions and declare the other players' description as normal (i.e., declared true by the consensus), mad self-descriptions can deviate on the level of both form and content. A different distinction is made between I and environment. A set of typical psychotic symptoms can be explained and understood as the result of a world view, the inner and outer borders of which deviate from the norm. In addition there are also deviations in the temporal organization of consistency and change. On the level of content, in particular, the distinctions between active and passive, strong and weak, good and bad (i.e., of cause and blame), which are characterized by feeling, are attributed to inside and outside in a different way. The shifting and crossing of boundaries discussed in reference to mad thinking are also, or particularly, made when using the concept "I." The boundaries of the hopscotch square labeled "I" become blurred or its content changes.

When, for instance, someone hears voices speaking to him, while all other people in his environment only register an oppressive silence, the person concerned is localizing events on the outside (i.e., outside himself) that in the opinion of all others occur somewhere inside—the famous little man in his ear, that is, within himself. He experiences his fantasies, ideas, desires, and fears as outside and perceives them as aspects of outer reality. These deviating perceptions are regarded by the others in his environment as wrong perceptions and are called hallucinations. Thinking his thoughts expand and are accessible and audible to everybody can be understood as an expression of a self-description in which the certainty of the distinction between inside and outside has been lost and there is a risk of disintegration of his own boundaries, that is, self-disintegration. Anyone who practices a distinction between self and non-self in such a way will attract attention by his odd and anxious—immensely perturbed—behavior. If he gives an account of his perceptions he will probably be diagnosed as schizophrenic.

If the distinction between self and non-self is made in accordance with the rules of the consensus, from a clinical point of view the emotional attributions of blame and cause play a decisive role. Whoever indulges in feelings of omnipotence during manic megalomania tacitly assumes that he controls processes which, according to the assessment (and in most cases the experience) of people who are close to him or have to diagnose him, are beyond his control. Procuring money is no problem; making contacts with the world's VIPs and solving problems with his eyes shut are quite easy for him. The same pattern of attributions explains the hardly bearable depressive feeling of guilt when responsibility—the other side of power—for all conceivable terrible events is claimed in a way that seems just as inappropriate.

A person's self-description can thus deviate psychotically from the rules of consensus in different ways, in content and in form. It makes an enormous difference whether the boundaries between I and environment follow the usual dividing lines and merely the contents deviate, or whether these dividing lines already take a different course. Someone who feels he is to blame for all the misery in the world because of all the sins he has burdened himself with, for example, takes it for granted that he himself is an acting entity. His family, which tries in vain to talk him out of this idea, also regards him as an entity, but sees him in regard to the misery of the world as not acting. They thus draw the same spatial boundary between him and his environment, but ascribe certain meanings (e.g., responsibility) differently. While the patient experiences (feels) himself as strong, active, and bad, he is described from the outside as weak, passive, and good or in the worst case as neither good nor bad. In contrast, someone who feels controlled from the outside by a sender sees himself as an entity, but not as acting; he ascribes the cause for his behavior to some perpetrator outside himself and sees himself as victim.

One such case of confusing inside and outside is the "projective identification" (Klein 1955) often described by psychoanalytical authors, in which the blame for one's own feelings, desires, motives, and thoughts is laid at somebody else's door. Systematized delusions can always develop when causes are ascribed to something deviating from the consensus. Or to put it differently, such a reality is called a delusion by all others, whereas their delusion is called reality. For even in the consensus on reality, cause and blame are ascribed, but in a different way. Patients whose subjective reality is organized in such a way that their personal boundaries between inside and outside are erected normally but the contents are ascribed in a deviating way attract attention by their behavior as well as by their frame of mind. In general they are more likely to be diagnosed as affectively disturbed or paranoid.

The third area in which the boundaries of the concept "I" can be used subjectively in a mad way is in the transitions between different contexts. Anyone who does not distinguish between them and tries to remain identical with himself regardless of context will inevitably violate the rules of direct interaction dependent on context.[6] For example, he will behave in public in a way one is only allowed to behave within one's own home, will walk through a shopping mall like a referee with a whistle, or will jump onto the stage in a theater to save Desdemona who is being threatened by Othello. His deviating behavior will attract attention.

The fourth area of deviations deals with temporal changes or nonchanges. The meaning of "I" derives from the distinction (i.e., the relationship) between environment and I. Both change in the course of time, but nevertheless the world is generally experienced as constant. If only the environment—or the part on which attention is focused—is experienced as changed, the feeling of living in an unreal world might develop (derealization). If, on the other hand, the "I" section of this distinction is experienced as changed, a feeling of self-estrangement might develop, a profound disconcertedness about whether one is the same person as before (depersonalization). One prerequisite of normality is to dissolve the human paradox already mentioned—*to remain the same in spite of all changes*—or, if this does not work, to fail discreetly so that nobody realizes it.

---

6. Erving Goffman's (1964) sociological definition of madness is the violation of the rules of direct interaction.

11

Family Realities

THE CROCODILE'S DILEMMA: VARIATIONS ON THE STORY OF A MOTHER WHO TRIES TO SAVE HER CHILD

A crocodile grabbed hold of a small child who was playing on the banks of the Nile. Its mother begged the crocodile to give the child back. "Okay," said the crocodile. "If you can predict exactly what I'm going to do, I'll give you back your child. But if your guess is wrong, I'll eat it for dinner."

"Oh, you're going to eat my child!" the despairing mother cried.

"Now I can't give the child back," the sly crocodile replied, "because if I give it back that will mean that your prediction was wrong, and I told you I would eat the child if you guessed wrongly."

"Oh no," said the clever mother, "it's the other way round. You can't eat my child, because if you do, I have told the truth, and in that case you promised to give me back my child. And I know that you're an honorable crocodile and will keep your word." [Falletta 1983, p. 84]

Variation I

A madness grabbed hold of a small child who was playing on the edge of normality. Its mother begged the madness to give back her child. "Okay," said the madness. "If you can predict exactly what I am going to do, I'll give you back your child. But if your guess is wrong, I'm going to keep it."

"Oh, you're going to keep it!" cried the despairing mother.

"Now I can't give the child back," replied the sly madness, "because if I give it back, that would mean that your prediction was wrong, and I threatened to keep the child if you guessed wrongly."

"Oh no," said the clever mother, "it's the other way round. You can't keep my child, because if you do I have told the truth, and in that case you promised to give me back the child. And I know that you are an honorable illness and will keep your word."

Variation II

A rather big child—from its age it was really an adult—grabbed hold of a madness while playing on the edge of normality. The mother begged her grown-up child to give up the madness. "Okay," the child said. "If you are a good mother and treat me as I need to be treated, I'll give up the madness. But if you are not a good mother and treat me in a way I don't need I'm going to keep it."

"Oh, you're going to keep it!" the despairing mother cried, and treated her child like a poor, dependent, sick person who cannot make his own decisions in life.

"Now I can't give up the madness," the grown-up child declared, "because if you treat me like a poor, sick, dependent person you are not a good mother, and I threatened that I would keep the madness if you behaved wrongly."

"Oh no," replied the worried mother, "it's the other way round. You can't keep the madness, because if you do I have behaved correctly; a good mother must take over the responsibility for her poor, sick child. And in that case you promised to give up this madness. And I know that you're an honorable child and will keep your promise."

Variation III

A rather big child—from its age it was really an adult—grabbed hold of a madness while playing on the edge of normality. The mother begged her grown-up child to give up the madness. "Okay," said the child. "If you are a good mother and treat me as I need to be treated, I'll give up the madness. But if you aren't a good mother and treat me in a way I don't need I'm going to keep it."

"Oh, you'll give it up all right!" said the confident mother, and treated her child like an independent, healthy adult who can make his own decisions about his life.

"Now I can't give up the madness," declared the grown-up child, "because if you don't treat me like a poor, sick person in need of help you aren't a good mother, and I threatened to keep the madness if you behaved wrongly."

"Oh no," replied the mother courageously. "You can't keep the madness, because if you do my behavior was right; a good mother must give up the responsibility for her grown-up, self-responsible, and independent child and even accept it uncomplainingly if this child decides to behave madly. And in that case you promised to give up this madness. And I know that you are an honorable child and will keep your promise."

Variation IV: Excerpt from a Therapy Session[1]

Therapist (asks the daughter): "What do you want to achieve with these sessions?"

Daughter: "I want to make my mother into a real mother."

Therapist: "And what would make you realize that your mother is a real mother?"

Daughter: "A real mother doesn't let her daughter tell her how she ought to be."

Mother (who looks as though she is in trance): "Ah."

---

1. This patient came to the session with her mother, for anorexia. The so-called anorexia is rather a mad matter. The patient distinguishes strictly between body and mind, so that both can be sent into the arena as enemies. The mind tries to defeat the body or rather hunger. When it finally manages this, it has lost.

Variation V: The Often-Practiced Aim
of Parental Education

"We want to make our child independent!"

CAN YOU MAKE SOMEONE MAD?
PROBLEMS OF FAMILY RESEARCH

We can acknowledge that dinosaurs are extinct, and one day we will probably be able to agree on an explanation for this extinction. Nevertheless we cannot say which living beings will survive in the course of evolution in the long term. Although we can establish the (Darwinian) conditions of not being fit, of inadequate adaptation, we cannot say which of the now living or not yet living creatures will fulfill them in the long term.

For the same reasons it is impossible to say what are the necessary conditions for and symptoms of health. Nevertheless we can establish symptoms and conditions of illness. Wherever survival is concerned, we can only establish the conditions of extinction, not those of survival. We know what is not possible, but not what is possible; we know what makes us ill, but not what keeps us healthy. In spite of this, we can, of course, take the appropriate steps in our own lives based on what we know about dying or getting sick. However, we are moving on the windy plain of statistics and probability calculus; these statements may be appropriate for a good average of examined persons, but may well prove absolutely meaningless in individual cases. After all, the average person does not generally wish to start up a health insurance company, for which these average data are important to establish the rates. We need to be able to decide whether it would be better to give up smoking or to take up jogging. We should not begin to mistrust all advice that promises health when we hear that Dr. Jim Fixx, who was the proponent of jogging as the basis of a (supposedly) more healthy way of life, fell down dead during his morning run. Nobody knows what makes and keeps us healthy. The only sensible advice that medical research can give us for our own way of life is to *refrain* from what harms us: "Stop smoking, because on average smokers die earlier!"

The same applies to advice deduced from the results of family research and therapy for the prevention of madness. Here too it is easier to deduce recipes not to do this and that—instructions to refrain from what is harmful—than instructions to do this and that, to do what is useful. "Don't hit your child, then it won't get (physical or mental) bruises!" Unfortunately we cannot conclude from such wisdom what we should, could, or must do with our child instead.

It is therefore not surprising that research results are often published about the (supposed) disturbance of families, but very rarely about the so-called normal family in which no symptoms are developed (Simon et al. 1985). We must mistrust all research results on the madness of families, as they are frequently based on cause-and-effect patterns, which are well tried and tested in everyday thinking yet are hardly useful—and even unscientific—in this case. Often reifications are made, according to which, for example, a schizophrenic family is like this, whereas a psychosomatic family is like that. When such formulations are used, there is a risk that once again the statics of the system are presupposed and that the therapist misunderstands himself as the rubber hammer coming from the outside who tries to bang the dents out of the family structure—instead of out of the personality structure as formerly—with as much strength as possible.

If we see the family as a living communications system, the description of its characteristics or its structural features is pushed into the background. Instead it is a matter of answering the question of which organizational processes are responsible for the emergence and preservation of such features and structures noticeable to the external observer. As no member of the family is in a position to force the others to behave in a certain way (there is no instructive interaction), no one can plan and form his own family like an engineer. Thus the family must also be understood as a self-organizing system that emerges from the interplay among its members, their mutual perturbation, and achieving a consensus.

The aim of this chapter is to present family rules, typical patterns of interaction, and the world view on which they are based—the interplay of prescriptive and descriptive rules—that can be connected with the emergence or preservation of madness from the (external) perspective and practical experience of the family therapist. Even if an attempt is made to deduce an explanation for madness from this connection, it must not be misunderstood as the cause of madness. It is merely a description of functional if/then links. Just as it is impossible to deduce from the link "if it is 8 P.M., the news starts on TV" that the clock is responsible for the news starting punctually, no causality or blame may be deduced from the connections depicted here.

However, the difference between the inner and outer perspective must be taken into consideration once again. Namely, for someone who is part of a system of interaction as the identified patient, a family member, or therapist, the neutral description of if/then links opens up the chance to change his description from the inner perspective and his own actions. For example, if you want to see the news, turn on the TV at 8 P.M.; if not, don't.

Thus someone who has got it into his head to make someone mad, as in some Alfred Hitchcock films, for example, may well be able to find recipes for carrying out his evil aims (e.g., obtaining someone's fortune) from the experiences of systemic family research. This is yet another example of the fact that it is easier to give instructions on how to disturb order (normality) than on how to create order. However, to come to the most important point first, it is one of the paradoxes of life that order establishes itself without the well-aimed intention of those concerned, whereas the attempt to create order consciously often leads merely to madness, disorder, and chaos. At best, those affected by madness (patients, relatives, therapists) can deduce advice on what should be refrained from in order to reduce the probability of madness emerging. That means they should simply avoid what someone who wants to make someone mad in Hitchcock's sense has to do.

We must explicitly point out once again a further difficulty of any family research, although it ought to be obvious in view of the difference between harder and softer reality, between greater or less dependence of the observed on the observer. We cannot measure families or can do so only to a small degree; it is impossible to gain data free of interpretation. Of course families also have hard data, but on closer contemplation these turn rather soft. Let us take the death of a spouse as an example. For many this is a great loss connected with pain, stress, and mourning. Life changes completely. However, we cannot presuppose this meaning as obvious, as after all most murders take place within families. Someone who has been trying for years to do away with his partner (by cooking toad soup, for example) will react differently to the sad news that his partner has had a heart attack while jogging than someone who found his only sense in life in the partnership.

Thus family research has more in common with ethnology or political science than with organic medicine. For the observer families are always native tribes or even foreign states, the customs, traditions, laws, and economic system of which are unknown to him. However, the greatest mistake a family researcher can make is even more basic—to believe naively that he could understand the language of a (foreign) family. Even if it sounds similar to the language spoken by him and his family, he still knows nothing about all the unspoken meanings, about this particular family's specific connotations that accompany every word and give meaning to every gesture. These form the expression of family history in the present.

The descriptions of families in the following paragraphs are the result of therapeutic work with families in which one or more members produced some form of madness or other symptoms. As no two families are exactly the same, these depictions are idealizations, in which the attempt is made to filter out what is typical and common and to imagine away what is not typical, that is, cars in the Alps.

This long introduction to the description of family dynamic aspects of madness seems necessary in order to preclude the terrible simplifications that emerge all too easily and that assign the family the blame for the madness of one of its members. Many psychiatrists come to the obvious conclusion that families ought to be acquitted of guilt (I agree!), and for this reason no family research should be conducted in this area (I object!). If these certainly well-meant suggestions were followed, we would deprive all affected, the patients as well as their relatives and the therapists, of the chance of using all the if/then rules, which can only be described from the perspective of the external observer, in order to influence the fate of someone who behaves, thinks, or feels madly.

REALITY THAT IS TOO HARD AND/OR TOO SOFT: PSYCHOSOMATIC, MANIC-DEPRESSIVE, AND SCHIZOPHRENIC PATTERNS–I

Then followed the usual fingerprinting and photographing ritual, fingerprints and photos en face and in profile were taken, and finally I was locked up in a single cell.

There I sat for three days without anyone bothering about me, except for the watery cabbage soup that was pushed through the hatch twice a day. Instead there was a loudspeaker in my apartment, and that was the worst thing, as it couldn't be turned off. It repeatedly screeched out the same sentences over and over again: LANGUAGE IS UNAMBIGUOUS. ANYONE WHO DOUBTS UNAMBIGUITY IS MAD OR A LIAR. ANYONE WHO GIVES WORDS DIFFERENT MEANINGS IS COMMITTING A CRIME AGAINST THE LANGUAGE COMMUNITY. HE SHOULD BE SILENT, SILENT, SILENT. LANGUAGE IS UNAMBIGUOUS. WE KNOW WHAT WORDS MEAN. WE KNOW ALL THE MEANINGS. WHOEVER BELIEVES US LIVES IN SECURITY. HE IS HAPPY, HAPPY, HAPPY. LANGUAGE IS UNAMBIGUOUS. [Bemmann 1984, pp. 114–115]

This terrifying vision of a prison in a totalitarian state springs from the fantasy of a writer and obviously has nothing to do with communication in families directly. However, it does so indirectly, as there are families in which similar beliefs on the role of language are put into *practice*. We find no dictators and no language surveyance offices, no prisons in families, and as a rule they do not often have cabbage soup. Yet, the connection between such families and the fictitious state in the novel is the assumption that language–

talking and communication—can and must be unambiguous. When such descriptive and prescriptive rules are followed by a family, group, or institution, structures of organization develop that—observed from the outside—have a great similarity to extremely limiting, compulsive state structures. In these systems of inter-action the consensus on reality becomes very hard: there is only one unambiguous truth that is free of contradiction. It cannot be changed; everyone has to obey its values and constraints. If he obeys, he is promised security and happiness. This promise need not come from some kind of dictatorial ruler; it follows logically from the presumption of an unambiguous reality. That suggests the possi-bility of doing everything right and threatens those who do anything wrong.

This hard world view arises and is preserved only when all par-ticipants in such a system of interaction comply with the rule that the focus of attention in communication must always be kept con-centrated merely on what is "really" essential. If they follow the ideal of a denotative language that names the objective facts, and try to exclude all connotative aspects, they confirm the validity of such communication rules. No one perturbs or disturbs the other in this pattern of interaction; no one can or must question the con-sensus on reality. There is no cause for worry.

This kind of world view proves its worth as long as it is dealing with the harder reality of the inanimate environment. In this case it makes sense for a nonswimmer, for example, to reckon on getting more than just wet feet when attempting to walk on the water of a lake. The hardness of physical laws (descriptive rules) makes it possible to invent a boat or a raft and to reach the other shore with dry feet, that is, to develop prescriptive rules that are useful for survival.

Applying this hard appreciation of the rules to the much softer sphere of interhuman relationships and feelings becomes problem-atic. Social rules are then dealt with in the same way as laws of nature. The family tradition of having the evening meal at 7 P.M. every day is considered just as binding and unchangeable as the force of gravity.

From the inner perspective the world seems rigid and unchange-able. Those who feel comfortable in it do not get into difficulties because of their point of view. However, when someone does not feel comfortable, he can have no hope that everything may turn out all right in the end either. The harder and more unchangeable reality seems, the more a black-and-white picture of the world emerges, and the clearer it seems to function in accordance with the all-or-nothing principle, the either–or pattern.

People who subjectively live in such a hard reality often have good chances of successful careers as mathematicians, physicists, chemical scientists, engineers, or even as missionaries or govern-ment officials. Nevertheless, in the messy private world of feelings, in their relationships, families, or partnerships they are often in a tight spot; in this hard reality ambivalence is not allowed, and that really is hard for them. Either all or nothing is the demand they must make of themselves and their partners if they comply with the rules. Once involved in a relationship, they are caught up in it forever. Binds are always eternal; the demand for mutual loyalty is too. Partnership is something like buying a house; ownership of the partner is recorded in the land register. You can feel safe and happy for the entire future and must ensure that the partner or the other family members also feel secure. Change is not provided for nor is dropping out of the relationship.

From the outer perspective of the therapist we can establish that in such a culture, such a hardened social reality, psychosomatic symptoms[2] develop frequently. However, as physical symptoms are usually interpreted as signs of a disturbed body, their existence does not question the assumptions on the world, but rather confirms them; still there are no grounds for worry.

Such patterns are to be found not only in families but wherever people interact with each other. Charitable or reforming institu-tions that place high moral demands on themselves and whose members gain a great deal of self-esteem and a feeling of identity

---

2. On the relationship between family patterns of interaction and the formation of spe-cific symptoms see in more detail Simon (1988).

from their work frequently follow these very rules. The difference between families and other organizations usually is that it is not so easy to drop out of the family or give notice as one can with a job, for example. The bind is greater. However, if the job or the workplace, the institution or the group, becomes an important factor for personal identity, or if for other material or ideal reasons permanence or another form of relationship for life exists, these apparently relevant institutions such as clinics, firms, or authorities become more and more like the family in their organization and culture. Religious sects are usually like the family from the outset.

We can, however, describe a second body of symptoms connected with such a very hard reality, namely, manic-depressive behavior. In times when no one behaves strangely, families in which one member manifests manic and depressive behavior seem like the families in which psychosomatic symptoms are formed. These symptoms are often combined.

For example, two sons and one daughter of the M. family suffer from asthma, Mr. M. has an indefinite heart complaint, and Mrs. M. is hospitalized because of severe depressions. After her depressive symptoms subside, she starts being more and more active, and her mood improves to an almost unbearable extent for the family. Finally she is brought back to the hospital and diagnosed as manic.

These combinations of symptoms are rather frequent. It often happens that the same person first develops physical complaints and only behaves madly later on, or there are oscillations between physical complaints and strange behavior.

However, we can describe an important difference between manic-depressive behavior and exclusively psychosomatic patterns: in phases when a family member behaves maniacally the hard consensus on reality is annulled. There is a kind of time-out; it can be compared to carnival time in otherwise prude neighborhoods when all-limiting regimentation is reversed. In the same way there now comes a time for the whole family in which the descriptive and prescriptive everyday rules are no longer valid. Even the patient's relatives occasionally allow themselves to behave in a way they would not permit themselves at other times—respectable bank directors hitchhike across the country to visit their poor, sick daughters in an institution somewhere; mothers who believed for years that it was their duty to do everything for their children suddenly begin, very timidly, to think of themselves too and go on vacation alone. The security of hard reality is questioned; no one knows any more which behavior means what. Does the patient mean what he says ("You stupid idiots, leave me alone!"), or is it an expression of his illness? The unambiguity of language is no longer valid, and this is experienced (at least temporarily) as liberation.

On the other side of the spectrum, patterns of communication and organization can be described in which attention is barely focused and communication deviances, context mixing, and all other forms of mutual confusion manifest themselves. Here the consensus on reality is very soft, and everything is and remains possible. Language is ambiguous; it is now concrete and limited and then vague, woolly, the words mere husks or full of bubbles. Accordingly relationships cannot be established definitely, and liberty seems to have no limits, but the other side of the coin is a lack of security, the unreliability of relationships and of the whole world. These patterns can often be observed in families with a member diagnosed as schizophrenic. Here, too, no cause–effect relationship can or should be described. The mad behavior of a family member apparently stabilizes the structure of communication, and the structure of communication stabilizes mad behavior.

If we compare the structures of interaction connected with psychosomatic and manic-depressive symptoms with a totalitarian state in which police records departments, thought police, and other inquisition authorities try to survey and control whether each individual thinks, feels, and does the right thing, we have to compare the system of interaction that brings forth this madness with a state in which civil war reigns. We never know who is fighting with whom against whom. It is never obvious who rules which part of the country or city at a certain moment and for how long. No one can say whether defeats are really defeats or merely tactical retreats. There are no reliable arrangements; there can be a marksman behind every hedge. Life becomes extremely complicated. Northern Ireland or Beirut are good examples of places where there are such struggles for control. Chaos and the unpredictability of coexistence, insecurity, and violence are the result of the attempts of different parties to determine one-sidedly what the rules of coexistence should look like. They are attempts at instructive interaction; an attempt to control relationships of which one is an element; the unsuccessful application of a kind of thinking based on the distinction between subject and object, although one is an element of the object (the relationship) oneself. Inevitably paradox develops from this dissolving of the distinction between inside and outside; *the attempt to create order leads to disorder and chaos.*

These two patterns—on the one hand, totalitarian limitation, and on the other territorial struggles for power—however, are merely the extreme (and in this case extremely exaggerated) ends of a spectrum of intermediate and mixed forms. And—this point has to be emphasized yet again—these patterns can change.

HARMONY AND/OR CONFLICT: PSYCHOSOMATIC, MANIC-DEPRESSIVE, AND SCHIZOPHRENIC PATTERNS—II

The metaphor of the totalitarian state or civil war is so apt because it points to the fact that control of interaction is a question of politics even where the rules of families are concerned, or the other way around, namely, that even in politics this control is a matter of development, preservation, and the transformation of rules.

If we take a look at the psychosomatic, manic-depressive, and schizophrenic rules described in the earlier section, we find even more possibilities of describing the rules of interaction. We can, for example, distinguish among families in which conflicts are mainly emphasized and exaggerated, families in which they are denied or played down for the sake of harmony, and families in which both occur.

If we once again exaggerate in order to make differences and similarities clearer, we can then say of families in which the occurrence of psychosomatic symptoms is likely that the preservation of harmony is granted a high value. Differences between the individual family members are not acknowledged, that is, they make no difference. Unity and similarity, one's whole life revolving around the greater community, is the supreme principle to which everyone tries to do justice. One for all, all for one. All are the best of friends. Everyone loves everyone else above all and equally, none more and none less. In order to do justice to this high ideal, possible conflicts, deviating wishes, and different feelings and thoughts must be denied or avoided. Not even differences in relationships, the formation of parties, alliances, or factions, are allowed.

In such families (or other political systems) the boundaries of normality are set extremely narrowly and may not be overstepped. The rule is not to attract attention. Only slight change is possible. "We've always done it this way" or "We've never done it that way" are the guidelines for coming to decisions. How can eternal truths change anyway? Votes always end with a 99.9 percent majority. There is no room for individualism or experiment. Adaptation to transformed environmental conditions is thus difficult.

In family research David Reiss (1981) coined the concept *consensus-sensitivity* to express this pattern as a result of his experiments on family decision-making processes. Each individual family member is considerably better able to solve problems alone than when the others are there too. The necessity to adapt sensitively to what the others might feel or think prevents quick and factual optimal solutions from being chosen in cooperation with them. In case of doubt, agreement with the others is generally preferred. In this way each blocks the other from making full use of his abilities.

The opposite extreme is formed by patterns of interaction that are "distance-sensitive." In this case—seen from the outside—the avoidance of a consensus seems to be the most important rule. The emphasis and exaggeration of conflicts demonstrate individual independence. By the expression of aggressive feelings, the boundaries between the people concerned are made clear, and distance is created between them. They avoid showing affection, as doing so could emphasize similarities and temporarily lead to agreement; if things came to the worst it might even lead to the dissolution of mutual boundaries. The independence of the individual who does not submit to external constraints, but rather emphasizes his own independence, is the ideal. This pattern of sensitive distance can be found above all in families in which one family member manifests deviating behavioral patterns that have brought him into conflict with the police and criminal prosecution authorities. Anyone who follows these rules contravenes the rules of the social consensus (outside the family). As he is considered responsible for himself and not sick, he is running a great risk of being labeled and treated as a criminal.

In each of these two extreme forms of interaction, one side of the possible ambivalent feelings between closeness and distance, between dependence and independence, is tabooed respectively. In the pattern sensitive to the consensus, it does not seem possible to express negative feelings associated with distance, separation, and independence; in the pattern sensitive to distance it does not seem possible to express positive feelings associated with closeness, fusion, and dependence.

In families in which one of the members behaves madly, in contrast, both sides of the ambivalence—sensitivity to distance and sensitivity to the consensus—can be described. They are combined differently, however, in the different forms of madness.

Families with manic-depressive patterns contain parties that have a different history and different values. One party (sometimes composed of only one member—one parent or one partner) has lived an unattached and free, sometimes even dissipated life until starting a family or a partnership. If he or she has not done this or that wild behavior, that person nevertheless feels the desire for independence. In the eyes of the partner or the other party (usually composed of several persons) such tendencies and impulses are an expression of untidiness that need strict control. The party of peace, closeness, order, and harmony normally predominates, so that in normal times the family lives more in accordance with the rules sensitive to the consensus. However, from time to time there are phases when the minority party predominates and determines the rules of interaction. This puts conflict on the agenda, and the party of order attempts to take control. There is a struggle for power. As in the case of individual ambivalence, the contrary tendencies of sensitivity to the consensus and sensitivity to distance are ordered one after the other by the family as a whole; here too we may speak of diachronic dissociation. The actions of the identified patient are exemplary of this chronological splitting. Either he demonstrates his independence and ensures distance (in the manic phase), or he manifests his dependence and thus causes the others to come closer (in the depressive phase).

To the observer schizophrenic patterns seem to be split in a different way; both sides of the opposing tendencies or ambivalent feelings are lived out simultaneously. Feelings and actions not only oscillate rapidly between the desire for closeness and distance, between love and hate, conflict and harmony, but also different persons in the same family can take over different tasks. Thus any member of the family can take on the distance-sensitive part and cause conflict when too much closeness and harmony ensue and threaten the feeling of independence of those concerned; doing so helps everyone secure their detachment and autonomy. Then, when conflicts threaten to boil over, he can take over a mediating and conciliatory role in the next moment. In this way the family's balance can be maintained on the whole by a kind of division of labor rotating between various persons. While in the manic-depressive pattern, with the exception of the patient, the same person always takes on the same roles; in the schizophrenic pattern anyone can take on any role. For this reason there can be no formation of fixed parties.

For the phases of harmony or animosity in such families Lyman Wynne and his colleagues (1958) coined the phrases "pseudo-harmony" and "pseudo-hostility" in order to make it clear that neither hostile nor harmonious behavior is unambiguous. Harmony is only comprehensible in the realm of hostility and hostility in the realm of harmony.[3] From the outside all three patterns—psychoso-

---

3. The contemporaneity of the opposing tendencies suggests here too, as in coping with individual ambivalence, the concept of synchronic dissociation.

matic, manic-depressive, and schizophrenic—seem to be stable and constant. The psychosomatic pattern arouses the impression of continuous, rigid lifelessness. The manic-depressive pattern gives this impression at some times, but this pattern is interrupted by phases of uncontrolled, gushing liveliness. The role patterns of the family members are fixed, and it is difficult to distinguish between role and personal characteristics. In this case the view from the outside is not very different from the picture from the inner perspective.

The situation is quite different in the schizophrenic pattern. From the outside a stable pattern can be recognized. There is always someone to take over the functions of ensuring distance and correspondence with the consensus, but who that is in each case has not been determined. Any third party interferes as savior or disturber. This suprapersonal stability of the system can only be recognized from the outer perspective, however. From the inner perspective, on the other hand, the takeover of different tasks and roles cannot be ascribed indefinitely to certain persons. Forming an individual identity and ascribing it are difficult, as none of the persons concerned seems identical with himself for any length of time.

POWER AND/OR IMPOTENCE: WHO DECIDES WHAT IS TRUE AND REAL?

"Knowledge is power," we say. Of someone who does not do his homework properly and does not know what he ought to know in an exam we say, "He has not mastered the subject matter." Someone who knows how to repair a car, can do it—someone who can do it knows how. The idea of knowledge is closely connected with the idea of knowing how, the potential, the possibility of achieving something. The idea that knowledge is power is the idea that man can gain control over his environment. If you *know* the laws of nature you can rely on them and behave accordingly. The biblical phrase "Be fruitful and multiply, and replenish the earth, and subdue it!" means "Learn to master it; control it!" When we are dealing with inanimate systems such as a car, this idea of power seems quite practicable. Anyone whose car runs off the road has lost his mastery over it and thus cannot control it properly any more.

However, if such ideas of power and knowledge are transferred to the interpersonal area, several typical patterns of interaction—often connected with madness and the formation of physical symptoms—can ensue. These patterns include hierarchical, totalitarian power structures, power struggles, or a rhythmic alternation between the two. In the first case—the psychosomatic pattern—the control model seems to be converted successfully into reality; in the second case—the schizophrenic pattern—there is a struggle for the position of power; in the third—the manic-depressive pattern—control and struggle for control alternate.[4]

The fact that the application of linear cause–effect thinking—for the idea of controlling one's fellow men (or oneself) like a car is nothing else than that—must lead to the development of such patterns of interaction becomes clear when we keep in mind the difference between living and nonliving systems, between harder and softer reality. There is no such thing as instructive interaction; we cannot foresee the effect of our own behavior on another living being, its inner structure, and behavior—and therefore we cannot control it purposefully. Instructive interaction does not even hold true in relation to cats, and much less so in relation to human beings. You say something to someone and cannot determine what meaning he gives to what he hears. And yet from the outside it often seems as though such control were possible and as though people and their behavior could be controlled by others. Seen from the inside, this interpretation also seems to be confirmed. Some people feel powerful, others impotent; some give orders, others obey. "I was only acting under orders" is a frequently heard attempt at an excuse in war crime trials. Power and impotence are experienced. They are (self-) descriptions of people who behave as though they could control or be controlled.

---

4. There are other struggles for control connected with the formation of symptoms, as in alcoholism, for example. However, I refrain from depicting them here so as not to extend the focus of attention too far.

How can we explain the development of such structures of apparent control and such struggles for the role of the one who has control and determines the course of others? From the outer perspective of systems theory, it can be determined that a purposeful direction of behavior in human interaction is not possible. After all, everyone determines the living conditions of all the others; order ensues from the combination of all concerned, not from the commands of one ruler. Every person is autonomous and behaves according to his inner structures. The environmental conditions (socalled rulers are a part of these conditions) can merely perturb, disturb, or stimulate and thus narrow the range of possible behaviors. It is always the living being himself who determines how he behaves. Anyone who wants to gain power over others must somehow entice them to do what he commands of their own free will. This naturally sounds paradoxical at first, but it is possible.

This possibility makes the concept of power as a description of human systems seem useful from a systemic perspective. However, power must not be equated with control. The foundation of power relationships in interhuman areas is formed not by the possibility of instructive but by destructive and constructive interaction, the ability of human beings to perturb one another, to limit or extend their living space, and if need be to kill each other. As we cannot control others directly, our only chance is to entice them indirectly to behave the way we want them to. The first strategy of power can be characterized by the formula "Your money or your life." The victim of a mugger who, with stiletto in hand, gives him the choice of relinquishing his wallet or his life *and* his wallet, has, as an autonomous creature—if we describe the situation in the terms of the free will model—the freedom to decide for or against his life. To put it radically, he gives the gangster his money because he wants to. He might also have let himself be killed, but obviously does not want to or thought it stupid, uneconomical, too soon. . . .

The mugger or violence strategy of power is based on the fact that another person's range of decision is extremely limited. Anyone who *wants* to keep his life has to give up his wallet. The threat connected with the mugger's dagger ensures a hardening of reality.

It ensures that the pedestrian fearing for his wallet and his life describes his situation according to a quite unmistakable if/then, if not/then, if/then not, or if not/then not rule and deduces the prescriptive rules for his actions from this description. It is the shadow of the future, the expected consequences, that finally lead him to *want* to give away his wallet.

Governmental power functions according to the same principle. Someone who does not want any points on his driving record, does not want to pay a fine, or does not want to be put into jail ought not to drive much faster than permitted within restricted areas and should not allow himself to get caught doing so.

In interaction, wherever one can limit the options of the other in such a way that he has no or few options left, a power relationship has developed. From the outside and from the inside the impression can arise that people can control one another. Feelings of power or impotence can ensue.

This method of gaining power, which is based on the application or threat of violence, rests on the limitation and restriction of the individual's range of action. It is therefore much more successful in preventing someone from doing something than in inciting him to do something. It thus leads to the *suppression* of individual actions, to the passivity of the one who finds himself in the position of impotence. What ensues is a social system in which everyone is concerned only with avoiding doing anything wrong. Creativity, individual initiative, and willingness to take risks cannot be expected.

However, this is not the only successful power strategy; there are other, much more elegant ones. They all arise from the same mechanism that enables the development of a consensus on reality, namely, mutual sensitivity and mutual understanding. For even the threat of imprisonment or the use of physical violence is based on the fact that we, as beings sensitive to pain, can assume that other people will react similarly and, in case of doubt, will rather choose the painless or lifesaving way out. Where people are prepared to accept pain and death, violence loses its effect as an instrument of power. Gandhi's campaign against British rule of India is a prime example (Erikson 1969).

However, it is not only sensitivity to the fears and cares of others, their desire to avoid unpleasant feelings and experiences, that opens up the chance to establish a power relationship. Even their desire for pleasant feelings and experiences and all the other personal values can be exploited. Next to suppression, *seduction* is a reliable power strategy. People can be corrupted by promises of money, affluence, respect, reason, knowledge, sexual fulfillment, and so on. Even commonly accepted social values gain their effectiveness from the seduction model. If someone works himself to death of his own free will or sacrifices himself, he does so because he has been promised fame, honor, money, paradise, or anything else that has a value for him—or even better, because he expects to achieve that aim. Contrary to the suppression model, the shadow of the future is not black but pink in this case. Not fear but hope leaves its mark on expectations. For this reason other people can be activated and motivated in a power system based on temptation. They use their creative potential to achieve the promised aim. Wherever people free themselves from such values and desires, seduction as a power strategy is no longer or so easily possible.

Knowledge of the fears and desires of another person, of the descriptive and prescriptive rules guiding his actions, enables the exercise of power in both the suppression and the seduction pattern. As everyone behaves autonomously and independently of others in accordance with these inner structures, any power must be based on the use of these descriptive or prescriptive rules. In the case of seduction and suppression, given rules determined by the necessities of a harder (biological) reality are exploited. The reactions of different people to pain, hunger, thirst, or sexual desires are similar enough to be reckoned with.

There is, however, a third method of gaining power. It is based on laying down the descriptive rules. The person who can decide what is to be considered true and real does not need to suppress or tempt anyone personally. It is the putative constraints that cause someone to obey of his own free will. Wherever proclamations of the truth and holy scriptures exist, the person who has this truth on his side has power. Thus popes and ayatollahs determine what are the contents of the consensus on reality. However, even their power is based on the fact that it is given to them by their believers and subjects. When the consensus breaks down, holy wars develop. Where the validity of revelations is doubted, claims of power are legitimized by (supposedly) scientifically established truths. It is no longer a person who cannot lie, but a scientific method that apparently cannot lie that legitimizes power. If such truths are not accepted as part of the consensus on reality, there is a dispute between schools, which is only to be distinguished from holy wars by the weapons used.

The depiction of these power structures and their dynamics has been given so much space here because they can also be described in families in which madnesses develop and, vice versa, because the patterns of interaction in these families can be explained very well as an aspect of a power structure or struggle for power.

In the psychosomatic pattern of a more hardened reality, all have accepted the same truths. There is no conflict about what is true or false. Every individual tries to do or say nothing wrong. It is impossible to determine where this truth comes from and who established it. In these families there is generally no dictator, no politburo, no party that is always right. As everyone subordinates himself to the given and unchangeable family view of reality, everyone limits himself and all others in his freedom of choice. If power struggles develop, they appear to be more an escalation of avoidance. In this pattern it is easiest to manipulate others by triggering feelings of guilt. Physical illness can thus gain powerful interactional meaning. It is a question of a family culture based on (self-) suppression.

The opposite picture presents itself to the observer of the schizophrenic pattern. Here everyone seems to be fighting with everyone else about what is really true. A consensus is impossible or, to put it differently, it remains vague, undecidable. The consequence of any commitment would be that one of the participants would feel powerful or impotent. The worry of giving up one's own independence prevents agreement on an unambiguous truth. The diversity of reality in the schizophrenic pattern enables every individual to feel powerful, or at least not impotent in his coexistence with the

other family members, as there is no clear definition of relationships. Seen from the outside, what emerges can be depicted as
follows:

> An absurd game in which the players have resolved to win, whilst the
> most important rule of the game is the ban on winning or losing.
> However, it is permissible and is even clandestinely suggested (to one
> at a time, so that no one is disheartened) that each should *believe* he
> has won, although you can only believe it in secret and have no way
> to prove it. A game that cannot end because the participants are forced
> into extreme tension that guarantees constant repetition. Each single
> player is tied up by the hubristic illusion, "As long as the game goes
> on I still have a chance to win"—and yet is subjected to the ban on
> declaring openly that he really wants to win or really has won. [Selvini
> Palazzoli et al. 1975, p. 35]

This game cannot end because each participant has a right of veto;
each has the possibility of refusing to agree to certain truths. The
power struggle of the schizophrenic pattern is a struggle for the
position of the one who decides what is real and true. The parallel
to holy wars and civil war situations is thus probably not accidental.

In the manic-depressive pattern, as in the psychosomatic pattern,
the family view of reality is rather hard and unchangeable. All subordinate themselves to the authority of superior truths. However,
there is a deviation from this rigid pattern insofar as phases of
(self-) seduction alternate with phases of (self-) suppression. The way
out of this restriction in the relationship to one or more persons—
for example, the family of origin, Mother, Father—is opened up by
seduction by another, the partner, for example. Anyone who is involved in two competing relationships has no need to feel subjected
or impotent in either. Thus the hardened reality of the psychosomatic pattern is softened a little, and the definition of the relationships becomes—as in the schizophrenic pattern—more unclear, less
restrictive, and less binding. The fear of loss of autonomy can thus
be lessened without the risk of the relationship's breaking up.

In this way all three typical patterns described here can also be
understood as the result of power strategies, as the result of the

attempt to make others behave as you want them to behave and to establish the reality of relationships one-sidedly.

OPEN AND/OR CLOSED: LOVE AND OTHER VIOLATIONS OF BOUNDARIES

Incognito ergo sum—I'm unknown; therefore I am—we might joke with Descartes, as a way of summing up the positive aspects of not being understood. Thoughts and feelings are only free so long as they cannot be guessed, and no one can know them. The sphere of our own experience and feelings, which is only accessible from the inner perspective, guarantees that a person can feel free. Anyone who allows himself to be seen through puts himself in the power of others because he is predictable, that is, can be seduced or suppressed. The autonomy of the individual is based on the fact that no one else knows what is going on inside him due to the boundary between inside and outside.

Every relationship in which someone allows someone else insight into his mind must be connected with ambivalent feelings regarding his own independence. Opening ourselves up to someone else is always connected with the risk of subjection to this person, who might use his knowledge shamelessly. This is valid not only for a relationship to a loved one but also for one to a psychotherapist. That is why some people only permit themselves to talk openly about themselves to bartenders; they can be certain that they will never meet them again so the threatening shadow of the future is short.

However, opening up too much and being understood too well are not the only dangers to one's own independence in a close, emotional relationship. Anyone who falls in love can be seduced and suppressed. Someone who wants something from somebody else—whether tenderness, love, sex, or appreciation—gives this person power over himself. Thus falling in love is always connected with a threat to one's own autonomy.

Someone caught in the fear of being left and having to live alone will not show his feelings and will suppress all behavior that he assumes will chase his partner away. He "closes up," as it is called so nicely in psycho jargon, and at the same time tries to empathize with the other as well as possible in order to fulfill all his wishes and thus make himself attractive, that is, powerful. Empathy has a second aspect, however. It should prevent someone from doing something wrong by mistake. Such a rule of setting up boundaries can be described in the psychosomatic pattern. Each tries to open the other up, to "crack" him, but closes up himself at the same time. If everyone does this, an atmosphere of suppressed feelings emerges in which everyone reads thoughts and thinks the other is the same as he.

Anyone who only wants the best for a loved one and uses all his sensitive abilities to empathize in order to understand the other violates his own boundaries. The other party (partner, child) often experiences this empathy as usurpation. The dynamics of escalation of wanting to understand and not wanting to be understood can be described thus: the one comes too close to the other and gets rejected. As long as he starts from the assumption that he has to understand the other person, he interprets such rejections as a sign of a lack of understanding and tries even more to understand, only to reap even more rejection.

What gives the observer the impression that no one can speak about his feelings or even perceive them[5] is actually the inability to speak frankly. People spare each other and do not want to burden each other. Empathy should guarantee the certainty of doing everything right and thus prevent guilt.

The ambivalence between fear of solitude, isolation, and loneliness on the one hand and fear of lack of freedom, dependence, and feeling restricted on the other determines the schizophrenic pattern. One's own borders are opened and closed alternately and thus become unpredictable for others. This changing between opening and closing leads to a general uncertainty about how someone really is, how he feels or thinks. Moments of closeness and mutual under-

---

5. The concepts of psychosomatics assume that these patients are not able to comprehend their own feelings and give this supposed deficit the names "pensée operatoire" and "alexithymy" (de M'Uzan 1974, Sifneos 1973).

standing can change from one second to the next into misunderstanding and distance; feelings of power toward somebody else can
abruptly be replaced by feelings of impotence.

The identified patient's mad self-dissociation and refusal to make
contact, known as autism, can be understood as a radical attempt
to sort everything out with oneself and to evade usurpation by others; at least it has this effect seen from the outside.

In the manic-depressive pattern we once again see a rhythmic
alternation, one after the other (diachronic), of various procedures
of forming boundaries. During the time free of symptoms, and without mad behavior, the manic-depressive pattern corresponds to the
psychosomatic pattern. During the symptomatic phase the formation of boundaries becomes unclear. In the manic phase the identified patient manifests actively dissociated behavior; in the depressive phase he seems to open up. In both cases these offers of a
relationship are ambiguous, though; they disqualify themselves
because they leave the frame of normal behavior that is understandable for others. In both cases appeals are sent to the environment to
control the patient, to slow down his hyperactivity or increase his
lacking activity, to dampen down his exuberant zest for life or to
brighten up his despondency. These are invitations to power struggles.

Quite generally, every bond, every relationship in which one
person feels responsible for another, loves him, identifies with him,
is worried about him, and takes on responsibility for him, leads to
a dilemma, because it takes a great deal of understanding to do
justice to the needs of the other person; and a great deal of understanding is always connected with the risk of incapacitation and thus
frequently does not do justice to the needs of the other person.

THE PARADOX OF RESPONSIBILITY:
A DOUBLE BIND FOR PARENTS, CHILDREN,
AND/OR PARTNER

Parents are responsible for their children. They have to pay for
windows broken by their beloved little ones, and when these little

ones have grown up and do something criminal or crazy, it "always reflects on the poor parents."

Parents are confronted by an impossible task. They are assigned responsibility for decisions that they do not make and then the blame for deeds they have not committed. No one can guide another person in the same way that he steers his car, not even his own child. Nevertheless, the cause (i.e., blame and credit) for the way their children develop is always sought for and then found, or even invented, in the parents. If children were as inanimate as cars, it would be no problem to demand that the owner or owners—their parents—not only wash and service them carefully but also steer them carefully, considerately, and responsibly. Children, though (unfortunately or thank God), are more unruly, not so easy to care for, more stubborn and contrary than cars.

So long as parents and all other educators are content with doing justice to their legal responsibility to care for their children, they need only set limits for their children. It is sufficient for them to *prevent* them from doing anything stupid. They can confine them to the house, for example, lock them in, or curb their range of activity in some other way. Parents' options are the same as those of other social controllers. Their power is based on the possibility of delimitation and exclusion—a form of suppression. Suppression is the power strategy, tried and tested in many large-scale political experiments, to prevent undesired activities. I will not speculate here on how satisfying such a relationship between parent and child can be. However, although very negative meanings are associated with the colloquial concept of "suppression," I use it only in the context of setting limits. Within these limits there is complete freedom of decision. Whether this form of social execution of power is to be assessed as positive or negative ought depend not only on the perspective but also on how big the remaining freedom is. Although the principle remains the same, it does make a difference that makes an enormous difference where the limits of individual freedom are set and where suppression of nonconforming behavior begins.

However, anyone who wants to bring up children is not usually satisfied with preventing their worst misdeeds. He wants to bring them up, which means he wants to bring them somewhere. Where he brings them depends on his idea of the finished product, namely, well-brought-up children. Parents love their children, sense their duty to care for them, and thus generally wish to do what is best for them. They want something better for their children than they had themselves, do not want them to have to go through the same bad experiences, want them to be able to have all the good and pleasant experiences, want them to have certain values, do not want them to head for disaster, want them to be independent, and so on.

This is a form of love described by Bertolt Brecht (1967, p. 386) in the following words: "What do you do," Mr. K. was asked, "when you love someone?" "I make a sketch of him," said Mr. K, "and make sure he resembles it." "Who? The sketch?" "No," said Mr. K., "the person."

We often find this kind of love in parents who take their task and responsibility seriously. The more concrete and clear their aims, the narrower the limits to their success are set, and the greater the risk of failure for parents and children. Thus not only should most children learn to read and write but some should also play the first violin in the Berlin Philharmonic Orchestra, win the Olympics in the shotput event, or become senior administrator of a hospital[6]; others should under no circumstances become bricklayers like their fathers, should be successful as good Christians but not as intellectuals, left-wing political scientists, or indeed prostitutes; they should take over parental transport or building companies or even the role of cheerleader for the Chicago Bulls. Sometimes these pictures are very precise; sometimes they merely hint vaguely at the direction. In the words of a father, "Son, you can be what you want, even a priest—but a bishop at the very least." In the words of a mother, "I've always known that you'd either be something really great or end up under a bridge in Paris."

Parents who develop less clear ideas about their children's future are better off. They only need to know what they will not per-

---

6. Helm Stierlin (1978) coined the concept of "delegation": parents set their children specific tasks. But the children must also accept them in order to have them.

mit and where they want to set limits. Anyone who has more concrete ideas for the life of his children has to use some kind of seduction strategy or try to establish reality in the sense of his own values and aims. If, as can often be seen in the households of some preachers, psychiatrists, or lawyers, he even has a higher, infallible authority on his side—God, science, or the law—he can, as their representative on earth in the family lay claim to and gain extreme power of definition over the other family members as to what is really true and really good and really beautiful. He does not even need personal lust for power to do this. It is quite sufficient that he wants the best for his children and thinks he knows how to get it. Under these circumstances conflicts about his view of the world and his values cannot be discussed on a level of equality. It is not a matter of differing opinions, but of truth, of objectively correct, reasonable, moral behavior. Independent of all individual claims to power, a difference in power ensues. After all, what can responsible parents do but orient themselves on their own values and truths in dealing with their children? Whoever thinks he knows which is the right future for his child must—this principle seems to be prescribed by the inevitable logic of parental care and responsibility—try to guide him in this direction.

As children are mainly dependent on their parents during the first years of their lives, this type of child rearing seems to function without any great problems at first. The parents have harder reality on their side. The physical survival of the infant is in their power. This balance of power shifts with the increasing physical and mental independence of the child or juvenile; the parents (or rather their educational success) become dependent on the child. If they commit themselves to aims for their children and if it is of great value to them that they are described as "good parents"—by strangers, their children, but above all by themselves—they are governed by their children. They give them much more power than indifferent or disinterested parents or even more than those who consciously give their children a lot of freedom. It is either not so important for such parents or they do not even care what becomes of their children, or they have come to the conclusion that they cannot live their children's lives for them. They are thus not dependent on their children's cooperation to the same extent. After all, it is they who train for the Olympics, lead a morally faultless life, or have to struggle for a place to study medicine.

When parents identify too much with the weal and woe of their children, there is a great risk of an ensuing power struggle for the child's autonomy. However, it is impossible to decide who has more power in the long run, either from the outside or the inside, as parents feel at the mercy of their children at least as much as children feel at the mercy of their parents. What is fatal about this power struggle, above all, is that confusion of the individual distinction between inside and outside can come about. No consensus can be reached on the question of whose motives are behind whose actions. The parents think they are only acting in the interests of the child, and the children are convinced that whatever they do is only done for love of their parents. As both are right according to their own view, power struggles for reality are inevitable if they think there is only *one* indivisible truth.

Unfortunately these power struggles often take a self-destructive course, in accordance with the motto "It serves my mother right that I've got frostbite in my fingers. Why doesn't she buy me gloves?" Where the boundaries between parents and children become blurred because mutual identification is so great, self-destruction—up to the point of suicide—becomes the greatest imaginable aggression that one can inflict on the other.

Normally the transition from the irresponsible role of infant to the self-responsible adult status occurs in small steps. In daily coexistence small boundary conflicts and experiments are carried out, and the child is given more self-responsibility or less self-determination. In a society in which there are no distinctive rituals of transition that are binding for everyone to establish the gradual change in identity from child to adult, the great leap is dissolved in a lasting crisis, in a painful process lasting years of negotiating the relationship between parent and child anew over and over again.

What is surprising and tragic about this struggle is that it is the more difficult and strenuous the greater the emotional bond between those concerned. Children whose parents or parents whose children are indifferent to them never try to save or manipulate each other for the best interests of the other. They thus respect the other's boundaries far more. The process of detachment from a close bond has to be extremely ambivalent. It is far more difficult to leave caring and loving parents on whose benevolence one can rely than to detach oneself from neglectful or abusive parents. This leads to the paradoxical situation that, in the task of opening up their children's path to independence, the "best" parents are the ones who are not so "good." Bad parents are good parents, and good parents are bad parents. Best—that is, most beneficial for the development of the children in the long run—parents are probably the indifferent good or bad parents who provide their children with a healthy measure of neglect—neither too much nor too little. The only problem is, who tells the poor parents where the limits of too much and too little lie?

It is particularly difficult for parents to let their child run wild sufficiently if he has been a problem child from early on. If he has been sickly since birth, for example, or was born with even the slightest handicap, a parent–child relationship is established from the very beginning in which interaction is not determined by the natural expectation of a normal childhood like development, but by the worry and fear of illness and deviation. There is a danger that the usual policy of wringing out independence in small steps has no effect, but for a long time a care relationship, free of ambivalence and conflict, determines the way parents handle their child and the child his parents. In family reality there can be no consensus on mutual boundaries. This dissociation conflict is then deferred to the age of juvenility and puberty, when the social environment or its norms demand that the young adult finally make his own way outside the family.

Seen from the outside, the ensuing family struggles between parents and child seem like wars of independence. The sides seem to be clear. The poor, suppressed children, robbed of their freedom, who seem to be fighting for their legitimate right to independence, are on the one side, and the parents who will not let them go are on the other. However, such a description does not do justice to the situation. It reflects unambiguous aims of both parties, which do not exist. Both are extremely ambivalent. The children want to be treated as adults, yet do not want to relinquish the advantages of the child role, the security and care of the family; the parents are only too happy to give up the burden of responsibility for their children, yet can only do so with a good conscience if they are convinced that their children can live on their own. The apparent clarity and unambiguity only come from the fact that the ambivalence is divided between two parties in accordance with the either–or pattern. As long as the parents seem to keep a hold on the juvenile, he need not be aware of his wish to stay at home; and as long as the juvenile or young adult strives to be away from home, the parents need not be aware of their desire to be released from the responsibility; this is similar to the collusion concept of Willi (1975). The positions can be changed at any time. When the parents try to throw their child out, he fights to be able to stay in the family, and when they try to keep him in the family, he fights for the right to leave. Seen from the outside, both sides of the ambivalence seem to remain balanced in the family as a whole simultaneously (or at least rapidly oscillating) in accordance with the both–and pattern. What kind of relationship the family members have with each other remains vague.

Therefore, no one can be the winner, as any outcome of the conflict to the advantage of one party or the other could only do justice to one side of the ambivalence. When these struggles are never decided, the ambivalence need not be decided either. The *struggle for independence* thus becomes an optimal compromise in which both sides of ambivalence can be enacted.

This is the pattern of detachment and border conflicts that can be observed in families with young adults who behave madly and are finally diagnosed as schizophrenic. As neither side capitulates and admits defeat, escalations to the degree of states of agitation and violence can result. The emotional climate is strained, and negative and positive feelings find their expression in exuberance and excess. When the seductive effect of demonstrative affection fails, all that is left is the helplessly bitter attempt to influence one another by mutual devaluation.[7] The mutual weakening of individual boundaries and individual self-esteem becomes ever stronger, until finally the psychotic breakdown, in which the distinction in the sense of the consensus on reality between inside and outside no longer exists, leads to a (temporary) neutralization of the power struggle.

The mad behavior of the child, who according to his chronological age is already quite grown up, establishes the unclarity of the relationship. If he could be clearly described as bad, the patient would have to be treated as an adult. If he could clearly be recognized as ill, the patient would need paternal care. The fact that he cannot be classified as either bad or mad ensures that the transition phase, the phase of social death between childhood and adulthood, becomes chronic. Childhood does not really come to an end; adulthood is not really begun.

The logic of the schizophrenic pattern results from the paradoxical link between the descriptive and prescriptive rules of the family members. The parents try to make their children independent, and the children prove their independence by manifesting their dependence. Anyone who feels controlled by others when he is controlling himself can only control himself when not controlling himself. This is a game without end, unless the assumption that humans can control each other is dropped.

In the psychosomatic and manic-depressive pattern of interaction, we can observe a similar measure of mutual care, love, responsibility, and—in connection with this—a violation of boundaries. These qualities are found in the relationship not only between parents and children but also between partners who become involved in a close emotional bond to each other. As the communication style in this pattern is more unambiguous and the mutually developed consen-

---

7. See the so-called expressed-emotion studies, by which a connection was proved between the amount of negative feelings expressed in the family and the relapse quota and inpatient hospitalization of patients diagnosed as schizophrenic (for a survey of the relevant literature see Olbrich 1983).

sus on reality is harder, the border conflicts take a different course. Power is exercised less by seduction, but more by limitation, by spoken or unspoken moral bans and laws. The well-being of each is made dependent on the well-being of all the others. The prescriptive and descriptive rules to which everyone seems to conform seem to declare that "I only feel well when you are well." It is not permissible to demand anything for oneself. "Love your neighbor *more* than yourself" is the rule. Only one possibility remains to assert ideas deviating from those of the others, for only the one who is objectively worst off at the moment has the right to think of himself. This rule means that only the one who is sufficiently badly off can feel well. We can often observe competition for the status of the one who is most ill. Although there are also phases in which all feel well, they usually do not last very long, as every worry extends over all personal boundaries and everyone's problems are dispossessed by all the others. One result is an escalation of allowing oneself to feel ill. When the husband feels bad, the wife feels bad because she notices that her husband feels bad. When the husband notices that his wife feels bad because he feels bad, he feels even worse than before. When the wife sees that her husband feels worse, and so on. Each tries to hide his feelings for his own protection.

This hard care pattern is also valid for the manic-depressive family. The future patient detaches himself from his family by looking for a partner who has just as hard a picture of reality and the same ideas of demanding and promising perfect neighborly love. In a situation in which two people compete in perfect solidarity and loyalty, the detachment of one from the other can always be justified by the demands of the other. The possessive demands of the husband are rejected because of the no less exacting demands of the mother, and vice versa; solidarity toward the wife enables detachment toward the lover hoping for marriage, and vice versa. Should one of the two partners at the corner of the triangle try to achieve an unambiguous definition of the relationship and fight for an exclusive partner relationship, the balance of the triangle is threatened. If, for example, the husband attempts to force his wife to decide between him or her mother or the wife tries to force her husband to choose her or the other woman, a struggle for control over the other ensues. In the frame of the ensuing escalation, the mad behavior of the patient in the manic-depressive pattern also results in neutralization. It is impossible to decide whether it is the patient who is behaving madly or whether the illness is the cause of his behavior.

The illness thus becomes a new partner in interaction and makes the formation of an alliance against a mutual enemy possible. You can fight against the illness, you have a piece of harder reality—so you think. And for as long as the illness is maintained as a new member of the family, the old boundary conflicts need not be negotiated. The question always remains open as to whether it is the patient to whom the responsibility for his behavior can be ascribed.

Patterns of behavior that others cannot understand form an unbridgeable boundary, a method of distinction between inside and outside, a mad form of individuation.

NOTE: ONE FAMILY = MANY FAMILIES

There are as many families as there are family members. Everyone lives in his own, quite private family that need have no resemblance to his partner's, his brothers' and sisters', children's, grandmother's, uncle's, or aunt's family. The family environment of each person is quite unique and individual.

There is no such thing as *one indivisible* Smith family, but rather the Smith family from the inner perspective of Mr. Smith, the Smith family from the inner perspective of Mrs. Smith, the Smith family of their daughter, of their son, and so on. The conditions of survival are different for each family member, and the picture each develops of his family need have no resemblance to that of one of the others. It merely has to fit that of the other members, that is, it should not be disturbed too much by unexpected behavior on the part of his relatives.

The descriptions of family patterns of interaction and communication given in the various sections of this chapter can be distin-

guished from the family members' descriptions by the outer perspective of the observer. The psychosomatic, manic-depressive, and
schizophrenic patterns described arise from the fact that each family member sees the family the way he sees them and behaves the
way he behaves from his own inner perspective. These patterns are
not static and unchangeable; they can and usually do change. The
interaction of a family can—again seen from the outside—follow a
psychosomatic pattern for a while and then, for whatever reason,
can turn into a manic-depressive or schizophrenic pattern. As an
example we frequently observe families in which a psychosomatic
pattern determines the family rules of the game for a long time until
a daughter starts a hunger strike and becomes anorectic. Now the
family's reality, so hard up to this moment, softens up; everyone
becomes uncertain how to deal with the daughter/sister and how
to assess her. Is she responsible herself, or is she ill? The ever-thinner
daughter's appeals for help put the parents in a double bind, for
the daughter experiences every attempt to take over responsibility
for her as rape. Communication becomes ever more vague and
unclear, family interaction and its power struggles resemble the
schizophrenic pattern more and more, and sometimes even the
symptoms change—the daughter manifests psychosis.

However, the formation of symptoms does not always lead to a
change in the patterns; the symptoms can also have a confirming
and intensifying effect. When physical illness occurs in a family
functioning according to psychosomatic rules, it does not perturb
or disturb these patterns, nor does it stimulate further development.
On the contrary, the illness forces everyone to concern himself even
more with the poor ill person in the sense of the rules, to subordinate their own needs even more, to express their own miserable state
even less, and so on.

The fact that everyone lives in his own, very private family also
explains why it is possible that in one and the same family (this
formulation naturally assumes the outer perspective again) different symptoms can occur. One family member manifests psychosomatic disturbances, another behaves first manic and then depres-

sive, one gives up his physical complaints or strange behavior, and at the same time another develops some symptoms. We can only say that the symptoms, or rather their evaluation and consequent behavior, must fit together, that is, they may not disturb each other. Some fit less well together, and others better, as, for example, in psychosomatic and manic-depressive patterns.

Another important factor must be mentioned here. The patterns described here gain more importance for individual development the stronger the outer boundary of the family is closed to the rest of the social environment. When there are only few or no important emotional contacts outside the nuclear family, when internal family values cannot be questioned by the values of the world outside, the family members, and their opinions, respect, and judgments, become overvalued. The family is then the only important world, the rules of which must be adapted to by everyone. The greater the difference between these family rules and those outside the family, the greater the crisis will be when the young adult gets or has to get involved in a close and emotionally important relationship to other people outside the family of origin; for example, when he falls in love or needs to prove himself at work.

The path to madness only too often opens up the way back into the family of origin. The son or daughter, an adult according to age, who is identified as ill can/must go on playing the role of a minor; the parents of a sick child can/must take on the role of responsible people who take care of this child. The softened reality in the transition phase, in which no one knew which role he had to play or what he had to do, gives way to the clarity and certainty of the hardened reality of the illness. All concerned can now fall back on the old pattern of parent–child interaction; it is reinforced as the process of chronicity is already marked out. At best the parents and children bow to their fate over the years; they then sit at home together and eat cake. At worst the struggle for power goes on forever with the revolving door rhythm of hospitalization and return to the family.

Such forms of chronicity can be prevented if—spontaneously,

accidentally, through the frequently observed fatigue of those concerned over the years, through incalculable external events, or even
in the frame of therapy—a process of development is activated
through which the family and individual patterns of interaction and
communication, thought, feeling, and action are again perturbed,
that is, disturbed and stimulated.

12

Chaos: A Formal Model of the Development of Madness

SEARCHING FOR THE ROOTS: SONGS AND SUMS

You probably know several songs like the following:

There's a hole in my bucket, dear Lisa, dear Lisa,
There's a hole in my bucket, dear Lisa, a hole.
Then mend it, dear Henry, dear Henry, dear Henry,
Then mend it, dear Henry, dear Henry, then mend it.
With what shall I mend it, dear Lisa, dear Lisa,
With what shall I mend it, dear Lisa, with what?
With a straw, dear Henry, dear Henry, dear Henry,
With a straw, dear Henry, dear Henry, with a straw.
The straw is too long, dear Lisa, dear Lisa,
The straw is too long, dear Lisa, too long.
Then cut it, dear Henry, dear Henry, dear Henry,
Then cut it, dear Henry, dear Henry, then cut it.
With what shall I cut it, dear Lisa, dear Lisa,
With what shall I cut it, dear Lisa, with what?
With a knife, dear Henry, dear Henry, dear Henry,
With a knife, dear Henry, dear Henry, with a knife.
The knife is too blunt, dear Lisa, dear Lisa,
The knife is too blunt, dear Lisa, too blunt.
Then sharpen it, dear Henry, dear Henry, dear Henry,
Then sharpen it, dear Henry, dear Henry, sharpen it.
With what shall I sharpen it, dear Lisa, dear Lisa,
With what shall I sharpen it, dear Lisa, with what?
With a stone, dear Henry, dear Henry, dear Henry,

With a stone, dear Henry, dear Henry, with a stone.
The stone is too dry, dear Lisa, dear Lisa,
The stone is too dry, dear Lisa, too dry.
Then wet it, dear Henry, dear Henry, dear Henry,
Then wet it, dear Henry, dear Henry, then wet it.
With what shall I wet it, dear Lisa, dear Lisa,
With what shall I wet it, dear Lisa, with what?
With water, dear Henry, dear Henry, dear Henry,
With water, dear Henry, dear Henry, with water.
In what shall I fetch it, dear Lisa, dear Lisa,
In what shall I fetch it, dear Lisa, in what?
In a bucket, dear Henry, dear Henry, dear Henry,
In a bucket, dear Henry, dear Henry, in a bucket.
There's a hole in my bucket, dear Lisa, dear Lisa,
There's a hole in my bucket, dear Lisa, a hole!

The same principle of never-ending verses is also the basis of the following problem:

Take a calculator, switch it on, and feed in a number with as many digits as your calculator permits. This initial number shall be called x_0. Example: x_0:75, 369, 521

Now press the button for the square root. The result of the calculation now appears on the screen of the calculator. The square root of the number you put in shall be called x_1. In our example we now get x_1: 8, 681.5621.

Repeat this, that is, find the square root of the square root. You get x_2: 93.1749.

Repeat this, that is, find the square root of the square root of the square root. You get x_3: 9.6527146

Repeat this, that is, find the square root of the square root of the square root of the square root. You get x_4: 3.1068818.

Repeat this, that is, find the square root of the square root of the square root of the square root of the square root. You get x_5: 1.7626349.

Go on doing this, that is, find the square root of the result of the square root. In our example you get the following values:

x_6: 1.3276426, x_7: 1.1522337, x_8: 1.0734215, x_9: 1.0360605, x_{10}: 1.0178705, x_{11}: 1.0088956, x_{12}: 1.0044379, x_{13}: 1.0022164, x_{14}: 1.0011075, x_{15}: 1.0005535, x_{16}: 1.0002767, x_{17}: 1.0001383, x_{18}: 1.0000691, x_{19}: 1.0000345, x_{20}: 1.0000172, x_{21}: 1.0000085, x_{22}: 1.0000042, x_{23}: 1.0000020, x_{24}: 1.0000009, x_{25}: 1.0000004, x_{26}: 1.0000001, and x_{27}: 1.

If you go on finding square roots long enough, you will always end up with the same value: x_{28}:1. The result is a stable value: x_∞:1.

Even if you start out with a value smaller than 1, this process of calculating the square root of the square root of the square root will sooner or later lead to the value $x_\infty = 1$. The only exception is if you begin with $x_0 = 0$. Then you always get 0 as the stable value. But even the slightest deviation from this value will inevitably and unavoidably gravitate toward 1.

Now imagine that the energy supply for your calculator is linked to finding square roots; every time you press the square root button, the battery recharges, for example. Then you have a model for the processes through which living—physical, mental, interactional—structures develop and maintain themselves. Their apparent statics—the recurring value 1 on the screen—is the result of a developmental process in which the same operation (calculating square roots) is constantly repeated on the result of the operation (square roots of square roots of square roots and so on). Starting from any point you like, the stable end of development is reached over a series of intermediary steps. This does not end the dynamics of the process, however, as without the continuation of the operation the end value achieved would fade: the energy supply of the calculator would fail.

This admittedly simplistic experiment illustrates the already often-explained principle of operational closure, the development of autonomous structures, and the basis of normality and madness.[1]

---

1. I would like to thank Heinz von Foerster for the idea of this experiment.

EIGEN-VALUE, EIGEN-BEHAVIOR, ATTRACTOR

Mathematical formulas seem to entail something extremely repellent for most normal human beings. Just as you can give car tires, vacuum cleaners, and briefcases a certain sex appeal in advertising by the addition of women's legs, you are likely to trigger attacks of panic and attempted flight in book readers with anything that even vaguely resembles mathematics. Although fully aware of this risk, I now wish to attempt a formal explanation for the development of madness and normality.

The reason for using a mathematical viewpoint derives from the characteristics of mathematics, as it is not concerned with specific contents but with forms, relationships, functions, and instructions for action. As madness is a question of *forms* of thinking, feeling, and behavior that deviate from those of normality, of *functions* being changed, of different *things being related to each other*, and different *prescriptive rules* being followed, a mathematical viewpoint seems appropriate, as it entails no risk of allowing oneself to be distracted by the respective contents of mad thought. Adopting this viewpoint opens up the opportunity to deduce formal characteristics of normality or madness from formal principles. (For the consolation of the reader the formulas presented here ought to be comprehensible to anyone who can read and write.)

Let us begin with the example of square roots. It follows a similar recipe to the development of living systems—in this case the development and maintenance of mental structures. Man applies certain operations to himself (to put it less mathematically, he thinks and feels), and he applies the same rules of thinking and feeling to what comes out of them. The result of one's own thinking and feeling as one's own thinking and feeling about one's own thinking and feeling remains within the sphere of one's own thinking and feeling.

This phenomenon, known as operational closure in analogy to mathematical concepts, can be seen as the basis of the autonomy of mental processes. It is the formal principle by which the self-organization of living processes can be described.

Heinz von Foerster (1977) cites the mathematician David Hilbert, who presents this process by means of the following mechanism:

> Let x_0 be a mode of behavior, a structure, a function, a value, or a situation (i.e., a "primary argument"; in our example this would be the value 75369521); Op symbolizes an operation performed on the respective value x (e.g., calculating square roots); x_1, x_2, x_3. . . . x_n stand for the successive results of the operation.
>
> The following series of equations ensues from these definitions:
> $x_1 = Op(x_0)$ (i.e., x_1 is the result of the operation on x_0)
> $x_2 = Op(x_1) = Op(Op(x_0))$ (i.e., x_2 is the result of the operation on x_1, which in turn is the result of the operation on x_0)
>
> $x_3 = Op(x_2) = Op(Op(Op(x_0)))$
> .
> .
> .
>
> $x_n = Op(Op(Op(Op(Op \ldots x_0))))$.
> If the infinite succession of operations on operations on operations. . .is called x_∞, this results in the recursive function:
> $x_\infty = Op(x_\infty)$.

The resulting values for x_∞ are the so-called Eigen-values of the operator Op. For Eigen-value we can substitute Eigen-function, Eigen-behavior, or Eigen-structure, depending on whether a function, behavior, or structure was used as the starting point. The term "attractor" is often used in recent literature, but may lead to misunderstanding, as it suggests that a given value (1 in the calculation of square roots) exerts an irresistible attraction. However, we are not dealing with the effect of some magical force or cause, but merely with a feature of certain (not all) self-referential functions, the so-called recursive functions.

This formalism describes the logic of the process by which some variables or structures preserve themselves. A system that organizes itself is in a position to perform operations, the initial premises and results of which are identical (1 in calculating square roots).

Not all self-referential functions result in an Eigen-value. Some have a variety of different Eigen-values, others none at all, and others oscillate. On the behavior level this can correspond to the generation and maintenance of stable behavior patterns in a changing environment, on the psychic level to the stability of certain affective–cognitive schemata. It is the principle by which realities—mad as well as normal—are confirmed.

THE LAWS OF LIVING FORM OR
THE EVOLUTION OF HOPSCOTCH SQUARES

Mathematical formulas and equations are a bit like cooking recipes. You take a certain amount of ingredient x, do this or that to it, and the meal y is ready. The same applies to our construction of reality. You take an initial situation, a pattern of the activities of the nervous system, a meaning; then you make a distinction, and the new activity of the nervous system, the new meaning, is ready. You repeat this until nothing changes any more. When nothing more changes in spite of continuing to make distinctions, a stable meaning, a stable and apparently static reality ensues. The operations leading to the structuring of systems of meaning and symbols are distinctions, distinctions of distinctions, distinctions of distinctions of distinctions, and so on.

The meaning of a symbol, a concept, a word, or sign can be understood as the Eigen-value, or, to put it more clearly, the Eigen-meaning of a self-referential, infinitely successive process of distinction.

Formally this can be illustrated thus:

x_0 stands for a certain initial meaning; Dis stands for a distinction performed on the respective meaning (x); x_1, x_2, x_3. . . . x_n stand for the respective meanings arising from the ever-narrower limitations resulting from the distinctions.

The result is the following series of equations:

$x_1 = \text{Dis} (x_0)$ (i.e., x_1 is the result of the distinction performed on x_0)

$x_2 = \text{Dis} (x_1) = \text{Dis} (\text{Dis} (x_0))$ (i.e., x_2 is the result of the distinction performed on x_1, which is the result of the distinction on x_0)

$x_3 = \text{Dis} (\text{Dis} (\text{Dis} (x_0)))$

.

.

.

$x_n = \text{Dis} (\text{Dis} (\text{Dis} (\text{Dis} (\text{Dis}. . .(x_0)))))$.

If the infinite series of distinctions on distinctions on distinctions is called x_∞, the result is the recursive function:

$x_\infty = \text{Dis} (x_\infty)$.

With each of these distinctions an area of meaning is narrowed down, that is, one of our famous hopscotch squares is drawn. Certain events, phenomena, or objects are ascribed to a certain characteristic (it is localized within the hopscotch square) or not (it is localized outside the hopscotch square). Everything within the boundaries of the distinction is made up into a parcel of meaning, in which each element of the whole parcel gives all other contents its own meaning as connotation (in the same way as, in a parcel in which chocolate and herrings are packed up together, the chocolate eventually takes on a fishy taste).

Meaning develops as a progressive limitation or narrowing down of hopscotch squares (areas of meaning) to an extent that communication—mutual understanding on the basis of similarly limited areas of meaning—becomes possible. From the host of distinctive features some are selected as meaningful for interaction and others are discarded as meaningless. By this process the boundaries of the respective area of meaning are narrowed more and more without ever actually coming to a single unambiguity.

Generally speaking, the possibility of limiting an area of meaning lies between "one sign means everything" (= everything inside the hopscotch square) and "one sign means nothing" (= nothing inside the hopscotch square). To illustrate this range of possible attributions of meaning or, more precisely, the limitation of meaning, mathematically, insert 1 for the extreme case in which there is no limitation of the meaning of a sign or symbol (extreme polysemy—the whole world is merged into one single hopscotch square), and 0 for the other extreme in which every meaning is excluded. In this way the whole spectrum between too much and too little meaning (i.e., overinclusion and overexclusion) can be covered.

If x_t stands for the range of meaning of a sign at a time t (the range of the hopscotch square), then $(1 - x_t)$ can be used to represent everything that does *not* belong within the range of meaning of the sign. How great the range of meaning of a hopscotch square (x_t) is at a time (t) depends on how great it was before the last distinction at a time $(t - 1)$, that is, which meanings have been included (x_{t-1}) and which excluded $(1 - x_{t-1})$.

We can illustrate this by the following mathematical equation:

$$x_t = f(x_{t-1}(1 - x_{t-1}))$$

Referring to the meanings (x_{t+1}) to be developed in the future $(t+1)$, this equation can be formulated thus:

$$x_{t+1} = f(x_t(1 - x_t))$$

The value or values resulting for x_∞ in the long term are the Eigenvalue or values of this function; its attractor, the *Eigen-meaning* of a word, symbol, or sign.

The unambiguity or ambiguity that signs or symbols gain for a person depends on the unambiguity or ambiguity of his interaction with the respective environment. His more-or-less loving fellow beings and also the living world or inanimate nature limit the possibilities of drawing hopscotch squares; their reality is hard or soft to varying degrees, and you cannot tie all meanings up into a parcel. The harder the reality, the narrower and more unambiguous the hopscotch squares; the softer the reality, the more extensive and ambiguous the boundaries of these areas of meaning.

The behavior of the living and inanimate environment—the one we have to deal with every day—has a perturbing effect, disturbs the application of meaning, and stimulates its development. How great this influence is depends on whether, where, and how offense is caused, that is, which boundaries can be felt.

Assuming the idealized case that other people's style of communication remains unambiguous or ambiguous to the same extent over a period of time, the effect of interaction can be expressed by the perturbing factor s (for "softness"). As it has a limiting effect on meanings, it must also have a value between 0 and 1. When it gravitates toward 0 it represents interaction and communication in a very hard consensus on reality—the psychosomatic pattern. When it gravitates toward 1, it stands for the effect of a very soft consensus on reality and of very vague and diffuse communication—the schizophrenic pattern.

In mathematical terms the connection between the individual development of meanings and style of communication, between private and public unambiguity and the ambiguity of symbols or other signs, between harder and softer reality can be expressed by the following equation:

$x_{t+1} = 4sx_t (1-x_t)$ in which the factor 4 guarantees that the value for x lies between 0 and 1

In the area of verbal communication a low value for s (s is smaller than 0.5) corresponds to a use of words or other communicative signals that gravitate toward concretism. In this case the connotative content declines in relation to the denotative content. A high value for s (s is greater than 0.5) corresponds to a high connotative factor; the use of words is more ambiguous. The mutual focusing of attention can be regarded as an interactional mechanism within which this limitation of meaning occurs. A high value for s stands for a broad, barely limited focus of attention; a low value for s, for a narrow, extremely limited focus of attention.

Without such a disturbance or stimulation from the world outside, no meaning or sense would develop at all. If the perturbing parameter s is omitted in the equation (s = 1), the result of the sum is always 0 in the long run, that is, meaninglessness. This equation has also been used to explain dynamic systems in various areas of research; for example, for the fluctuation in the increase or decrease of the population of certain animal species in which case s stands for the amount of food supply as a limiting factor.[2] The area of mutual attention, the range or narrowness of its focus as meaningful food supply, is rather a nice image.

CHAOTIC MEANINGS

The invention of the computer was necessary in order for the esthetic attraction of self-referential (recursive) equations and functions to be acknowledged. Before computers no one dreamed that such infinite calculations might lead to meaningful results. Self-reference was a suspiciously regarded phenomenon that led to paradoxes and ought to be forbidden rather than researched. The possibility of letting machines carry out these calculations without a foreseeable end opened up the chance to examine their characteristics and carry out imaginary experiments.

If the self-referential equation derived from the preceding section can serve as a model for the process of the individual development of meaning, it ought to be possible to confirm the connections (claimed as a result of clinical observations) between communication and madness in the model. And we can. As soon as s, which stands for the hardness or softness of the communicated meanings, exceeds a certain critical value in the equation, chaotic values for x are the result. If we transfer this to the level of thinking and feeling, it corresponds to an absolutely unpredictable application of meaning that is characteristic for mad cognition (Simon 1989).

x_t : range of meaning of a subjective sign at time t
s : range of meaning of the sign used by the partner in communication

Figure 12–1 illustrates the magnitude of the restriction of individual semantic fields (x_∞ = the size of the hopscotch square) in

---

2. In chaos research this concept became known under the name "logistical equation of differences" or as "logistical map" (Feigenbaum 1980, Gleick 1987).

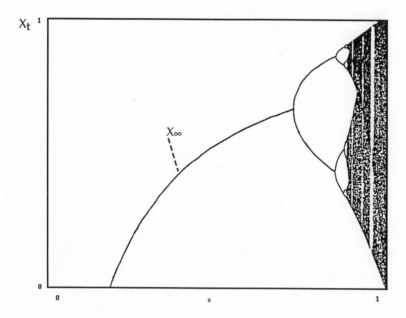

X_t ¹

X_∞

0

0   s   1

Figure 12-1

subordination to s. It shows that x_∞ (the stable meaning of a sign, symbol, or term) changes continuously within a broad range of s values. The differences between more or less unambiguous behavior and extremely ambiguous behavior on the part of the partners in interaction—the area in which s values range between 0.3 and 0.71—correspond to a slightly higher or lower connotative meaning content, a slightly narrower or broader meaning of a symbol, a slightly harder or softer view of reality on the individual level.

From a certain critical level of s (when s becomes greater than approximately 0.72) onward, a bifurcation results, that is, meanings split off and oscillate between two different areas. From one moment to the next, the area of meaning changes in such a way that different meanings with alternately extremely high or extremely low connotative content result. If communication becomes even more ambiguous (if s gravitates toward 1), a further splitting of

Eigen-values, an oscillation between four, eight, sixteen, etc., semantic fields that are split off from one another takes place and finally
results in a completely unpredictable and unordered chaotic succession of an almost infinite number of (too) narrow and then (too)
broad meanings; the structures of subjective reality disintegrate with
the meanings of the symbols. During this process the subjective range
of meaning fluctuates from one moment to the next between
overinclusiveness and overexclusiveness. The long-term range of
meaning is characterized by a chaotic attractor, a chaotic Eigen-
value.

Clinically this corresponds to ambivalence, on the one hand, and
to the alternation between concretist, too limited thought with
merely a low connotative content (i.e., x_∞ gravitates toward 0) and
vague, diffuse, too indistinct thought with a high connotative content in the phase of acute madness (i.e., x_∞ gravitates toward 1), on
the other hand.

The clinical relevance of these functional interrelations becomes
obvious once we realize that double binds represent the extreme
case of a high s value. Paradoxical communication corresponds to
an s value of 1. All distinctions between inside and outside are suspended, the dogma of impermissible contradiction is no longer valid,
and any application of meaning is possible.

We may safely assume that not all signs, symbols, or concepts
and their respective meanings are of equal relevance for the onset
of madness. However, let us imagine communication between two
emotionally close and mutually dependent people, for example,
about their personal identity, their mutual and individual boundaries, the respective inside–outside distinction between self and non-
self, the dissociation between I and we, between responsibility for
the other and lack of responsibility for the other. When communication becomes extremely ambiguous or even paradoxical, a chaotic or psychotic oscillation of the personal distinction between inside
and outside can ensue. With the fusion and disintegration of individual boundaries, communication itself is threatened.

The difference between the manic-depressive and the schizophrenic pattern can be explained by a different time rhythm. If,

when s is high, the speed of oscillation is so fast that a jump between different meanings takes place in short intervals, we are dealing with the schizophrenic pattern. If, when s is also high, the speed
of oscillation is slow and takes months, for example, instead of split
seconds, the meanings the person gives over long intervals seem to
remain the same as in the psychosomatic pattern (low s) in the harder
area of reality (x_∞ much smaller than 0.5) and then suddenly jump
to the softer reality (x_∞ much greater than 0.5) and remain there,
this is a manic-depressive pattern. Ambivalence and ambiguity thus
split temporally in the sense of an either–or pattern.

What is fascinating about this mathematical contemplation of
the process of the distinction of distinctions of distinctions is that
the diverse variations of human views of the world, the variety of
madness and also of normality can be deduced from one single
principle of structuring, namely, *making distinctions*. Normality and
madness thus present themselves as the results of using the same
(cooking) recipe. The same prescriptive rules that enable consensus and communication between man also ensure the breakdown
of communication and leaving the consensus. You do not become
mad if your own mental processes work differently from other
people's on principle, but only if they function in exactly the same
way. Madness does not develop when the rules of normal thinking
and feeling are given up, but only when they are applied. However,
I must warn you that in this mathematical model the value s, standing for disturbance by the environment, cannot stand only for the
influence of the social environment. The body or rather physical
processes are also a part of the environment with respect to the
process of development of meaning described here. In order to
achieve an effect similar to the communicative softening of reality,
it is possible according to this mathematical model that quite unspecific physical influences can suffice to disturb the focusing of
attention.

13

When the World View Does Not Fit the World: Epistemological Errors and Traps

MAYBE: THE STORY OF A HORSE

This is a popular Chinese legend about a farmer whose horse ran away (Watts 1975).

In the evening the neighbors gathered and felt sorry for him because of his bad luck. The farmer said, "Maybe." The horse came back the next day and brought six wild horses with it, and the neighbors came and declared what good luck he had. He said, "Maybe." And the next day his son tried to saddle and ride one of the wild horses. He was thrown off and broke his leg. Again the neighbors came and pitied him for his bad luck. He said, "Maybe." The next day officers came into the village to recruit young men for the army, but the farmer's son was deferred because of his broken leg. When the neighbors came in and wanted to tell him that everything had taken a turn for the better, he said, "Maybe."

TO ERR IS HUMAN: A LIST OF UNWHOLESOME ASSUMPTIONS ABOUT THE WORLD

"There is this much connection certainly between scientific truth, on the one hand, and beauty and morality, on the other: that if a man entertain false opinions regarding his own nature, he will be led thereby to courses of action which will be in some profound sense immoral and ugly" (Bateson 1960, p. 265). Gregory Bateson has coined the concept "epistemological error" for these false assumptions about the world. They are false because they presuppose characteristic attributes of man as well as of the world as a whole that are wrong, that is, do not fit. Although nobody can say what the world is really like, you can nevertheless establish what it is not like. Science is all about establishing what is false. When such epistemological errors become the basis of action, it is not wholesome for the world in the long run or for those who behave in accordance with those principles.

The questions raised by Bateson about the moral or esthetic value of epistemological assumptions are not taken into account here because the danger of becoming enmeshed in moralizing or estheticizing would simply be too great. Instead we only consider which of these particular errors contribute to the development of madness and mental misery.

World views are something like tools that have to be tested in daily use to prove their quality. If need be, you can even knock a nail into the wall with a saw; yet day-to-day experience shows that it is better and easier to do it with a hammer. If, however, you try to do it with a fountain pen—possibly with one of those outrageously expensive, snobbishly old-fashioned showpieces—the joke will be on you. Hand and shirt full of ink, the pen broken, and the nail still in your hand, not in the wall. The tool did not fit the job and hence was not appropriate for your intended task. Using the pen was a mistake.

Something similar can happen to each of us if the assumptions determining our behavior, feeling, and thinking do not fit our physical and mental state and the world in which we live. At best we and our fellow men are left with a black eye; at worst we and others experience something similar to the pen, as we and/or they break. The difference between wholesome and unwholesome world views, which can build up to the difference between normal and mad, exists less in the type of instruments employed than in the quantity, location, time, and consequence of their application. Although city maps are generally useful aids to orientation, it is simply stupid to look for the Eiffel Tower in Rome with a map of Paris and extremely dangerous to wander through the Gobi desert with a map of the world on a scale of 1:100,000,000.

Most of the epistemological errors resulting from the application of mechanical notions to living systems have already been presented in detail. For this reason they are merely summarized briefly and called back to mind. Their distribution in different assumptions about the world is relatively arbitrary, since they are all interconnected and can be deduced logically from one another.

Mistaking the Menu for the Meal

Quite consciously and purposefully I refrain here from any indication of the distinction between menu and meal—that is, between linguistic description and behavior—which should be sufficiently clear to the reader by now. Because the confusing and maddening dangers of language come from the fact that they allow the speaker to claim not to be doing something and thereby do it. Therefore nothing is written here about the fact that menus are hardly digestible and, if eaten, lie heavily on your stomach.

The Notion of One Indivisible Reality and Truth

Imagining the observer away suggests the assumption that only one reality and truth exists and is equally binding for everybody. No wonder that Olympic competitions develop over possession of this truth, particularly since this truth prescribes who has to do what and when and can be used as a means of power. However, this idea has even more consequences. It can lead to the error that knowledge of the world is something like a big soup pot that can be emptied sometime and somehow, provided you try hard enough. Anyone who attempts this is bound to run into difficulties, because he himself is the meat (sometimes somewhat more hard-boiled or well-done) in this soup.

The Principle of All or Nothing

Reason is often equated with logical thinking in the sense of binary logic and its either–or scheme. Such logic may be useful for operating computers, although even this seems questionable.[1] It is not useful, however, for developing human—in every sense of the word—world views. Living systems, human beings, families, and so on are ambivalent organizations. They must constantly balance and conciliate opposing tendencies. Where there is no room left for both–and and you can never answer "yes and no" instead of "yes" or "no," madness develops.

The Notion of Personal Identity

Closely connected with the application of binary logic is the assumption that always and everywhere, under all possible and imaginable conditions, regardless of historical changes and changing relationships, you could or must remain the same. Anyone who thinks or feels this way has to avoid new experiences; they might perturb him too much. He is like an actor who has to act the same play on the same stage for decades. He develops more and more routine, but his artistic and creative power is certainly not called for and encouraged. And it seems only logical that he tries to prevent the other players from learning, rehearsing, and enacting new roles too.

The Notion of Control

Applying linear cause–effect thinking to human relations presents the insoluble task of instructive interaction. Human beings are autonomous systems whose behavior is determined by their inner struc-

---

1. The development of so-called fuzzy logic shows that it can be an advantage not to distinguish between 0 or 1 in the logic of computer programming, but to use a value between 0 and 1 when ascribing meaning, as presented in Chapter 12 (See Zadeh 1968, 1978).

tures and can only be perturbed by the environment. Anyone who thinks he can control other people will be enmeshed in power struggles out of which he will most likely emerge with a feeling of impotence. What is worse, however, is the fact that he misses the chance of cooperating and robs himself of the opportunity to influence others. For to do so he would have to use his empathic abilities to establish the interests of the others in order to induce them to come to an independent decision that would make consensus with him possible, that is, would be in his interest too.

The Notion of Hierarchy

Inevitably the notion of control logically leads to the notion of hierarchy, according to which one gives commands that the other has to listen to, that is, obey. However, someone who listens does not have to act. Relationships cannot be defined one-sidedly. In relationships between the top and the bottom, the persons concerned also agree somehow on what kind of relationship they have or want to have with each other. Hierarchical structures develop where all concerned pretend that control is possible. Anyone who carries out someone else's orders does so either because he believes that he has no alternative or because he decides not to utilize all possible options. After all, there are situations where it is more useful for one's own survival to acquiesce in someone else's decisions (in the case of an emergency landing of an airplane it would not be very practical if every passenger personally concerned himself with the shortest evacuation plan for all the rest).

The options of self-organization are not used if the conclusion that there can be no order without hierarchical structures is drawn from the fact that, in certain situations, the directives of a dictator can lead to a form of order that serves the survival of the entire social system. A compulsive system develops that does not make use of its own resources. This principle applies not only to social interaction but also to each individual's dealings with himself. The assumption that you can plan and control your own life consciously leads to paralysis and obstruction of spontaneous development.

The Notion That the World Is Calculable

Chess players and warlords develop strategies in order to win. The aim of their action is determined clearly and simply. The better and more fitting their information and the better they can calculate the course of the game in advance, the more successful they are. The difference between a game of chess and life is the fact that you do not have to reckon with a sudden change of rules and the creation of something completely new with each move on the chessboard. In real life too, the aims and principles of winning cannot be established as clearly and simply.

Nevertheless, although it is obviously sensible to plan, one has to keep in mind that nobody can ever know what might be important in the future. Since every description of the world (of yourself, your own life, and so on) can change what it describes, planning can only be limited, as it changes its own prerequisites.

The Notion of Knowing What Is Good and Bad

Man develops desires, goals, and values on which he orients himself. They form the standard of his judgments and actions. We can only say whether everyday events are good or bad, whether we are lucky or unlucky, if we know what kind of long-term consequences these events will have. Once again it is the assumption that we have all the information about the game—the world—that leads to joy and sorrow, euphoria and depression, to the feeling that we have taken a further step to fulfilling our own values and achieving our goals. As you can never be sure whether the advantage will not prove to be a disadvantage in the long run, you should not count your chickens before they are hatched. In view of the self-organization of the world there is only one adequate answer to the question of good luck and bad luck, of good or bad in the long run, namely, "maybe."

Mistaking Active and Passive Negation

The example of hierarchy has already shown that, if order is not ensured actively, it does not mean that disorder will ensue, and if you actively do something against disorder, it does not mean that order really ensues. On the level of human behavior there are always three ways of behaving in regard to certain goals or values. In the first way, you can actively fight for them and try to promote them, for example, the ruling party or the political goals it represents. Logically this means that you try to negate the opposite *actively* (in this case the goals of the opposition party). In the second way, you can decide against this value or this goal and try to negate it *actively*. In this case you fight against the realization of this goal (in our example, against the ruling party and its program) and for the opposite (for the opposition party). The third way consists of *passive* negation. You act neutrally, and your own behavior neither serves nor harms the goal or value at issue (you neither fight for nor against the ruling or opposition party).

If you do not distinguish between these active and passive forms of negation, you will get into difficulties, particularly where there is a question of balancing ambivalence. You will often feel under pressure to act, although you could wait it out. You will feel subjected to mutually exclusive requests for action, and you will not be able to make use of the full extent of your decision-making options appropriate to a given situation, namely, to do one thing and forget the other, to do the other thing and forget the first, to do both, or to even forget both.

The Notion of Omnipotence and Impotence

This notion is merely a special case of applying the above-mentioned epistemological errors (e.g., the all–or–nothing principle and the notion of control) when people think that they have either no power or influence whatsoever or have enormous power and boundless influence. The human dilemma is that both are true. The world changes completely when someone changes his behavior, but nevertheless, no one can decide to change the world purposefully. Everybody is responsible for the whole world, but still cannot decide hierarchically what this world will look like. Anyone who only sees one side of this dilemma will end in despondency or megalomania and either over- or underrate himself, his own value, his responsibility, and his guilt.

None of these dilemmas and epistemological errors is new. They have run through mankind's history since time immemorial and have brought forth madnesses of all kinds. What is relatively new is merely that the consequences of these errors are being treated as illnesses. It is natural to suspect that doing so subjects us to the same errors and—tragically enmeshed—contributes to the preservation of madness.

TRAGEDY AND/OR ABSURD THEATER

Let us return to the bleachers to observe the game of madness from the outside once again. Anyone who has the opportunity to observe the family dramas that evolve around madness from close by, as therapist or in any other function, will not be able to evade the shock and emotion of witnessing tragic events. And indeed, the characteristics of tragedy are fulfilled.

"Everything 'tragic,'" Goethe writes, "is based on an unbalanceable contradiction. As soon as balance is achieved or becomes possible, what is tragic disappears" (Eckermann 1836). What matters is the insoluble contradiction, the clash of two orders, of two descriptive and prescriptive rule systems.

The observer in the bleachers sees the heroes of Greek tragedy in the same dilemma as the therapist sees the patient who behaves in a mad way and his family. It is the contradiction between the (self-)descriptions of the individual as perpetrator, autonomous, responsible, and culpable, or as victim, whose belief that he can determine his own life reveals itself as madness, since fate has decided differently and without compassion.

The dramaturgy of Greek tragedy emerged at a time when, in Greece, two world views came into conflict with each other, a mythical view symbolized by Homeric heroes and a logical one whose ideal was Socrates. The heroes of this myth did not know or need conscience, they could not make decisions, they were not acting individuals, but were *dependent victims* who had to perform what the powers of destiny had decided for them. It was not possible to ascribe to them personal responsibility or guilt for their behavior.

But myth was not the only available system of meaning. The triumphal march of logical thinking had already begun, and with it the separation of subject and object of cognition. When man can predict the world, he can choose to opt between different actions. He can decide to do something or refrain from doing it; he becomes his own master, an acting individual, a responsible perpetrator. Destiny seems deprived of power.

Oedipus provides the best example of the victory of reason over the mythical powers. It is he who liberates the city of Thebes from the frightening threat of the man-eating Sphinx, the strangler. Until her riddle is solved, she will carry off a new victim every day. Oedipus ends this endless series of victims by answering the Sphinx's big question:

> On the earth there is something with two legs and something with four legs called the same, and even with three legs. It is the only one of all the living beings moving on the earth, in the air and in the sea that changes its form. When it walks supported on most of its legs its swiftness of limb is slightest.
> "You mean man!" Oedipus cried out, "who, when still crawling on the earth, hardly born, uses four legs, but when he grows old and, with a hunched back and the burden of old age, uses a stick as a third leg, he then has three legs." [quoted in Kerényi 1966, p. 83]

Anyone who believes that, with this brain teaser, Oedipus had also solved the riddle of what it means to be human will soon be put right.

The hero of logical thought, Oedipus, who wants to take his destiny into his own hands experiences for himself that he fulfills it by trying to evade it. There was a threatening prophecy that he would kill his father and marry his mother. In order to elude this prophecy (negate it actively), Oedipus leaves the house he regards as his parents' house and the people he regards as his parents. And thus destiny takes its course. The tragic hero kills his "real" father and marries his "real" mother. A series of epistemological errors have brought about their paradoxical and tragic effects.

When Oedipus realizes that he has not just slain an old man but his own father, his self-description changes abruptly; he realizes his truth was only delusion, his freedom destiny. It is the presentation of the insurmountable contradiction between the notion of the individual who makes decisions according to his own free will and a world view in which the individual has to subject himself to the course of overall events that triggers a tragic shock in the outside spectator—but also in somebody experiencing it from the inner perspective. Man always requires this kind of double description—for example, free will *and* self-organization—if he does not want to be enmeshed in epistemological errors and wants to develop a world view fitting his own nature and that of the world. The essential lesson of Greek tragedy is "the basic knowledge of the unity of all that exists, the observation of individuation as the source of all evil" (Nietzsche 1871, p. 99).

The parallels of tragedy to the patterns of interaction in families in which madness occurs cannot be overlooked. They are the same epistemological errors that have a paradoxical effect and bring about disaster in spite of—and often because of—all attempts to do and give one's best. And just as in tragedy, there is an irreconcilable contradiction between a world view in which the individual is the perpetrator and another in which he is the victim, which determines the course of events and communication. As a result reality becomes

softer and softer, and any security about the meaning and sense of
your own actions and those of others fades away.[2]

If you ascribe the cause of madness to an illness, you make reality hard again and clarify things where there was unclarity before.
The price, however, is that now you are dealing with an imaginary
partner of interaction again, an unfathomable god on an inacces-
sible Mount Olympus. The illness takes its fateful course; the poor
madman is the victim strangled by it. This victim only has an opportunity to take his life into his own hands if he begins to see himself
as the perpetrator.

However, tragic shock is not the only form of experience that
grips the spectator on the bleachers when madness is being enacted.
At the same time you feel as if you are watching absurd theater.
Sisyphus rolls and rolls and rolls the rock, incapable of seeing himself and the absurdity of his actions from the outside. In this absurd and ridiculous play there are two leading roles, that of Sisyphus
and that of the rock. Both can say, "I am rolling and you are rolling," without coming to a consensus on which is active and which
passive, and both see themselves as Sisyphus, the other or others as
the rock. Yet at the same time they behave toward the other(s) like
the infamous rolling stone. All mutually confirm their epistemological errors. As everyone assures us plausibly and with a good
conscience, all this only happens from honest motives and for the
best of the other.

> "It's absurd" means "it's impossible," but also: "It's contradictory."
> If I see a man armed only with a sword attack a group of machine-
> guns, I shall consider his act to be absurd. But it is so solely by vir-
> tue of the disproportion between his intention and the reality he will
> encounter, of the contradiction I notice between his true strength
> and the aim he has in view. . . . I am thus justified in saying that the
> feeling of absurdity does not spring from the mere scrutiny of a fact

---

2. An extensive discussion about what tragedy and family interaction have in common in
dramaturgy can be found in my article, "Die Geburt der Schizophrenie aus dem Geist der
Tragödie" (Simon 1984).

or an impression but that it bursts from the comparison between a bare fact and a certain reality, between an action and the world that transcends it. The absurd is essentially a divorce. It lies in neither of the elements compared, it is born of their confrontation. [Camus 1965, p. 30]

The characterization of the absurd given by Albert Camus shows the family similarity of tragic and absurd patterns.

Common to both patterns is the contradiction between intention and result of human actions, between what can be observed from the inner and what can be observed from the outer perspective. These tragic-absurd contradictions are the origins of madness. The way out of this circle of continuous repetitions of absurd actions, the termination of this tragic game and the dropping out of madness, is to be found via the spectator's bleachers. The inner view of someone who is enmeshed in epistemological errors can change when he realizes how contradictory this game is and how ambivalent all acts and omissions are, i.e., when he allows himself a tragic shock and learns to laugh about it at the same time. This may not be the only way out of madness, but it is one of the most successful ones.[3]

ZEN *KOAN*: SIGNPOST TO THE DEAD-END STREETS OF LOGIC

Imagine that you are searching for the truth. What could be more natural than to ask one of the men who are called learned and wise because everyone thinks they have found the truth? Although or because (a difference that does not make very much difference in this case), it is in vogue right now, you go to see a Zen master. You soon realize that his task is to ask you mysterious questions that confuse (both) you and your logical thought. He will probably, which is quite typical for these people, stretch out his hand toward you

---

3. This assertion cannot, of course, be backed up by statistics, but is my personal opinion based on my therapeutic experience.

(the title "master" speaks of handicraft traditions) and ask: "What does a clapping hand sound like?"

If you come across a somewhat more radical master, who does not shrink from corporal punishment (perturbation) to help enlighten you, the following will happen. He shows you a stick, quite an unmistakable stick that can be immediately recognized as a stick by every normal person. It is clearly distinct from anything else you have ever seen in the hand of a master (for example, fried sausages and rolls, saws and sanders, brick trowels and screwdrivers, or gold medals and diplomas). You are immediately aware that it is a typical stick. However, your spontaneous security dwindles because the master admonishes you in a dignified and sober way, without any menacing undertone: "If you say this is a stick, I'll hit you with it! If you say this is not a stick, I'll hit you with it!"

A classical double bind. Whatever you answer, you will get a beating. You are requested to invent a third way beyond assertion and negation. You have to overcome the limitations of binary logic with its either–or pattern and inside–outside distinctions. The foundations of your linguistic conceptualization will be questioned radically by such a *koan*, the technical term for this kind of Buddhist double bind. Please do not believe that you could avoid the blows by offering your master some other concept with a similar meaning, such as cane or club.

Your master's tricks aim to shatter your pleasure and security in any conceptual thought: "Ever since the development of our consciousness we have been used to reacting to inner and outer states in a conceptual and analytical way. The practice of Zen consists in canceling out this basic activity once and for all and reconstructing the old spiritual framework on a brand new basis" (Suzuki 1939, p. 132). When using a concept we take the outer perspective of observation for granted; even when we say "I," we pretend we are facing talking about ourselves. The practices of Zen force us to preserve the inner perspective. They throw the pupil back to the necessity of feeling and behaving, even though he cannot explain: "Zen feels that fire is warm and ice cold, because we shiver when it is freezing and welcome the fire. Feeling is everything, as

Faust says, no theory affects reality. But here 'feeling' has to be understood in its deepest sense and its purest form. If someone even says, 'this is the feeling,' this is not Zen anymore" (Suzuki 1939, pp. 132, 56).

You should abandon all hope of *talking* your way out of it and *do* something. You could, for instance, take the club out of your master's hand and hit him on the head or some other valuable part of his body. This is certainly not the only way out of your dilemma. You could even—far less violently—simply break the master's stick. In both cases you have found an ingenious way out of the dead-end street of brooding into which the master has pushed you. You no longer worry about the "true" solution of the logical problem (= the level of the menu) but about the problem of the imminent thrashing (= the level of the meal), which is much more important in your life.

Of course, I do not want to claim that it is always a sign of enlightenment to give one's master a thrashing. Nevertheless, the form of the *koan* and its "solutions" make us aware that paradoxes and other logical problems resulting from the characteristics of language dissolve when you start acting.

Obviously no Zen master would accept such an interpretation of his actions for this interpretation also exists and remains within the sphere of linguistic description, whereas his aim is to transcend it. What all these sages really think and feel will remain concealed from us. But the tasks they set their pupils might also perhaps seduce us a little to meditate further on the dangers of mistaking logic for life and other inappropriate distinctions or nondistinctions.

And since it has nothing to do with the path to enlightenment but—quite modestly—with reconsidering the foundations of human normality and madness, we will not get very far without words. We must talk about something we cannot keep silent about.[4]

---

4. If you are still waiting for the bicycle announced in the title, it got there by way of displacement and condensation. The title really should read, *My Psychosis, My Auto, and Me* (after all, this book deals mostly with autonomy, autopoiesis, and such like).

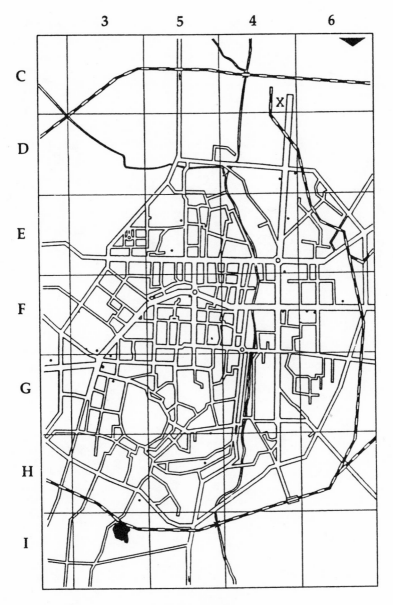

Figure 13–1

REFERENCES

Arieti, S. (1978). *On Schizophrenia: Phobias, Depression, Psychotherapy, and the Farther Shores of Psychiatry.* New York: Brunner/Mazel.

Aristotle. (1984). Metaphysics. 1011b and 1005b. In *The Works of Aristotle,* vol. 1. Encyclopedia Britannica.

Ashby, W. R. (1956). *An Introduction to Cybernetics.* London: Chapman and Hall.

Axelrod, R. (1984). *The Evolution of Cooperation.* New York: Basic Books.

Bateson, G. (1960). Minimal requirements for a theory of schizophrenia. In *Steps to an Ecology of Mind.* New York: Ballantine, 1972.

—— (1969). Double bind. In *Steps to an Ecology of Mind.* San Francisco: Chandler, 1972.

—— (1972). The cybernetics of self. A theory of alcoholism. In *Steps to an Ecology of Mind.* San Francisco: Chandler.

—— (1979). *Mind and Nature: A Necessary Unity.* New York: E. P. Dutton.

Bateson, G., Jackson, D., Haley, J., and Weakland, J. (1956). Toward a theory of schizophrenia. In *Steps to an Ecology of Mind.* San Francisco: Chandler, 1972.

Bemmann, H. (1984). *Erwins Badezimmer oder Die Gefährlichkeit der Sprache.* Munich: Goldmann.

Bergson, H. (1988). *Sur les données immediates de la conscience.* Paris: Presses Université de France.

Bleuler, E. (1911). *Dementia Praecox of the Group of Schizophrenics.* New York: International Universities Press.

—— (1916). *Lehrbuch der Psychiatrie,* 12th ed. Berlin: Springer, 1972.

Brecht, B. (1967). *Geschichten vom Herrn Keuner, Das Wiedersehen. Gesammelte Werke* Bd. V. Frankfurt: Suhrkamp.

Bowlby, J. (1969). *Attachment and Loss.* London: Hogarth.

Camus, A. (1965). *Der Mythos von Sisyphos.* Reinbek: Rowohlt.

Capra, F. (1982). *Wendezeit.* Bern: Scherz.

Carroll, L. (1865). *Alice in Wonderland.* London: Penguin, 1946.

—— (1897). *Symbolic Logic,* part I. New York: Dover and Berkeley.

Ciompi, L. (1988). *Außenwelt-Innenwelt.* Göttingen: Vandenhoeck and Ruprecht.

Clark, E. (1973). What's in a word? In *Cognitive Development and the Acquisition of Language,* ed. T. Moore. New York: Academic Press.

Cooper, D. (1977). *Wer ist Dissident?* Berlin: Rotbuch.

de M'Uzan, M. (1974). Psychodynamic mechanisms in psychosomatic symptom formation. *Psychotherapy and Psychosomatics* 23:103–110.

Dell, P. (1986). *Klinische Erkenntnis.* Dortmund: Verlag Modernes Lernen.

Dörner, K., Egetmeyer, A., and Könning, K., eds. (1982). *Freispruch der Familie.* Wunstorf-Hannover: Psychiatrie-Verlag.

Eccles, J. C. (1989). Der Ursprung des Geistes, des Bewuβtseins und des SelbstBewuβtseins im Rahmen der zerebralen Evolution. In *Geist und Natur*, ed. H. P. Dürr and W. Zimmerli. Bern: Scherz.

Eckermann, J. P. (1836). Gespräche mit Goethe in den letzten Jahren seines Lebens, III. Teil. 28. März 1825. Leipzig: Brockhaus.

Eigen, M., and Winkler, R. (1975). *Das Spiel*. Munich: Piper.

Elias, N. (1984). *Über die Zeit*. Frankfurt: Suhrkamp.

Elster, J. (1979). Active and passive negation. In *The Invented Reality*, ed. P. Watzlawick. New York; Norton.

Erikson, É. H. (1946). Ego development and historical change. Clinical notes. *Psychoanalytic Study of the Child* 2:359–396. New York: International Universities Press.

—— (1959). *Identität und Lebenszyklus*. Frankfurt: Suhrkamp.

—— (1969). *Gandhi's Truth*. New York: Norton.

Falletta, N. (1983). *Paradoxon*. Frankfurt: Fischer.

Feigenbaum, M. J. (1980). Universal behavior in nonlinear systems. *Los Alamos Science* (Summer) pp. 4–27.

Fischer, H. R., and Simon. F. B. (1988). Kontextualitat und Transkontextualitat. Variationen eines Themas bei Wittgenstein, Schapp und Bateson. *Grazer Philosophische Studien* 31:59–83.

Freud, S. (1900). The interpretation of dreams. *Standard Edition* 4/5:1–626.

—— (1915). Instincts and their vicissitudes. *Standard Edition* 14:109–140.

—— (1926). Inhibitions, symptoms and anxiety. *Standard Edition* 20:77–174.

Geertz, C. (1973). Thick description: toward an interpretive theory of culture. In *The Interpretation of Cultures: Selected Essays*. New York: Basic Books.

Gernhardt, R., Bernstein, F. W., and Waechter, F. K. (1979). *Welt im Spiegel 1964–1976*. Frankfurt: Zweitausendeins.

Gleick, J. (1987). *Chaos: Making a New Science*. New York: Viking.

Goethe, J. W. *Faust: Der Tragödie erster Teil*. Hamburger Ausgabe. Band 3. München (Beck) II. Aufl.

Goffman, E. (1964). Psychic symptom and public order. Disorder of communication. Research publication. *Association for Research in Nervous and Mental Disease*, Research Publication 62:262–269.

Goldstein, M. (1983). Family interaction: patterns predictive of the onset and course of schizophrenia, In *Psychosocial Intervention in Schizophrenia*, ed. H. Stierlin, L. Wynne, and M. Wirsching. Berlin: Springer.

Haken, H. (1981). *Erfolgsgeheimnisse der Natur*. Stuttgart: Deutsche Verlagsanstalt.

Hegel, G. W. (1807). *Phänomenologie des Geistes. Werkausgabe Bd. III*. Frankfurt: Suhrkamp, 1970.

Heisenberg, W. (1989). *Ordnung der Wirklichkeit*. Munich: Piper.

Hempel, C. G. (1942). The function of general laws in history. In *Aspects of Scientific Explanation and Other Essays in the Philosophy of Science*. New York: Free Press, 1965.

Hofstadter, D. (1979). *Godel, Escher, Bach*. New York: Basic Books.

Jaeger, W. (1934). *Paideia, Buch I*. Berlin: DeGruyter.

Jantsch, E. (1979). *Die Selbstorganisation des Universums*. Munich: Hanser.

Jaspers, K. (1913). *Allgemeine Psychopathologie*, 9th ed. Berlin: Springer.

—— (1937). *Descartes und die Philosophie*. Berlin: DeGruyter.

Kant, I. (1789). Anthropologie in pragmatischer Hinsicht. In *Werkausgabe* Bd. XII. Frankfurt: Suhrkamp, 1977.

Kelsen, H. (1941). *Vergeltung und Kausalität, eine soziologische Untersuchung*. The Hague: Stockum & Zoon.

Kerényi, K. (1966). *Die Mythologie der Griechen*, vol. II. Munich: Deutscher Taschenbuch Verlag, 1987.

Klaus, G. (1964). *Moderne Logik*. Berlin: Deutscher Verlag der Wissenschaften.

Klein, M. (1955). On identification. In *Envy and Gratitude and Other Works*. New York: Delacorte.

Kraus, A. (1989). Der Manisch-Depressive und sein Partner. *Daseinsanalyse* 6:106–120.

Luhmann, N. (1984). *Soziale Systeme. Grundriβeiner allgemeinen Theorie*. Frankfurt: Suhrkamp.

MacLean, P. (1962). New findings relevant to the evolution of psychosexual functions of the brain. *Journal of Nervous and Mental Disorders* 135:289–301.

Mandler, G. (1982). Stress and thought processes. In *Handbook of Stress*, ed. L. Goldberger and S. Brenitz. London: Macmillan.

Maturana, H. (1970). Biology of cognition. In *Autopoiesis and Cognition: The Realization of the Living*, ed. H. Maturana and F. Varela. Boston: Reidel, 1979.

—— (1975). The organization of the living: a theory of the living organization. *International Journal of Man-Machine Studies* 7:313–332.

—— (1976). Biology of language: the epistemology of reality. In *Psychology and Biology of Language and Thought*, ed. G. Miller and E. Lenneberg. New York: Academic Press.

—— (1984). *The Tree of Knowledge: The Biological Roots of Understanding*. Boston: New Science Library, 1987.

Maturana, H., Uribe, G., and Frenk, S. G. (1968). A biological theory of relativistic colour coding in the primate retina. *Archivos de Biologia y Medicina Experimentales*, (supplement 1). Santiago: Universidad de Chile.

McConaghty, N. (1960). Modes of abstract thinking and psychosis. *American Journal of Psychiatry* 117:106–110.

Merton, R. (1965). *On the Shoulders of Giants: A Shandean Postscript*. Chicago: University of Chicago Press.

Morgenstern, C. (1985). Das Knie. In *Das Morgenstern-Buch*. Munich: Piper.

Morin, E. (1977). *La methode. I. La nature de la nature*. Paris: Seuil.

Nietzsche, F. (1871). Die Geburt der Tragödie aus dem Geist der Musik. In *Sämtliche Werke*, Bd. I. Stuttgart: Kröner, 1964.

Olbrich, R. (1983). Expressed emotions (EE) und die Auslösung schizophrener Episoden: eine Literaturübersicht. *Nervenarzt* 54:113–121.

Osgood, C., May, W., and Mison, M. (1975). *Cross-cultural Universals of Affective Meaning*. Urbana, IL: University of Illinois Press.

Petzold, H., and Paula, M., eds. (1976). *Transaktionale Analyse und Skriptanalyse*. Hamburg: Altmann.

Piaget, J. (1955). *The Child's Conception of Time*. London: Routledge and Kegan Paul, 1969.

Plato. (1984a). Phaidros. In *The Dialogues of Plato*. Encyclopedia Britannica.

—— (1984b). Symposium. In *The Dialogues of Plato*. Encyclopedia Britannica.

Popper, K. R. (1972). *Objektive Erkenntnis*, 4th ed. Hamburg: Hoffmann und Campe, 1984.

Reiss, D. (1981). *The Family's Construction of Reality*. Cambridge: MA: Harvard University Press.

Russell, B. (1903). *The Principles of Mathematics*, 7th ed. London: Allen Unwin.

—— (1912/13). On the notion of causes. In *Mysticism and Logic*. New York: Doubleday Anchor.

Schöne, A. (1982). *Aufklärung aus dem Geist der Experimentalphysik Lichtenbergsche Konjunktive*. Munich: Beck.

Selvini Palazzoli, M., Boscolo, L., Cecchin, G., and Prata, G. (1975). *Paradox and Counterparadox: General Models of Psychotic Processes in the Family*. New York: Jason Aronson, 1978.

Sifneos, P. (1973). The prevalence of alexithymic characteristics in psychosomatic patients. *Psychotherapy and Psychosomatics* 22:255–262.

Simon, F. B. (1984). *Der Prozeß der Individuation*. Göttingen: Vandenhoeck & Ruprecht.

—— (1988). *Unterschiede, die Unterschiede machen. Klinische Epistemologie: Grundlage einer systemischen Psychiatrie und Psychosomatik*, 2nd revised ed. Frankfurt: Suhrkamp, 1993.

—— (1989). Das deterministische Chaos schizophrenen Denkens. *Familiendynamik* 14:236–258.

Simon, F. B., Stierlin, H., and Wynne, L. (1985). *The Language of Family Therapy: A Vocabulary and Sourcebook*. New York: Family Process Press, 1985.

Simon, F. B., Weber, H., Stierlin, H., et al. (1989). "Schizoaffektive" Muster: Eine systemische Beschreibung. *Familiendynamik* 14:190–213.

Spencer-Brown, G. (1969). *Laws of Form*. New York: E. P. Dutton, 1979.

Spitz, R. (1954). *Die Entstehung der ersten Objektbeziehungen*, 3rd ed. Stuttgart: Klett, 1973.

—— (1965). *Vom Säugling zum Kleinkind*, 2nd ed. Stuttgart: Klett, 1972.

Stierlin, H. (1959). The adaptation to the "stronger" person's reality. *Psychiatry* 22:143–152.

—— (1978). *Delegation und Familie*. Frankfurt: Suhrkamp.

Suzuki, D. (1939). Die große Befreiung. In *Buddhistische Geisteswelt*, ed. G. Mensching, pp. 132 and 156. Baden-Baden: Holle.

Szagun, G. (1986). *Sprachentwicklung beim Kind*, 3rd. rev. ed. Weinheim: Psychologie Verlags Union.

Tienari, P., Sorri, A., Lahti, M., et al. (1988). Family environment and the etiology of schizophrenia: implications from the Finnish adoptive family study. In *Familiar Realities*, ed. H. Stierlin, F. Simon, and G. Schmidt. New York: Brunner/Mazel.

van Gennep, A. (1909). *Übergangsriten*. Frankfurt: Campus, 1986.

Varela, F. (1979). *Principles of Biological Autonomy*. New York: North Holland.

—— (1981). The creative circle. In *The Invented Reality*, ed. P. Watzlawick. New York: Norton, 1984.

von Aster, E. (1932). *Geschichte der Philosophie*. Stuttgart: Kroner.

von Domarus, E. (1944). The specific laws of logic in schizophrenia. In *Language and Thought in Schizophrenia: Collected Papers*. Kasanin: University of California Press.

von Foerster, H. (1972). The responsibilities of competence. In *Observing Systems*. Seaside, CA: Intersystems Publications, 1984.

—— (1973). On constructing a reality. In *Observing Systems*. Seaside, CA: Intersystems Publications, 1984.

——, ed. (1974). *Cybernetics of Cybernetics*, 2nd ed. San Jose, CA: San Jose State University, 1986.

—— (1977). Objects: tokens for Eigen- behaviors. In *Observing Systems*. Seaside, CA: Intersystems Publications, 1984.

—— (1988). Abbau und Aufbau. In *Lebende Systeme*, ed. F. B. Simon. Berlin: Springer.

von Glasersfeld, E. (1981). Introduction to radical constructivism. In *The Invented Reality*, ed. P. Watzlawick. New York: Norton, 1984.

von Wright, G. H. (1963). *Norm und Handlung*. Königstein: Scriptor.

—— (1971). Erklaren und Verstehen. Königstein: Athenäum.

Watts, A. (1975). *Tao: The Watercourse Way*. New York: Vintage.

Watzlawick, P., Beavin, J., and Jackson, D. (1967). *Pragmatics of Human Communication*. New York: Norton.

Werner, H. (1957). The concept of development from a comparative and organismus point of view. In *The Concept of Development*, ed. D. B. Harris. Minneapolis: University of Minnesota Press.

Whitehead, A. N., and Russell, B. (1910–1913). *Principia Mathematica*. Cambridge: Cambridge University Press.

Whorf, B. L. (1942). *Language, Thought, and Reality*. Cambridge, MA: MIT Press.

Wickler, W., and Seibt, U. (1977). *Das Prinzip Eigennutz*. Munich: Piper.

Willi, J. (1975). *Qie Zweierbeziehung*. Reinbek: Rowohlt.

Winograd, T., and Flores, F. (1986). *Understanding Computers and Cognition: A New Foundation for Design*. Norwood, NJ: Ablex.

Wittgenstein, L. (1921). *Tractatus Logico-Philosophicus*. London: Routledge and Kegan Paul, 1955.

—— (1958). *Philosophical Investigations*. Oxford: Blackwell.

Wulff, E. (1972). *Psychiatrie und Klassengesellschaft*. Frankfurt: Athenäum.

Wynne, L. C., Ryckoff, I. M., Day, J., and Hirsch, S. J. (1958). Pseudomutuality in the family relations of schizophrenics. *Psychiatry* 21:205–220.

Wynne, L. C., and Singer, M. (1963). Thought disorder and family relations of schizophrenics. *Archives of General Psychiatry* 12:187–212.

Zadeh, L. A. (1968). Probability measures of fuzzy events. *Journal of Mathematical Analysis and Applications* 23:421–427.

—— (1978). Fuzzy sets as a basis for a theory of possibility. *Fuzzy Sets and Systems* 1:3–28.

INDEX